The Politics of San Antonio

Edited by David R. Johnson, John A. Booth, & Richard J. Harris

The Politics
of
San Antonio

Community, Progress, & Power

University of Nebraska Press

Lincoln & London

Chapter 8 was first published as "Democratic
Change in the Urban Political Economy,"
Texas Journal of Politics I (Fall 1978): 4-31.

Copyright 1983 by the University of Nebraska Press
Manufactured in the United States of America

The paper in this book meets the guidelines for
permanence and durability of the Committee on
Production Guidelines for Book Longevity of the
Council on Library Resources.

Library of Congress Cataloging in Publication Data

Main entry under title:

The Politics of San Antonio.

Includes bibliographical reference and index.
1. San Antonio (Tex.)–Politics and government–
Addresses, essays, lectures. 2. Political participa-
tion–Texas–San Antonio–Addresses, essays, lectures.
I. Johnson, David Ralph, 1942- . II. Booth,
John A. III. Harris, Richard J., 1948- .
JS1425.2.A2P64 1983 320.8'09764'351 83-5766
ISBN 0-8032-1178-3
ISBN 0-8032-6068-7 (pbk.)

Contents

John A. Booth and
David R. Johnson

Preface

Community, Progress, and Power in San Antonio

Our purpose in this volume is to demonstrate how the ideas of community, progress, and power have contributed to the growth of San Antonio. Different versions and applications of each idea have contributed to San Antonio's development since 1836. At each stage of the city's growth various groups, but most especially local social and economic elites, have used political power to implement their version of San Antonio's future.[1] San Antonio's public policy makers have usually operated within a set of ideological constraints that, with little public consent, maximized governmental support of the local economic elite's interests. This tradition began with the first political machine organized by Bryan Callaghan II (1885–99). Callaghan, a prime mover in San Antonio's first period of major growth and development, pursued public policies that strongly favored local businesses. Later, from 1914 to roughly 1925, a "reform" government drawn largely from the city's economic elite vigorously expanded public works. Their goal was to reestablish subsidies for city services (street paving, street lighting, and the like) whose costs had previously been borne by private developers. A third era of heavy city government subsidy for private business interests occurred between 1955 and 1975, when the Good Government League (GGL) ruled San Antonio. City councils dominated by the GGL made policy within a set of guidelines established by the GGL leadership.[2]

The degree of elite economic and political control, however, has varied cyclically since the nineteenth century. In 1885–99, 1914–25, and 1955–75 the city's socioeconomic elites dominated much of what went on in both the economic and political arenas. But during the periods 1899–1912, 1925–52, and since 1975, disunity among the socioeconomic elites, demographic changes in the city's electorate, changes in the national economy, and other factors have led to a greater dispersion of power. In these periods, key political decisions rested in somewhat different hands from those of major economic decisions (see Chapters 1, 5, 8, and 10). Indeed, many of the city's major political conflicts have pitted the city's economic elite against middle-class and lower-middle-class people who had achieved political power and who had different conceptions of community and progress. From 1905 to 1914, political decisions rested in the hands of a lower-middle-class political machine. The 1912–14 commission government reform movement represented the socioeconomic elites' effort to reassert their views. Between 1925 and 1952, a middle-class political machine controlled city and county government in San Antonio. The contemporary power struggle in San Antonio is more complex than earlier struggles, but remains a contest over the concentration of economic and political influence. The demise of the GGL in 1975 and the shift to a district-based city council system in 1977 dispersed political and economic power, with a certain amount of political decision making slipping away from the now divided economic elites to a variety of other groups. This decline of the economic elites' twenty-year political hegemony has brought a strong challenge to its economic decision-making power as well. A shifting coalition led by Communities Organized for Public Service (COPS)—a lower- and lower-middle-class, largely Mexican-American community improvement pressure group—has attempted, with some success, to place major economic development and growth policies on the public agenda.

Regardless of their differences, all the groups that have sought or exercised power in San Antonio share a commitment to progress, a vague but powerful ideological concept that implies a universally beneficial developmental process. For San Antonians, as for boosters elsewhere, progress has meant population growth, better public services, and economic development. Each of these interrelated elements has critical implications for capitalists. Growth of population expands the size of local markets, increasing the potential profitability for local business and demands for new services. Expansion of the public service network represents a critical element for attracting and holding new population, thereby indirectly subsidizing local business interests. Furthermore, public services provide a direct subsidy to certain businesses, especially real estate developers, by lowering the cost of their product. Third, economic development (defined as increasing the per capita investment in the local economy, increasing per capita income, and expanding the city's economic hinterland) provides a magnet for further population growth and still greater opportunities for local capital. All in all, then, there are ample reasons why San Antonio's economic elites have historically intervened so vigorously in the political arena in the name of "progress."

The pursuit of progress is one thing; its distribution is another. The power to distribute the benefits of progress has rested in a relatively small number of hands. During the periods when economic and political power have been most concentrated, the benefits of the city's progress have gone disproportionately to the elites. Thus, during the GGL's dominance, public service spending was largely directed toward subsidizing suburban development on the north and west sides of San Antonio, where middle- and upper-class immigrants attracted by expanding businesses, schools, and medical facilities were settling. Simultaneously, however, the GGL councils directed capital expenditures away from older, poorer areas where services were deteriorating under the pressures of dealing with the increasing flow of poor Spanish-speaking migrants (see Chapter 9). In the long run, such discrimination in the distribution of progress has had important repercussions for community in San Antonio.

Several major ethnocultural and racial communities make up San Antonio's population. The major (though not all) ethnic, cultural, and racial groups have vertical social groupings, cutting across class lines and internally united by shared cultural, religious, and linguistic traits.[3] *Mexicanos,* Spanish speakers with roots in the Spanish colonial system and independent Mexico, were among San Antonio's major nineteenth-century ethnic/racial groups. Anglo-Saxons (English, Irish, Scots), usually from the southern U.S. states, began migrating to the city in the 1820s and became a flood by the late nineteenth century. Black slaves came with the Anglo-Saxons, establishing the nucleus of a small but important population in San Antonio. French settlers were a significant element especially during the early 1800s, but they were gradually overwhelmed numerically by other nationality groups. Germans initially arrived in San Antonio during the 1840s and, along with the Mexican Americans and the Anglo-Saxons, eventually became one of the three major cultural groups. Other elements— Chinese, Italians, Greeks, and Poles, to name but a few—came as well, but in lesser numbers.

These communities have not remained stable in proportion to one another. The Mexicanos, a majority in the early nineteenth century, were roughly equalled in numbers by both Germans and Anglos in the late nineteenth century owing to heavy immigration by the latter two. But beginning in the mid-twentieth century, increasing Mexican-American immigration and higher birthrates enabled this ethnic group to achieve majority status again by the mid-1970s. During the twentieth century many of the cultural and linguistic barriers among the groups of northern European origin diminished as Germans, Czechs, Poles, and Italians began to assimilate into the dominant English-language culture. The process, though still far from complete, has proceeded to the degree that the term "Anglo" in the area's vernacular now refers to almost anyone neither Chicano nor black. In fact, in the political arena, one might well argue that this "Anglo" or "white" element is emerging as a new community in and of itself. Despite such trends, many of the original ethnic communities persist and receive nurture through organized religious and cultural celebrations which perpetuate their groups' traditions.

Although ethnic, cultural, and racial communities cut across class lines in San Antonio, the city's ethnocultural communities do not share equally in wealth, status, and power. One dramatic demonstration of this comes from comparing U.S. census education and income data on blacks, Hispanics, and whites in the San Antonio area.[4] The median income and educational attainment for Hispanics and blacks are far below those for whites. Equally interesting is the disparity between Hispanics and blacks. While the blacks in both 1970 and 1980 were more educated than San Antonio Hispanics, their median income level was less. A San Antonian's ethnocultural background or language substantially influences his chances for political, economic, educational, and occupational success (see Chapters 3, 4, and 7). From the statistics, or from even a cursory glance at the everyday reality confronted by San Antonio's diverse communities, any observer can see that the Chicano majority and the black minority live in much less advantageous situations than the Anglo minority. Much of this disparity stems from long-standing discrimination by economic and political decision makers.[5]

"Community" also involves San Antonians' identification with their place of residence and with each other. This includes several nuances—affection for the city, mutual respect among its citizens, a sense of shared destiny, and so forth. This type of community might be best described in terms of people getting along with each other. San Antonians often congratulate themselves on the city's harmony and its lack of conflict. Indeed, over much of its recent history the city has been remarkably quiescent in comparison with other U.S. cities, many riven by overt racial, class, and political conflicts. However, we believe that much of what San Antonians have interpreted as community has in fact been an enforced quietude that masks many pronounced tensions.

We thus argue that it would be a great mistake to interpret such controlled calm as evidence of this second type of community among San Antonians. Indeed, in recent years, the city has experienced increased conflict as established mechanisms of political and economic control have deteriorated. When in the early 1970s the ruling elites of San Antonio, incarnate in the Good Government League, lost their internal cohesion and eventually fell from power, the consequent power vacuum permitted a series of strong challenges to the established political elite, as well as to extant political and economic development policies. These challenges came from several new organizations embodying the dissatisfaction of many previously silent, but obviously discontented groups. Perhaps no organization better exemplifies this trend than Communities Organized for Public Service. COPS was born of the frustration of a group of Mexican-American home owners with poor services, and by employing a variety of tactics to gain access to the public agenda COPS has won a series of important policy victories (see Chapter 9). Elements of the declining old political elite have attacked COPS as radical and as a threat to social peace and competence in government. This attack has further politicized the differences between Mexican Americans and Anglos, threatening the city with further interethnic polarization and hostility.

San Antonio is thus a city once again in the midst of major political, social, and economic changes. The key to solving crucial problems in the community's future development lies in the formation of a new political consensus which can, for the first time, distribute power among competing groups, so that progress will not come, as it has too often in the past, at the expense of community.

Acknowledgments

The editors would like to thank a number of people for their valuable assistance and encouragement in the writing of this book. Several of our secretaries responded generously to our entreaties for help. We would especially like to thank Martha La Roque, Elisa Valderas Jimenez, Anne M. Hardy-Holley, Bettie E. Karter, and Marjorie Present. Caroline Luna, a work-study student, also cheerfully typed portions of the manuscript. In addition, several of our administrative colleagues, especially Dwight Henderson, Thomas Greaves, Thomas Bellows, and Raymond Baird, eased the way by providing funding for photocopying and graphic work, for which we are grateful. Last, we would like to thank our contributors for their interest in and enthusiasm for this project.

Part I: The Setting

John A. Booth and
David R. Johnson

Chapter One

Power and Progress in
San Antonio Politics, 1836–1970

The people of American cities, San Antonians among them, have always regarded growth as the key to prosperity. Growth of population and economic activity have been synonymous with prosperity. Because of competition for population and economic resources, city dwellers have not assumed that growth was inevitable. Urban boosters have equated a marginal population increase, or economic difficulties, with failure and even death.[1] Indeed, urban development in the United States has been quite uneven. From the frenetic city-building era of the nineteenth century to the present there have been many examples of stagnation and of outright failure. Recent theories of urban development argue that transformations of the national capitalist economy are largely responsible for the problems and opportunities of every city. Nationwide economic changes have had "profound effects upon the relative prosperity and rates of growth in different metropolitan areas."[2] Shifting patterns of capital accumulation and the resulting rise and decline of productive specialties, the evolution of labor relations, and changing regional terms of trade have shaped American urban development for two centuries.[3]

But within these constraints, local elites have shaped the fate of specific cities. In order to promote growth, local leaders have sought to attract new population and stimulate urban development. Broadly construed, development took two forms. The first involved economic initiatives to give one city a competitive advantage over its rivals. Transportation connections with good markets were important in the rise of the northeastern mercantile cities from 1800 to the 1860s. Later, the expansion of dynamic industries concentrated in the younger cities of the Midwest provided new opportunities for growth. Since the depression of the 1930s, new trends in capital accumulation, markets, federal spending, energy resources, agriculture, and tourism have boosted the urbanization of southern cities.[4] Urban services have constituted a second form of development. Police and fire protection, paved streets, adequate public utilities, and good schools enhanced the living conditions of a city and made it attractive to prospective settlers and local investors.

In their decisions about such matters as investments in transportation, loans to new businesses, and purchases of real estate tracts, elites have exercised direct control over the first type of development.[5] But decisions regarding urban services were the public's business and lay in the realm of politics. The interests of an economic elite represented only one of many demands which politicians had to weigh. While the majority of any city's inhabitants believed that growth and development were necessary, ideas about how to promote and to finance them often differed along class lines.

Local urban politics, therefore, has involved more than just battles over patronage or conflicts between honest reformers and corrupt politicians. It has also been an arena, bounded by national economic trends, in which people with competing visions of progress and with divergent class interests clashed for control over the decisions that shaped a city's future. The socioeconomic elite have not always prevailed, and their shifting fortunes can in many respects help explain the nature and context of urban politics.[6] This may be especially true of cities such as San Antonio, which aspire to greater success than they already have.

The Formation of the San Antonio Social and Economic Elite, 1836–77

Since 1836, San Antonio's elite has intervened at critical junctures in the city's evolution, either to provoke major economic, social, and political changes, or to set the agenda "determining which questions are considered at all and which are not."[7] Elites are not necessarily unified, first of all because there are different areas of activity in society. San Antonio's social, economic, and political arenas most concern us here, and unity both within and among those elites has varied substantially since 1836. The extent to which San Antonio's leaders have exhibited unity and self-awareness and marshalled power has shaped the progress of the city.

Since Texas independence the larger economic environments of the United States and Republican Texas set the boundaries within which the city would develop. From the 1830s to the 1850s the mercantile cities of the Northeast, by dint of canal and railroad construction to lower freight rates, expanded their economic hinterlands throughout the West and South and thus broke the mercantile power of the Mississippi port of New Orleans. By thus restraining southern mercantile growth, "this new transport network fostered uneven development and allowed northern prosperity to occur simultaneously with deepening southern poverty."[8] San Antonio, an outpost on the frontier of the North American commercial system, was thus limited in its potential for capital growth.

The economy of San Antonio just after Texas independence was in ruins. The Creole forefathers, the city's upper class, found themselves in a village of a few thousand whose population consisted overwhelmingly of poor Mexicans, plus a handful of Anglos of varied backgrounds, some Creole landowning families, and a smattering of other Europeans. Smuggling, once an important part of San Antonio's prosperity, had been curtailed by the efforts of the Mexican government in retaliation for Texas independence. The economy began to recover after 1844 through the resurgence of smuggling into Mexico and the development of a fledgling commercial establishment which supplied finished goods from the Northeast to the new ranches and farms of central and south Texas.

Though San Antonio grew larger than other major cities around the state in the 1840s and 1850s, its rivals, Galveston and Houston, were more strategically located and kept San Antonio the poorest in terms of trade. It was not until the Civil War, in fact, that trading experienced a real boom, once again through smuggling. The war temporarily broke the thrall of the northeastern commercial centers in the South, stimulating sudden opportunities for capital accumulation. Texas's cotton was greatly in demand abroad but was embargoed by the South and blockaded by the North. Enterprising local merchants smuggled this precious contraband to Mexico along a "Cotton Road" from San Antonio to the Rio Grande. By the end of the Civil War the fruits of both the legal and illegal Mexican trade had put the city's commercial elite firmly on its feet. Commission companies supplied the now-burgeoning cattle industry with needed goods. The town's new banks—most formed with the profits from mercantile houses or directly from smuggling—supplied capital for the expansion of ranching. The city also served as a collection point for the northward cattle drives.[9]

By 1865 some families had already established the basis for their economic, social, and political dynasties. Four ethnic groups contributed to this development. First were the Creoles, prosperous landowning families descended from the original Spanish and Canary Island settlers. Next, a very small number of French families arrived, becoming important merchants after independence. Some Anglo members of the future elite began to trickle into Texas even before independence. This Anglo trickle became a steady flow after 1836. Germans began to filter into San Antonio after Baron von Braunfels' colonization scheme in surrounding Central Texas disintegrated in the mid-1840s. Like the French, the Anglo and German newcomers concentrated their investments in commerce, acting as the village's link to the outside world. Intermarriage among these diverse national groups created a unified multiethnic social elite. While the Germans intermarried less than the other ethnic groups, their growing numbers and economic strength foreshadowed their integration into the new ruling class shortly after the Civil War.

As this social and economic elite formed, it sought to enhance its growing prestige and wealth with political power. The Republic of Texas granted San Antonio a municipal charter in 1837 under which the city established an eight-seat board of aldermen, each member elected from a separate ward. The first councilmen, supporters of Texas independence, all had Spanish surnames. The first mayor, however, was John W. Smith, an Anglo whose election was a portent of things to come. He had arrived in Texas in 1826 and had married into the Delgado-Curbelo family, one of the original families of San Antonio. Beginning with John Smith, the newcomers to San Antonio insinuated themselves into roles of influence, soon taking control of politics. By 1845—in a scant eight years—the Germans, Anglos, and French had squeezed the Mexican Americans from their dominant position on the board of aldermen.[10] Mexican Americans would not regain significant influence on the city's governing body until the 1970s (see Chapter 5). Although the foundations of a unified social, economic, and political elite were laid prior to 1865, its consolidation occurred only in the twenty years after the Civil War. The merchants of San Antonio, who had prospered during the war, now possessed the essential ingredient for putting their power to work—capital. All the banks which would control that capital sprang from trading activities prior to 1865. Merchants with names still familiar to San Antonians today—Oppenheimer, Gross, Frost, Brackenridge, and Maverick—started banks in the period after the war. These men invested in development enterprises as diverse as a produce exchange, trolley companies, a water system, several breweries, a fair association, and barbed wire, a technological marvel that transformed cattle raising into a profitable business. Thus, the war strengthened San Antonio's mercantile enterprises and also led to some industrial development.

But the key investment by San Antonio's economic leaders was in railroads. In the early 1870s a group of merchants and businessmen persuaded the county government to help finance a rail line connecting San Antonio to Galveston. By 1885 two more lines had been completed, placing San Antonio at the center of a steel web stretching from northern Texas into Mexico. The rails brought prosperity from two directions. Cattle driven to the railroad from the surrounding ranches gave rise to the livestock commission business and, somewhat later, to meat packing. And as the cattle and beef were shipped out, tourists were shipped in. San Antonio's healthful and pleasant climate attracted throngs of visitors. The city grew at a spectacular rate because of these initiatives. In the twenty years following the Civil War, its population increased by 208 percent, to 37,600.[11]

Although these were years of great prosperity for San Antonio, the economic elite which directed this growth was not at first united because of tensions that had arisen during the war. The German community, though economically powerful, had remained distinct socially because of its reluctance to intermarry prior to the war. When the war began, the Germans refused to support the South and thus became social and political pariahs. But at the end of the war, Texas's Republican governors rewarded the loyalty of San Antonio's Germans by appointing them to most public offices. With most Democrats disenfranchised, Germans dominated the board of aldermen for nearly twenty years thereafter.[12]

San Antonio's opportunities blunted the bitterness engendered by the Civil War. In many other Southern cities the racial passions inflamed by Reconstruction drove a searing wedge into the community, but the small size of the black population of the Alamo City kept this issue from aggravating the partisan cleavage. Furthermore, business leaders on both sides saw that the town had too much potential for wealth to waste energy on infighting. Recognizing that cooperation would reap greater profits than conflict, they buried the partisan hatchet. German businessmen entered into partnerships with Anglo-French entrepreneurs to promote San Antonio's growth. The railroad to Galveston provides a prime example of this cooperation. The Frenchmen François Guilbeau and Honoré Grenet joined Germans James H. Kampmann and Ed Steves and Anglo Willy Harvey Maverick, among others, to promote that railroad. Similarly, the city's earliest streetcar company, authorized in 1874, was jointly owned by a number of influential Germans and Anglos. Spurred on by San Antonio's opportunities, the various factions within the elite—Germans, Anglos, and French, Republicans and Democrats—began to cooperate for their mutual benefit.[13]

The Socioeconomic Elite and Politics, 1877–1914

At about the same time San Antonio began its post–Civil War expansion, other cities in the country started to industrialize rapidly. These cities, mostly midwestern and certain smaller northeastern centers, had begun, much like San Antonio, as mercantile outposts. But following the Civil War, their entrepreneurs began to invest in new industrial processes and products that the dominant merchants of the time largely ignored. Soon the new industrial cities established independent economic bases, began to grow rapidly, and expanded their own hinterlands dramatically. But the South, laboring with Reconstruction, one-crop agriculture, discriminatory freight rates, and eventually, ownership of many key means of production by northern investors, failed to experience comparable industrial urbanization.[14] San Antonio's growth during this period occurred as a secondary mercantile development coupled with some industrial expansion. The expanded commercial activity, beef shipping and packing, brewing, tourism, and the maintenance of an important U.S. Army post provided the most vital sectors of the city's economy—sufficient for rapid growth but not for substantial, independent, and self-sustaining capital accumulation.

Having invested so much effort and money in promoting prosperity, the city's now quite unified socioeconomic elite sought to protect its status. Their position in the community momentarily insured that their interest would be served, but any changes in San Antonio's economy which shifted development away from the primary concerns of the elite, or threatened to undermine the city's competitive position *vis-à-vis* Houston and Dallas required attention. Hence their concern about politics.

San Antonio's social and economic leaders seem to have had little taste for day-to-day political life. Corruption, for example, never appeared as a major issue in local politics before 1915. Police protection of prostitutes and gamblers' participation in political affairs seems to have passed largely unnoticed. Nor did battles over patronage greatly concern the city's leading citizens. But the members of the upper class did concern themselves with public policies that affected the city's ability to grow and to prosper. Factions within the elite occasionally differed about particular policies, but they generally agreed upon the necessity for political programs which would perpetuate their self-interests—which they regarded as equivalent to the best interests of San Antonio.

The original Republic-era structure of local politics served well for many years primarily because San Antonio's first important machine politician, Bryan Callaghan II, created an organization which could implement policies favored by the city's socioeconomic leaders. His credentials for San Antonio politics were nearly impeccable. Callaghan not only had the language requirements—he was fluent in Spanish, French, German, and English—but he also had the requisite social background and commitment to urban growth. His parents, Bryan Callaghan and Concepción Ramón, belonged to the socioeconomic elite. Callaghan, Sr., had been a dry goods merchant, alderman, and mayor in 1845. His wife was descended from original settlers of the region. Bryan Callaghan II married Adele Guilbeau, daughter of a family whose patriarch belonged to the same mercantile elite. These family connections not only cemented Callaghan's social standing among the city's best citizens, but also made him popular among lower-class Mexicans, who regarded him, as they had his father, as their patron. This honor was no small matter, since Mexican-Americans constituted the largest voting block in San Antonio before 1900.[15]

Ties to the upper class and to an important segment of the city's lower classes gave Callaghan a solid base for a political career. He enhanced this position by his attitudes toward progress. Recognizing that San Antonio needed a large number of public improvements if it were to fulfill its economic promise, he advocated urban service development, a program welcomed by the city's elite.[16] Callaghan's political machine—a multiethnic, multiclass organization which was nominally Democratic—took shape between 1885 and 1889, as Callaghan used his powers as mayor to build a traditional organization based on patronage for the faithful and solid policies for the elite. Miles of streets were paved and lighted; franchises for streetcar companies were granted; fire hydrants were installed in business and some residential areas. Callaghan also paid attention to symbols of urban pride and progress: he built a handsome new city hall, moving the government from shabby quarters referred to locally as "the cave,"[17] and later built the new Bexar County Courthouse. Although the city was growing rapidly, thereby expanding the potential tax revenues, Callaghan preferred to stimulate growth by keeping taxes low while he borrowed against the future. Bond issues and loans from local banks (at unregulated interest rates) financed the expansion of urban services, while city funds were often held in interest-free accounts.[18]

Although he was an adroit politician and a near-perfect embodiment of socioeconomic elite interests, Callaghan could not always satisfy everyone. Nor could he control the impact of larger issues and trends, which began to unsettle local politics in the 1890s. Fissures began to appear as some social and business leaders criticized his spending policies as profligate, while others, paradoxically, felt Callaghan was not doing enough. Tourism, for instance, was becoming increasingly important to the city's economy, but Callaghan neglected San Antonio's growing health problems by neglecting to improve the sewer system. Epidemics in the eighties and nineties endangered both the local populace and the growing tourist industry and alienated leading doctors.[19]

Moreover, the ethnic balance of San Antonio shifted during the nineties. With further urban growth, more Anglos than ever before poured into the city, and by 1900 they had become the dominant ethnic group. Their culture and values differed from those of the ethnic groups with whom Bryan Callaghan had worked. For example, by the 1890s much of the substantial new Anglo ethnic bloc was Baptist and favored prohibition. The temperance advocates hoped by prohibiting liquor to purify the behavior of certain "undesirables"—especially Mexicanos and Germans—who refused to conform to their stiff-necked definition of "normal" Victorian middle-class morality. Prohibition thus pitted Baptists against Catholics and Anglos against Germans and Mexican-Americans, providing a basis for community factionalism that Callaghan ultimately could not control.

These problems made the nineties a difficult decade for "Boss" Callaghan. When he resigned as mayor in 1893 to assume a county judgeship, his organization lost the mayoralty to Dr. George Paschal, scion of one of the city's first Anglo families. Paschal and his supporters attacked Callaghan's free-wheeling spending priorities and neglect of health and sanitation needs. These reformers, embodying a fundamental division of the previously unified elite, adopted more conservative funding procedures and shifted priorities to previously neglected urban services. They managed to hold office for four years before Callaghan recaptured the mayor's office in 1897. Callaghan's victory was tenuous: he won only a plurality, not a majority, of the votes cast in a race among four candidates.

The problems of 1897 spelled doom for Callaghan in 1899. In that election the elite's anti-Callaghan coalition mobilized Republicans and county politicians. Callaghan developed another problem when, to repay a political debt, he supported the gubernatorial candidacy of James Hogg, who had the reputation of being protemperance. This pared away Callaghan's support from his traditional Mexican and German ethnic allies because of their antitemperance sentiments. Finally, Callaghan's organization had not kept abreast of demographic changes in the city's most rapidly growing wards, where a lack of organization caused him to lose votes and forced the "Boss" to retire from active leadership for the next six years.[20]

Callaghan's defeat, however, did not mean that San Antonio's social and economic elite had lost its influential role in local politics. Quite the contrary. The group that defeated him in 1899 drew its leadership from the ranks of the city's best citizens. Unlike the reformers of 1893, however, these men were not opposed to Callaghan's urban policies and fiscal ideas, for they also advocated a broad-ranging program of improvements and liberal spending policies. They had eventually come to differ with Callaghan, however, because he remained committed to decentralized, ward-based politics, and they, in response to national progressive reform ideas, were beginning to favor centralization.[21]

It is not clear why ward-based politics lost the support of the elite of San Antonio. One crucial reason may have had to do with the shifting composition of the city's socioeconomic leadership. The elite was not a static group. As the city grew, the economic elite acquired new members from among recent arrivals whose business and social activities conformed to accepted patterns of behavior. Marshall Hicks, the successful candidate for mayor in 1899, was a product of this recruiting process. Hicks had lived in San Antonio only since 1895. A lawyer, he became involved in an extensive real estate business soon after his arrival. Like many of the Anglos who moved into San Antonio in the 1890s, he was a college-educated, native Texas Baptist. His values, emphasizing law and order, efficiency in business and government, and a dislike for Catholicism and foreign immigrants, were new ideas which established members of the elite had to accommodate because of the growing economic and political power of Hicks' ethnic group.[22]

From 1899 to 1905 reformers like Hicks directed city affairs and sought to increase honesty, efficiency, and centralization of power. They created an independent, nonpartisan school board and a police and fire commission staffed by persons elected separately from other city officials. Performance and disclosure rules governing the financial activities of various city departments sought to insure more faithful, open conduct. These reforms struck at the complex interrelationships of ward politics by undermining the basis for compromise and favoritism characteristic of that system. Practices like Callaghan's habit of awarding contracts to his friends while he served simultaneously as mayor and president of the school board would presumably no longer be possible.[23]

The campaign to change the city's political system so that it would serve the interests of the business community more efficiently received a severe jolt in 1905. Callaghan returned to the public arena with a vengeance, winning the campaign for mayor at the head of an organization whose voting prowess rivalled its record prior to 1893. The precise nature of Callaghan's political activities between 1899 and 1905 is very obscure, but he and his supporters had obviously not been idle. Yet, the new political elite of 1905–1912 had changed markedly in its class origins. Unlike his first machine, the Boss's second organization drew its leadership from the working and small business sectors: there were plumbers, electricians, and even a barbecue stand operator, but very few of the socioeconomic elite. This machine's philosophy was also markedly different from its predecessor's. Perhaps reflecting the parochial concerns of his supporters, and unchecked by the necessity to heed the interests of the now-excluded social and economic leadership, Callaghan had become an advocate of moderate fiscal policies and pay-as-you-go urban improvements. The new machine, in other words, espoused ideas which directly contradicted the interests of San Antonio's economic leaders.[24]

Callaghan's resurrection could not have come at a worse time from the standpoint of the city's socioeconomic leaders. San Antonio had become the largest city in Texas, and new citizens and businesses flowed into the city in increasing numbers. The city's population increased 81 percent between 1900 and 1910, to a total of 96,517. Those newcomers represented myriad opportunities to those who controlled real estate development, housing construction, bank loans to new businesses, and other aspects of the local economy. Growth had brought prosperity, and typically, the two phenomena had become interchangeable to those most directly interested. Presumably, lack of growth would result in lack of prosperity. Less tangible considerations also figured into the growth-prosperity equation. San Antonio had its prestige and pride to maintain; the state's largest city needed to act her part. Inadequate urban services threatened San Antonio's continued growth, prosperity, and status.

But inadequate services is what Callaghan's organization provided. By 1911 his street improvement record was becoming a symbol of the problem inherent in Callaghan's moderate spending program. Nearly half of the city's 410 miles of paved roads had been paid for out of private funds. Between 1907 and 1911 real estate developers had opened forty-six new suburban areas. All the utilities which served these areas, including paved streets, sidewalks, sewers, and gas mains, had been installed by the developers and donated to the city. Private initiatives in creating conditions for orderly urban growth had far outstripped those of urban government. Citizens were laying streets, sewer lines, and gas mains at the rate of 52-1/2 miles per year while the city was building only 19-1/2 miles of these services per year. The downtown—center and symbol of San Antonio's progress—suffered from poor streets and congestion.[25]

Callaghan viewed this situation with an equanimity which indicated he now had a less grandiose vision of San Antonio's future than did the elite. He thought the prospects for economic development were less than they had been in 1900 and stressed the need for low taxes, a good credit rating, and fewer bond elections. Steady growth and fiscal conservatism now typified the machine's outlook for San Antonio. So long as the city remained under the organization's control, the prospects for continued growth and prosperity looked dim.[26]

Some members of San Antonio's social and economic elite set out to rectify this situation. Thomas L. Conroy, a director of the Civic Improvement League, member of the Real Estate Commission, and director of the Publicity League of the Chamber of Commerce, founded the Commission Government League in February 1911. Conroy's initiative, supported by several others, splintered the socioeconomic leadership of the city. The Commission League, and the Citizen's Party which grew from it, were not simply ploys to attack Callaghan and his organization in a traditional sense. Rather, these reformers proposed to change the local political system, an idea which apparently made many important people uneasy. Powerful figures in the Chamber of Commerce, local banks, and politics abandoned their pro- or anti-Callaghan stands over the commission issue. W. A. Wurzbach, a former party chairman for Callaghan, switched to the Citizen's Party; J. H. Kirkpatrick, an important realtor, businessman, and opponent of Callaghan, now became one of the mayor's supporters; Ferdinand Herff, Jr., vice-president of the San Antonio National Bank and previously city treasurer under Callaghan, now moved into the Citizen's Party camp. In founding the League, Conroy had polarized the economic elite over the issue of decentralized, democratic government, and it was clear that a significant proportion of that group had only tenuous loyalty to that system.[27]

The battle over the structure of urban government lasted three years. Opponents of the commission idea rallied around Callaghan. The mayor was forced to call a special election in February 1911 to put the issue before the voters, but he conducted a vigorous campaign to defeat the reformers. Interest in this election ran high, indicating that many recognized the issue's importance. Voters turned out in record numbers—exceeding any previous municipal election—and Callaghan's organization won by 168 votes out of 14,292 cast. One critical element in his victory may have been the special police Callaghan appointed to watch the polls. They arrested fifty-five persons—all commission supporters.[28]

Backers of the commission idea viewed this defeat as a temporary setback and planned to wrest the mayoralty from Callaghan in the spring elections. J. E. Webb, a leading spokesman for commission government, challenged

Callaghan, and the Citizen's Party fielded a full slate of aldermanic candidates. Callaghan won in another record-turnout election, but just squeaked by in the canvass. The mayor had lost the Anglo wards, but his organization produced an impressive vote in the working-class, Mexican-American areas. Although Webb lost, several of his party's aldermanic candidates defeated Callaghan supporters.[29] City council debates became considerably more acrimonious after the spring of 1911, as proponents of civic improvements and commission government harassed the mayor.

Acrimony, however, did not produce a commission form of government. The stalemate in council, which aggravated the city's service problems for one year, ended when Callaghan's death in July 1912 removed the most effective opponent of change. After a decent pause to honor one of San Antonio's most powerful and charismatic figures, commission supporters resumed their campaign to unseat the lower-middle-class political leaders and their conservative policies. In the spring elections of 1913, Clinton Brown, businessman, prominent attorney, and heir of the founder of the Alamo National Bank, headed a ticket pledged to solve the city's problems through bond issues and a commission government. Brown did not specify just what improvements he favored. Rather, he asked the voters to give him a mandate for change and trust him to do the right thing. This open-ended approach allowed the social and economic elites and a majority of voters to rally around Brown, and the reformers triumphed.[30]

Once in office, Brown pushed vigorously for civic improvements, but he ignored the issue of structural change. Late in 1913, advocates of commission government began agitating for an elected committee to write a new charter for San Antonio based on the commission government system. Brown and his supporters, who had more interest in urban services than in a commission government, decided that this demand could be manipulated to obtain their goals *and* to perpetuate their power.[31] Brown moved quickly to control the direction and content of reform. Ignoring the request for an elected committee, Brown had the city council appoint its own committee to consider commission government. He sidestepped criticism of this procedure by inviting the principal proponents of reform to help draw up the council committee's report. That report became the basis for the February 1914 election, which approved a commission government for San Antonio. Curiously enough, however, all the major ideas which advocates of commission government suggested were dropped from the final report. For example, instead of presenting the voters with a completely new city charter, Brown and his supporters offered them a series of long, technical, and sometimes contradictory amendments to the charter. In the election itself, the complete text of each amendment did not appear on the ballot, and no copies of complete texts were available for public perusal. Civil service, an idea dear to progressive hearts, was not even mentioned in the final report. Brown apparently had no intention of abandoning patronage politics as long as he controlled the city government. Nor did he intend to dilute his powers. The mayor retained substantial authority in the new government—a situation at odds with the commission idea. Among his most important powers was a veto over financial expenditures, a provision which gave him a powerful voice in the direction of civic improvements. Finally, Brown's supporters ignored a proposal that commissioners could not serve more than two terms. Rotation in office thus went the way of other basic reforms which would have undermined the power of advocates of progress and growth.[32]

In sum, the change to a commission government concentrated power in a few hands without most of the attendant restrictions in its use which were characteristic of such progressive reforms elsewhere in Texas and the nation. This betrayal of their intentions caused the original proponents of reform considerable grief. Brown had outmanuevered them as skillfully as Callaghan had ever done, hoisting them by their own petard by offering the form but not the substance of commission government. Factionalism continued within the elite, but there were too few purists with too little practical influence or power to defeat Brown. He advocated growth, civic improvements, and "reform" in a package so attractive as to distract the public from his opponents' ideas. Under Brown's guidance, city government was once more responding to the elite's needs with policies which promoted growth and prosperity. Minor differences over particular ideas seemed less relevant than that overriding consideration.

The Commission Machine and Its Challengers, 1914–41

The commission government reformers promoted progress through better services but did not long retain control of local politics. They were soon replaced by lower-status professional politicians, many from the Callaghan days. For example, Clinton Brown was succeeded in 1919 by San Antonio immigrant John W. Tobin, former Callaghan alderman, fire chief, city treasurer, and Democratic sheriff of Bexar County. Tobin was followed in turn by another former county machine politician and small businessman, C. M. Chambers, and then by C. K. Quin, also a professional politician. Albert Steves, of the economically powerful old German family and a stalwart at-large anti-Callaghan councilman for years, was the first police and fire commissioner (1915–18). He was succeeded by Democratic professional politician Phil Wright, who retained the post until 1938. Wright had come to San Antonio in 1887 and became a fireman, eventually rising through the machine's ranks to become fire chief.[33]

Similarly, reformers Clinton Kearney (1915–19) and L. Heuermann (1919–23) served as the first two street commissioners, to be succeeded by former bartender Paul E. Steffler, who retained office until 1947. Saloon keeper J. R. Lambert, formerly a strong Callaghan supporter, was elected commissioner of parks and sanitation from the outset in 1915. Ex-Callaghan men apparently also controlled the tax commissioner's post. James Garland (1915–19) had been city assessor under the old machine. In 1923 voters elected as tax commissioner Frank Bushick, a gambler and professional politician, who would serve until 1948.

Thus, within a decade, the socioeconomic elite's reformist leaders had been supplanted by professional politicians of lower-status backgrounds, many of them immigrants to the city. This group then developed with county politicos yet another city-county political ring. By 1925, the class basis of the political elite had shifted once again. The social and economic leaders, perhaps through complacency or a loss of self-awareness, had relinquished their political control to representatives of a different class. The main interest of these professional politicians was to perpetuate themselves in office. Their instrument for doing so was patronage, its use facilitated in both governments by the lack of civil service systems and by the commissioners' control of city and county public employment.[34]

The votes needed to retain control of such powers were manipulated through several devices: (1) In order to obtain a government job, one had to demonstrate to his potential employer that he had poll tax receipts—not only for himself, but for as many other people as possible (family members and friends). (2) The ring padded the city and county payrolls with superfluous personnel, used mainly to vote for the machine. (3) Voting as ordered by one's boss was a condition for retaining employment; sympathetic poll watchers could verify compliance. (4) Machine operatives would sometimes collect poll tax receipts from employees and vote in their stead. (5) At times the dead left the graveyard to haunt the polls. (6) Political "influentials" were cultivated; among them, Charles Bellinger, black gambler and bootlegger, who built a network of manipulable votes through poll tax purchases and gifts to churches whose pastors shepherded their flocks where Bellinger wished on election day. Bellinger thus mobilized votes in exchange for official blindness toward his illicit businesses.[35]

San Antonio prospered during the early years of commission government. The socioeconomic and political elite, following a tradition already fifty years old, assiduously and successfully persuaded the federal government to expand its military posts. This strategy gave a continuous boost to the economy as Fort Sam Houston grew, first during the Mexican Revolution and even more during the First World War. Also during the war, the Army Air Corps established its training center at Fort Sam Houston; the corps later moved to Randolph Field, a site donated by the city.[36] Brewing, cottage-industry pecan shelling, light manufacturing, and meat packing were the city's major industries. Larger structural trends presented obstacles to rapid industrialization, however, and ultimately caused the city's growth to falter. During the two decades prior to 1920, Houston's entrepreneurs had promoted the state's major rail hub in that city, and by 1914 the Houston Ship Channel was completed. These initiatives, when combined with the dynamic growth of the East Texas oil fields, transformed Houston into a late-blooming industrial center.[37]

With the expansion of the Houston economic hinterland, San Antonio's growth flagged. By 1930 San Antonio's population had risen to 231,542, but it rose by only 22,000 over the next decade, as Houston and Dallas quickly surpassed it. During the next ten years San Antonio's economy failed to support adequately the city's population. Poverty afflicted many of the city's residents, concentrating disproportionately among Mexican Americans and blacks, a grim legacy that continues to this day. (See Chapter 3.) The Depression greatly aggravated the city's poverty,[38] because San Antonio lacked strong financial and industrial links to the burgeoning oil industry that cushioned the effect of hard times on other Texas cities. Lacking oil-related jobs, the city's laboring class sank into worsening poverty.[39]

The commission ring was unable to cope adequately with even mundane public service problems, not to mention the effects of a national depression. Members of the ring, as representatives of the lower middle class, apparently lacked the concern for rational planning and service development that has traditionally marked the economic elite's defense of its interests. Furthermore, as professional politicians, the ring tended to regard the delivery of services mainly as an instrument for promoting its own longevity—to be manipulated to curry support—rather than as a tool for promoting urban development. In consequence, the rapid population growth of the 1920s had greatly taxed the quality of basic public services. During the 1930s several disputes arose over the city's providing free fire and police protection and sewer service to unincorporated suburbs, and over the declining quality of services provided by privately owned gas and electric utilities.[40]

Dissatisfaction with this state of affairs began to sharpen among the socioeconomic elite, eventually taking the form of a campaign for honest government. Against the backdrop of machine politics, economic stagnation, and the growing service malaise, a group of San Antonio business leaders raised once again the banner of municipal reform. An independent tabloid, *The Bexar Facts,* appeared in late 1929 denouncing the corruption of the city-county ring: "The Bexar County machine can give Tammany Hall of New York lessons when it comes to holding crooked elections."[41] At about the same time the *San Antonio Light,* a Hearst paper, began publication, presenting an independent critical voice (the *Express* and its sister publication, the *News,* consistently supported the machine in this period).[42] In 1930 several business leaders began to organize, among them Walter W. McAllister, owner of the San Antonio Building and Loan Association (now San Antonio Savings Association), and Maury Maverick, a young attorney and real estate developer-builder who, despite his solid elite status, had strong populist proclivities. An informal committee, known as the Wednesday Club for its midweek meetings at the Menger Hotel, served as a brain trust for the incipient reformers. The Wednesday Club gave birth to a larger organization known as the San Antonio Citizens League, the electoral arm of the elite.[43]

The league first tilted with the machine in 1930 for the school trustee elections and then over a $5 million bond proposal, losing the first but winning the second narrowly despite extensive fraud.[44] Citizens League leaders, "all substantial citizens, business man types,"[45] then began a modestly successful challenge to machine candidates in city, county, and legislative races from 1931 to 1936, electing Frost Woodhull as county judge, Albert Hauser as sheriff, and Robert Uhr and Albert Maverick, Jr., as commissioners.[46] A very loose coalition fueled mainly by antimachine sentiment, the league saw several of its early allies drift over to the ring, including Commissioner Uhr and eventually Sheriff Hauser.[47] Thus, this upper-class reform coalition never achieved great unity of purpose. The Citizens League, having forced the machine to clean up and become somewhat more responsive and circumspect, disintegrated in 1936 when members split over policies concerning organized gambling and a two-term limit for league officeholders.[48]

Frustrated from 1931 through 1935 in its struggle to make inroads on the municipal government through the Citizens League, the Wednesday Club continued its efforts, eventually coming close to its goal in the late thirties. One of the committee's ends was to "bring about change and improvements in city government through charter revision"[49]—specifically, to implement the council-manager form of government. Commission government was criticized as ineffective because commissioners failed to promote technical expertise in their departments and hired unqualified employees through patronage.[50]

The Wednesday Club turned to the fiery Maury Maverick as the key to placing a council-manager charter revision before the city's voters. Maverick had defeated machine mayor C. K. Quin in the 1934 race for Congress, but Quin and the machine had settled the score by ousting Maverick in 1938. Later that year, the machine was unable to suppress indictments for election irregularities against Mayor Quin, weakening the organization's hold. Backed by the Wednesday Club, Maverick in 1939 ran for mayor on the Fusion ticket. Maverick stressed the need for clean and efficient government and for wiping out the ring. The reformers prevailed, putting Maverick in the mayor's seat and electing three of four commissioners.[51]

Maverick's term as mayor set a model for municipal reform for San Antonio. He revamped city records, tax assessment, and tax collection; reformed the sanitation, police, and fire departments; made important health and hygiene advances; and rebuilt La Villita, a small group of buildings constructed by early San Antonio settlers.[52] Maverick's administration was controversial, however, and he had many political enemies. His apparent "radicalism" and his failure to back charter reform proved fatal to his career as mayor. Although he placed a council-manager charter revision on the city ballot in 1940 as promised, Maverick reportedly ordered city employees to oppose the change, causing it to lose narrowly. This killed the charter reform effort for years because the war broke out soon afterward. Seeking revenge, the Wednesday Club aligned with conservative county Democrats and old city machine pols to back former mayor C. K. Quin, who defeated Maverick in his bid for a second mayoral term in 1941. The result, ironically, was the speedy rebuilding of the city-county ring that the upper-class reformers had so long opposed.[53] Much to the reformers' chagrin, the machine had received a ten-year reprieve.

Postwar Reform and the Good Government League, 1946–75

During the Great Depression and World War II, major changes in the national economy created conditions favorable to an economic revitalization for San Antonio. The desire of the federal government to stimulate recovery coincided with the need of the southern cities for major improvements as a precondition for new development. The power of southern congressional delegations, combined with the New Deal's growth policies during the 1930s to direct massive amounts of public capital into the South and Southwest, stimulated rapid growth. The region's cheap land and labor, low taxes, and lack of unions began to attract new private industrial investment. Expenditures for defense plants during World War II directed more federal monies into the Sunbelt, with dramatic multiplier effects. Finally, the most dynamic new industries of the mid-twentieth century found the Sunbelt advantageous: "In the post war phase of capital accumulation, six new pillars of growth—agriculture, defense, advanced technology, oil and natural gas, real estate and construction, and tourism and leisure—emerged as the dominant industries. All have chosen a Sunbelt location."[54]

San Antonio's problems before the war now became advantages. Located in the heart of the Sunbelt, the city became heir to the opportunities inherent in its location, so that the development strategies the socioeconomic elite had followed since the 1870s—encouragement of tourism and military establishments—suddenly and dramatically bore fruit. Despite the inability of the major businessmen to control city government during the thirties and forties, their economic initiatives began to pay off.

Tourism, long an important industry, was heartily encouraged by the local upper class. The resurrection of the Alamo and its transformation into a tourist attraction served as a model for subsequent efforts. Led by some of the city's wealthiest matrons, the San Antonio Conservation Society began rescuing such landmarks as the city's missions and the Spanish governor's palace. Federal government assistance from the Works Progress Administration and the National Youth Administration, attracted in part through Maury Maverick's ties to the New Deal, led to the construction of the San Antonio River Walk and the reconstruction of La Villita.[55]

While some manufacturing activity developed during this era, economic elites were quite particular about its character. For instance, during the 1930s Ford Motor Company had sought to build a factory in the city, but was rebuffed, reportedly owing to local businessmen's militant fear of organized labor and their concern that such "smokestack" production would damage tourism.[56] But though highly unionized heavy manufacturing was discouraged, wartime investment increased manufacturing plants by 50 percent (the work force in manufacturing nevertheless rose only to a low 12 percent).

The presence of a major U.S. Army post and the location of nearly all Air Corps training in San Antonio transformed the city's economy during the war. The Chamber of Commerce's military affairs committee lobbied energetically and successfully to expand military installations in the city. Civilian jobs on these bases attracted waves of immigrants, and during the 1940s the population jumped from 253,854 to 406,442.[57] Such growth produced tremendous suburbanization as new housing sprawled outside the incorporated city limits.

These changes reinforced the local economic elite's historic commitments to stimulating manufacturing, to boosting tourism, and to promoting the service sector. Though perhaps overstating the case somewhat, Arnold Fleischmann captures the spirit of the period: "San Antonio's economic boosters . . . put all their economic eggs in the basket of the burgeoning service economy."[58] There were other service-related efforts: to expand the city's air and surface links to Latin America and to attract a medical school. Trinity University was persuaded to relocate in San Antonio in 1942. A planning board, chaired by a major builder-developer, was established in 1944 and pushed for development of a coliseum, freeways, airport expansion, and public service improvements.[59]

Wartime growth transformed the service problems of the late 1930s into nightmares. The machine, notorious already for poor delivery of services, failed to improve things. Since 1930 so little new territory had been annexed by the city that much of the city's new growth had occurred in poorly planned, unincorporated suburbs which did not provide adequate services. Such service problems, combined with an apparent effort to segregate housing and schools (see Chapter 7), led to a suburban incorporation movement during the forties that threatened San Antonio's future growth and tax base. During the late 1940s the city did annex many of the suburban developments to defend its tax base and forestalled the expansion of other Bexar County municipalities. However, the city government failed to bring services in the newly annexed areas up to par. Problems with electric, gas, water, and sewer services continued, and residents grew increasingly angry.[60]

In response to these problems, reform-oriented community leaders, frustrated in 1941 and stymied by the war, began to regroup. Walter McAllister formed yet another group, the Council-Manager Association of San Antonio, and in 1946 the struggle was joined again. Led by hotelier Jack White, Chamber of Commerce president Charles Harrell, the owner of a large bookbinding enterprise, and McAllister, the association called for reform. When then-mayor Alfred Callaghan (son of Bryan Callaghan II) refused in 1948 to place a council-manager charter revision proposed before the voters, White ran against him as a council-manager advocate. In the campaign, White emphasized the need for progress, governmental efficiency, and service improvements. Accusing the machine of ineptitude, White called for hospital expansion, a massive health program, neighborhood improvements, a fumigation program, improvement of virtually all municipal services, disclosure of city spending, and industrial growth. Two further key issues reveal the concerns of White's backers. He demanded equal city services for newly annexed areas, a clarion call for orderly urban development. This issue was critical to real estate developers and their local investors. White also noted that San Antonio had lagged behind other Texas cities in its progress, as the gap between the city's large population and its still underdeveloped economy and public service infrastructure amply demonstrated.[61] Callaghan's counterattack correctly assessed the nature of his opposition: he urged the voters to "keep the city out of the hands of millionaires."[62] White won handily, but for two years faced a city commission hostile to his purposes. In 1951 White and his backers attacked the ring again, this time supported by a full slate of pro–council-manager commission candidates. All the machine's incumbents lost resoundingly, and a popular referendum for charter revision passed overwhelmingly. A charter revision commission (to be chaired by W. W. McAllister)[63] was also elected. Proceeding swiftly, the Charter Revision Commission placed a council-manager charter before the voters in October 1951, winning by a two-to-one margin.[64]

The new council chose Charles Harrell, stalwart toiler with McAllister for council-manager government, as the new city manager.[65] Moving swiftly to modernize city government, the council installed thousands of street signs, updated tax rolls, implemented a water conservation ordinance, expanded public health services, and annexed a whopping eighty square miles of new territory, doubling the municipality's total area.[66] But brambles soon appeared in the garden of reform. First, the annexations angered two oilmen whose estates were included; their opposition drove a wedge into the reform movement. Furthermore, as had happened previously with Mayors Bryan Callaghan II, Clinton Brown, and Maury Maverick, the mayor quickly grew fond of his power and tried to enhance it. The goals of the reform clique appeared threatened as White struggled with manager Harrell, seeking to centralize power in the mayor's hands, with the manager serving as a mere assistant. The dispute soon turned bitter; the reformers accused White of attempting to build a new machine. By the 1953 elections, Mayor White, now backed by many former commission machine figures and with $100,000 for his campaign from the anti-annexation faction, led a victorious slate of council candidates who advocated reviving commission government.[67]

Reacting swiftly to save council-manager government and its rationalization of planning and service delivery, the reformers chose a new strategy.

They knew that earlier "reform" mayors had proven reluctant to carry through their promises once in power, and that service- and tax-stingy machines had risen as phoenixes from the ashes of reform. Experience had made the elite distrustful of structural changes and the steadfastness of their cohorts' commitments to promoting continued growth. This distrust led to a major structural innovation in city politics. For the first time, reformers created a permanent political organization to transform a history of sporadic and transitory successes into longer-lasting control. President of the Chamber of Commerce Tom L. Powell convened sixty citizens in his home on December 7, 1954. Of these, 43 percent were owners of businesses, 17 percent were attorneys, 14 percent other professionals and clergymen. Three were heads of local business associations. The vast majority lived in the silk-stocking neighborhoods of the north side. Many were veterans of the Council-Manager Association, and over one-fourth had belonged to the Citizens League and Wednesday Club. This assembly voted to create the Good Government League, aimed at ensuring "stability and integrity in city government"[68] by defending nonpartisan council-manager government from White and his allies.

The Good Government League (GGL) quickly expanded its membership to 3,000 from diverse social strata, though most came from the city's prosperous north side, and even from the wealthy enclave municipalities of Olmos Park, Alamo Heights, and Terrill Hills. Despite its large membership, the organization's true power was concentrated in two groups: (1) the Board of Directors, whose members constituted "the economic and social elite of San Antonio";[69] and (2) the secret Nominating Committee, selected by the board. These nominating committees, from 1955 to 1971, selected in secret deliberations[70] slates of candidates for city council; the GGL won 77 of 81 of these seats.[71] Overall for 1955–71, the council candidates selected consisted primarily of Anglos (78 percent), although there were a few token Mexican Americans (one in 1955, two from 1957 to 1971, and three in 1971). From 1964 on, one black was always selected as well.[72] Sixty-five percent of the GGL council members came from northern San Antonio, even many of the Mexican Americans. The typical slate consisted of managers, retailers, doctors, lawyers, developers, real estate brokers, and bankers—in short, representatives of the socially prominent and the economically powerful.[73]

The Nominating Committee would select the mayoral candidate first; he could then veto other potential candidates. All candidates had to meet four criteria: be sufficiently prosperous to devote time to serving virtually without pay; lack further political ambition; demonstrate "civic mindedness";

and represent the "community as a whole"—that is, eschew strong partisan or ethnic allegiances and work for growth and economic expansion.[74] The harmonious nature of the GGL councils thus selected has become legendary, but it was the harmony imposed and very narrowly defined by the elite-controlled nomination process.

The GGL pursued its particular vision of progress, efficiency, and development throughout its eighteen-year reign by controlling the city council and by appointing GGL members to city boards and commissions. A unified socioeconomic and political elite's interest in orderly, rational growth and municipal service efficiency were well served by a mayor, council, and (often) city manager, City Public Service Board (gas and electric utilities), City Water Board, and Planning and Zoning Commission all composed of GGL members. The organization rebuffed several challenges to its hegemony in the 1960s by combining ardent appeals to nonpartisanship with manipulation of Anglo voters' fears of political "radicals" and racial minorities.[75]

The GGL, its hegemony so complete that it merited the label of "machine" in its own right,[76] also served well the economic interests of the elite. The tactic of attracting government services and capital investments dominated the boosters' development strategy. The promotion of Hemisfair, with state and federal support, greatly enhanced downtown property values, stimulated a construction boom, and revived the city's flagging tourist industry. The extension of utility lines to suburban housing developments at city taxpayers' expense and the promotion of freeways and an urban loop greatly enhanced the attractiveness and profitability of developers' investments. A successful foray into county and state legislative offices in 1966[77] laid the groundwork for the construction of the University of Texas at San Antonio and the University of Texas Health Science Center. (See Chapter 2 on recent changes in the city's economy.)

Despite two decades of virtually uniform enthusiasm for the GGL from the San Antonio mass media, many critics eventually surfaced. They decried the GGL's lack of representativeness, frequent appeals to ethnic fears, direction of city services and improvements to the north side to the systematic neglect of older neighborhoods, the apparently self-serving nature of such ventures as Hemisfair, and the economic development priorities. The GGL's political hegemony cracked in 1971, declined in 1973, and failed altogether in 1975, when it elected only three council members—a minority—for the first time since 1955 (see Chapter 5). The GGL formally disbanded in 1976. The group's decline stemmed in part from an internal split between the city's older monied interests, increasingly concerned to maintain the deteriorating center city, and north side businessmen and suburban developers who wished to continue the northwestward expansion of the city (see Chapter 8). The north side businessmen and developers split from the GGL in the early 1970s and began to run opposing candidate slates. The *coup de grace* was delivered in early 1977 by a coalition of neighborhood organizations and ethnic groups who successfully backed a charter revision (required by the U.S. Justice Department) that created individual councilmanic districts. Council-manager government was retained. Thus, factionalism within the economic leadership of the community contributed to a great decline in its political power.

Conclusions

Since the late nineteenth century, the city's socioeconomic elite, while apparently admitting some new members with changing economic trends, has been self-perpetuating. Many of the names and families in pre–Civil War economics and politics remain prominent to this day. This elite, with its multi-ethnic roots and bipartisan character, has consistently returned to development strategies and political tactics established during the nineteenth century. The city leadership crafted a late-blooming mercantile expansion in the wake of the Civil War at the same time that other cities were growing mainly because of industrialization. Promoting military and government services and tourism has paid off during both world wars and since. Old strategies for development, once not dependable for sustained growth, have now put San Antonio squarely in the mainstream of Sunbelt growth.

In the political realm, the socioeconomic elite's irregular involvement has been heavily marked by factionalism. When professional politicians with different class interests have jeopardized elite economic interests through inept public management, "reform" efforts have developed to put things back on track. Elites have mobilized to capture public office and make structural alterations in the city's government. These efforts, however, have usually succumbed in short order because of rapid organizational atrophy and opportunism or vacillation by the reformers' elected officeholders.[78] The elite has endured corruption with grace,[79] but what *has* provoked the increasingly lengthy periods of socioeconomic elite political intervention were threats to their economic interests in the form of public service, planning, and development crises that inhibit orderly growth and "progress."

In a century and a half of urban development, the economic and political fate of the city's black and Mexican-American population has too often been ignored. As elsewhere in the United States, the costs and benefits of San Antonio's urbanization have been distributed quite unequally along ethnic and racial lines.[80] While San Antonio's overall development has been conditioned at least partly by external forces, racial inequality has been determined in great measure by local elites.

At present San Antonio's blacks and Chicanos (6 percent and 51 percent of the population, respectively) suffer much poorer occupational status, educational attainment, income, public services, school systems, political participation, and representation in public office than the dominant white population. Lack of economic and political power among the (largely) lower-class blacks and Chicanos has insured the systematic subversion of their interests in city services to the class interests of the elites.

Whites (Anglos, French, and Germans) captured control of major city and county political institutions in the second quarter of the nineteenth century, leaving Mexicanos badly underrepresented politically until 1977. Blacks, mostly slaves until after the Civil War, were victims of a more formal and repressive discrimination until the 1960s. These groups, lacking an independent political voice, served as political objects for the dominant groups. Though never disenfranchised completely, San Antonio's black voters were curried by socioeconomic elite factions only when leadership was divided over politics (for example, during the contest to unseat the first Callaghan ring).[81] In the twentieth century Charles Bellinger brokered black votes to the city and county rings mainly to protect his own illicit businesses rather than to serve black community interests. Mexican Americans provided the base for Boss Callaghan's power, but at least his paternalism meant some reciprocal obligation and patronage in exchange for support. The commission ring, however, seems to have needed the Mexicano vote much less than Callaghan owing to the increased Anglo population in the twentieth century, so that its treatment of Mexicanos was more baldly manipulative and less distributive. In general, when the socioeconomic elite's reformers held political power, the Mexican-American populace received even less from the political system than under the machines.

The classic example of how the political and economic elites have distributed rewards comes from the reformers' promises in the late 1940s and early 1950s of west side drainage projects to gain Chicano support for bond issues. Even though such funds were approved and the projects authorized, the GGL-dominated council and city administration simply never built the projects.[82] Other examples abound. Chapter 7 reveals how the San Antonio Independent School District refused to consolidate with poorer, "browner" south side districts while absorbing wealthier, "whiter" ones.

Public services have been provided in San Antonio in conformity with a "racial model," so that blacks and Mexican Americans tend to "receive access to public services only after whites receive them, and then only . . . [when] all other demands on local government have been satisfied."[83] Over the long haul the result has been a consistent pattern of service discrimination in favor of Anglo, north side, and developer interests.[84]

In the economic arena the process has been similar. Blacks and Mexicanos, politically weak and poorly educated, have been unable to achieve or maintain significant occupational status and income gains (see Chapter 3 for details). The immigrant, lower-middle-class Anglos of the late nineteenth and twentieth centuries captured city government and utilized it to promote their economic mobility. At the same time, however, they froze blacks and Mexicanos out of the same opportunities. The economic elite appears to have resisted industrialization in strongly unionized sectors and repressed labor organization[85]—two factors that might have increased lower-class incomes in San Antonio—in order to maintain firm control of the working classes and to maximize profits. Growth has been promoted through tourism, defense, and service industries which generate mainly low-skilled and low-paying jobs for local workers. In these industries skilled positions (military officers, doctors, technicians, professors) tend to be filled by Anglos imported from outside the community (see Chapter 2), rather than presenting employment opportunities for local poor people.

Overall, then, major socioeconomic inequalities within San Antonio appear to have been partly originated and largely maintained by conscious decisions of community leaders. The cumulative effects of a century and a half of such policy stand in vivid relief from even a casual glance at life on San Antonio's streets. Recent structural changes may begin slowly to reduce such inequities. But most of these political and economic transformations have been imposed upon San Antonio from outside—by civil rights legislation, changes in voting laws, and restructuring of local government. These externally imposed transformations have set in motion still others—Mexican-American neighborhood activism, realignment of political leadership, political disintegration of the socioeconomic elite, dramatic development policy shifts—that promise still further change. Subsequent chapters of this book examine aspects of San Antonio's contemporary evolution and offer analyses of where they will lead America's tenth largest city.

Richard C. Jones

Chapter Two

San Antonio's Spatial Economic Structure, 1955–80

San Antonio is a city with one foot in the East and the other in the West, figuratively speaking. It lies on the boundary between the humid subtropical and the semi-arid steppe climates, and topographically, the Balcones Escarpment cuts through its northwestern margins to separate the Blackland Prairie from the Edwards Plateau. It maintains strong economic and social ties with both regions, and these are reflected in the sources of its recent growth. Here, I shall place San Antonio within the framework of Sunbelt growth in general and Texas growth in particular, investigating both population growth and growth in employment by sector.

San Antonio's Recent Growth Trends in Regional and National Perspective

San Antonio's recent growth, in both population and employment, is not atypical of large Sunbelt cities in the Southwest and Far West. The 1970–75 population growth rate of 10.5 percent for the San Antonio standard metropolitan statistical area (SMSA) was greater than the growth rates for Dallas-Fort Worth (6.3 percent) and Oklahoma City (6.8 percent), but smaller than those for Houston (14.4 percent), Albuquerque (15.4 percent), San Diego (16.7 percent), and Phoenix (25.8 percent). San Antonio's position has, in fact, improved since 1960–70, when its rate of growth was surpassed by all of these SMSAs.[1] Though average for the Sunbelt, San Antonio's growth rate from 1970–75 was rapid relative to comparable SMSAs in the Frostbelt.[2] The city's recent population growth probably reflects the Sunbelt growth phenomenon, which is largely attributable to extraregional factors—high wages and benefits, severe climate, labor union-ism, and government regulation in the Frostbelt states. The expansion of extraregional spatial linkages is something which San Antonio shares with many other Sunbelt cities, despite the fact that San Antonio's growth sectors are different from those of, say, Phoenix or San Diego.

The fact that San Antonio is in Texas, in recent years the fastest-growing Sunbelt state, weighs in its favor, given the city's relative isolation and lack of certain industrial prerequisites. Texas's steadily improving position in Sunbelt versus Frostbelt growth is illustrated by Table 2.1. Note that the 1970–75 period was a watershed, during which the Frostbelt states suffered abrupt growth-rate declines and the Sunbelt states (with the exception of California) enjoyed abrupt increases. The phenomena were of course com-plementary and interrelated, for this period brought a *de facto* energy crisis to the United States, making heating oil suddenly very expensive for Northerners as the oil companies switched to producing gasoline, and saw a debilitating series of labor strikes (notably, affecting General Motors and its subsidiaries) which encouraged industries to mechanize and to expand their operations outside the Frostbelt. These abrupt setbacks to the so-called foundry region were overlaid upon long-term trends, which included in-creasing return migration to the South and the increasingly "footloose"

Table 2.1: Average Annual Sunbelt versus
Frostbelt Growth: Selected States, 1950–77 (U.S. = 100)

Sunbelt	1950–60	1960–70	1970–75	1975–77
Texas	126	130	202	310
New Mexico	193	58	272	241
California	236	195	129	232
Arizona	335	258	519	208
Florida	347	265	474	82
Frostbelt				
Illinois	84	82	3	58
Michigan	118	106	69	d
Ohio	117	76	20	d
Pennsylvania	44	34	3	d
New York	73	68	d	d

SOURCE: Janet Rothenberg Pack, "Frostbelt and Sunbelt: Convergence over Time," *Intergovernmental Perspective* 4 (Fall 1978): 8–15.

NOTE: The letter *d* indicates absolute decline in population (e.g., New York lost 198,000 people between 1975 and 1977).

(transport-cost free) nature of new manufacturing firms, making it possible for them to locate anywhere (thus favoring amenity locations in the South and West). By these figures, one may conclude that Texas is becoming the "belt buckle" of the Sunbelt as congestion, high costs of living, and increasingly severe governmental restrictions inflict themselves upon Florida and the Far West. In addition, recent empirical analyses place Texas in the premier position among all the states in "business climate"—a favorable tax structure, lack of unionism, and general probusiness sentiments.[3] This unprecedented industrial and population growth in Texas has *not* been equally beneficial to all groups (see Chapters 3 and 7); it has often exacerbated inequalities between and within cities. Furthermore, Texas has a relatively low ranking among the states in per capita receipt of social services and educational benefits.

Has San Antonio's recent economic growth been led by the same economic sectors as in Texas as a whole? One might think otherwise, given San Antonio's unique history, ethnic mix (which in 1975 placed Hispanics in the majority for the first time since 1845), its traditional connections to the military, and its political evolution (see Chapter 1, 4–6, and 8). San Antonio is a city dominated by retail activities, services, and government employment; these sectors constitute 70 percent of San Antonio's labor force, versus 42 percent for the state. Some of San Antonio's uniqueness is due to the large military presence (some 70,000 military and base personnel, 18 percent of the labor force, which is three times the state's level) and to its low industrial profile for a city of its size (only 12 percent of the labor force is industrial, half the state's level). Despite its unusual structure, San Antonio's economic growth patterns across sectors of the local economy are quite similar to those of Texas.[4] Overall growth in employment over the period 1956–76 was close to the state's, with Bexar County growing 110 percent to the state's 100 percent (Table 2.2). Furthermore, the twenty-four most important subsectors of the local private-sector economy[5] grew at about the same relative rates as in Texas as a whole.[6]

An analysis of some of the most important subsectors in San Antonio's economy serves to underline the local-national growth linkages (Table 2.2). Medical and health services was the most rapidly growing subsector in both San Antonio and in the state, reflecting a national trend toward increasing life expectancy, a state and Sunbelt trend toward increasing numbers of inmigrant retirees, and, locally, a stimulus from the already established military medical facilities. Phenomenal medical growth occurred in San Antonio between 1962 and 1968, with the building of the 7,500-employee South Texas Medical Center, which has seven public and private hospitals.

Table 2.2: Percentage Change in Private Sector Employment, by
Selected SIC Categories: Bexar County versus Texas, 1956–76

	Bexar County		Texas		Location Quotients for Bexar County	
	% Change	Rank	% Change	Rank	1956	1976
Oil and gas extraction	17.3	22	−19.3	24	.297	.412
Total mining	15.5		0.7		.305	.311
Building construction	69.7	14	48.1	21	1.028	1.124
Total contract construction	153.8		111.4		1.132	1.298
Food manufacturing	46.8	20	34.6	22	1.476	1.537
Apparel manufacturing	39.2	21	154.0	9	1.692	.885
Printing and publishing	64.6	16	83.1	14	1.195	1.026
Fabricated metals mfg.	259.9	4	238.1	4	.630	.641
Nonelectrical machinery	208.6	6	170.0	8	.626	.683
Total manufacturing	83.9		86.6		.639	.601
Trucking and warehousing	54.8	19	56.2	18	.943	.893
Communications	110.4	9	88.1	13	1.220	1.304
Total transportation and public utilities	59.8		58.6		.778	.748
Total wholesale	62.8		89.8		1.255	1.028
General merchandise stores	55.5	18	64.4	16	1.425	1.277
Food stores	56.6	17	65.2	15	1.410	1.277
Auto dealers/service stas.	64.9	15	52.9	20	1.048	1.078
Apparel and accessory stores	−7.8	24	64.3	17	1.930	1.034
Eating and drinking places	182.8	7	188.9	5	1.339	1.251
Total retail	84.5		92.3		1.296	1.186

Table 2.2 Continued

	Bexar County		Texas		Location Quotients for Bexar County	
	% Change	Rank	% Change	Rank	1956	1976
Banking	219.3	5	171.1	7	.979	1.037
Credit agencies	98.0	12	150.8	10	1.917	1.445
Insurance carriers	106.3	10	53.7	19	1.408	1.805
Real estate	101.2	11	175.7	6	1.586	1.105
Total finance/ insurance/real estate	118.1		125.4		1.379	1.274
Hotels and other lodging	74.4	13	92.2	12	1.521	1.318
Personal services	12.7	23	8.9	23	1.359	1.343
Business services	315.5	3	518.4	2	1.682	1.079
Auto repair	138.9	8	124.0	11	1.448	1.475
Medical and health svc.	831.8	1	700.5	1	1.089	1.211
Membership organizations	593.2	2	511.1	3	1.161	1.257
Total services	240.4		253.0		1.350	1.243
Total private sector	109.9		100.4			

SOURCE: Data from U.S. Department of Labor, *County Business Patterns: Texas,* 1956 and 1976.

NOTE: The categories given in this table are those two-digit SIC (Standard Industrial Classification) categories for which Bexar County had employment ≥ 1% of total employment in 1976, plus summary categories and total employment.

Growth in membership organizations and in business services was responsible for much of the rest of the increase in services, in both San Antonio and the state. Growth in religious organizations, civic and social organizations, research and development laboratories, real estate appraisal, managerial consulting, and building maintenance were important elements of the increase. The emergence of these activities in San Antonio marks the city's transition to a more mature city, in that they foment redistribution of income and the integration of growth within the city. Business services such as real estate appraisal and managerial consulting, for example, enable existing firms to become more efficient in competing in the local market and enable them to consolidate gains already made. The substantial growth in contract construction has been largely due to the building of roads and highways and building construction. In this sector, San Antonio's growth rate was almost 40 percent above the state's, owing to the development of its extensive expressway system (second in mileage only to Los Angeles'), to the promotion in 1968 of the international exposition Hemisfair (which refocused development on the downtown and stimulated San Antonio's flagging tourist industry), and to the development of numerous public and private building projects, among them the University of Texas at San Antonio, the South Texas Medical Center, four regional malls, and several large downtown hotels.

Although growth in manufacturing employment was slightly below the growth rate of all employment in both San Antonio and Texas, certain subsectors grew rapidly. Employment more than tripled in fabricated metals and nonelectrical machinery because of the establishment of small and medium-sized plants in such industries as oilfield supplies (e.g., Bakerline, established in 1975), refrigeration equipment (e.g., Refrigeration Engineering Corp., 1960), prestressed concrete (e.g., Wolco Corp., 1958), and aluminum cans (e.g., Pearl Container Co., 1974).[7] Again, this growth marks the maturation of the San Antonio economy, for it is indicative of a move away from raw-materials processing industries (food and textiles, apparel) to more capital-intensive, higher unit-value types of operations, which also happen to be nonpolluting to the environment.

Recent trends in San Antonio's government employment category suggest either decline or stagnation—not surprising given the emergence of specialized service and industrial sectors. Military and base personnel suffered an absolute decline of 16 percent over the period 1971–76.[8] This mirrors a national trend in which military employment has been declining since the mid-1950s, with the development of more capital-intensive weapons systems and with the winding down of the Vietnam conflict. Nevertheless, in 1977 San Antonio, with four major Air Force bases, had approximately 14 percent of all U.S. Air Force military personnel serving in the continental United States. The nonmilitary government sector has in recent years been growing at a rate just below the city's average employment growth, but this may be misleading in that an absolute decline in federal employment has been countered by a substantial growth in local government employment, much of it supported by federal funds. The latter growth represents various planning, regulatory, and other professional personnel who are being hired to address the problems attendant to San Antonio's recent growth and change in orientation to the outside world.

Location quotients (LQs) for San Antonio over the period emphasize that economically San Antonio is becoming more like Texas, while retaining several of its most distinguishing growth characteristics (Table 2.2, final two columns). The location quotient may be defined as a place's employment proportion in a given economic activity divided by the employment proportion in that activity region- or nationwide. Here, only private-sector employment is considered, and the base region is Texas. A quotient above 1.0 indicates specialization in the activity relative to Texas; a quotient less that 1.0 indicates a relative paucity of the activity; and a quotient of 1.0 indicates an average level of the activity in the place. The quotients for major sectors show that in wholesale and retail trade, financial activities, and services, San Antonio is becoming more like the state (the quotient is closer to 1.0 in 1976 than in 1956). Only in construction and manufacturing has it become dissimilar. At the subsector level, five of the six activities with LQs less than 1.0 in 1956 showed increases in 1976, while eleven of nineteen activities with LQs greater than 1.0 showed decreases. Among the eight remaining subsectors (all of which had LQs greater than 1.0 and showed increases), the growth in medical services, insurance, and membership organizations were notable, in addition to construction and food manufacturing. In other words, for the most part San Antonio's trailing subsectors began to catch up with the state's, while most of its leading subsectors slackened off, the exceptions being a few specialized subsectors which have been in the lead for many years and which have widened that lead.

To summarize, San Antonio's economic structure, though quite different from that of the state, has become more like the state's over the last twenty years. In many ways the city's growth, with a lag of a decade or so, has followed that of Dallas and Houston, which have led sectoral changes in the state. For example, whereas Dallas-Ft. Worth showed stable or declining specialization over the 1956–76 period in such established activities as banking, medicine and health, machinery, and transport-equipment manufacturing, San Antonio showed rapid growth. Spinoff from Dallas and Houston is reaching San Antonio, as evidenced by the recent entry of two large firms—Hartford Insurance Company and Tenneco (oil and gas)—into the San Antonio market, chiefly because their Dallas and Houston branches had reached full capacity or diminishing returns.[9] San Antonio is thus establishing economic ties with other regions of the country while breaking certain regional and local ties, a trend which is investigated in detail below.

This summary suggests that San Antonio's economic growth is influenced to an important degree by regional economic trends outside of its control (Sunbelt vs. Frostbelt), and by its own particular but long-standing attractions (historic image, climate, location). The city's increasing attraction for specialized services and more dynamic industry—the recent growth generators—is chiefly a function of its favorable position in a national and regional growth matrix, rather than a function of local decisions. Admittedly, local decisions—the decisions of local political and public institutions—had important influences on the timing and pace of such growth. As is pointed out elsewhere in this volume (Chapters 1, 6, and 8), Good Government League council and mayoral candidates promoted Hemisfair, the South Texas Medical Center, the University of Texas at San Antonio (UTSA), new industrial growth, and other significant projects in San Antonio over the period 1955–71. It is doubtful, however, that a different political structure would have much affected the outcome. The outside forces which promoted San Antonio's development would have been compelling to San Antonio's elite, under the GGL or any other regime. This is not to say that the GGL did not have a significant effect on the distribution and pace of growth within San Antonio.

External Linkages and Internal Growth: Theories

A city or a region cannot grow by taking in its own laundry; unless it is completely self-sufficient, it must purchase goods and services from the outside, and this requires that it pay for them with exports of its own. Those activities that generate sales on the outside are referred to as the place's *economic base,* or *export base,* because one finds that through income circulation, export base income generates income for all non–export base (residentiary) activities.[10] For a large city, export base activities have regional or national markets. A city's growth is often explained by increases in its export base; similarly, increases in export base activities are frequently indexed by a spatial broadening of the city's economic as well as social links with the outside world. Geographers use the term *situation factors* to refer to functional linkages of a place to other places.

Once the determinants of growth have been identified in a place, the focus shifts to how this growth is distributed across its economic sectors and over the physical space within the place. There are several models of land-use change in cities, but perhaps the best verified is that of Homer Hoyt.[11] Hoyt argued that land-use changes in large American cities are characterized by outward expansion within relatively homogenous spatial sectors (wedges), beginning just beyond the central business district. These spatial sectors follow major transport arteries. The leading activity (that which focuses growth along an artery in the first place) according to Hoyt is high-quality residential development. Hoyt listed several factors which influence the initial location of high-grade residential areas, which in turn influence the direction of subsequent growth in the city:

1. The fastest existing transportation lines.
2. The existence of open country (uncrowded, scenic) and/or higher land (free from flooding, scenic).
3. The residential choice of community leaders.
4. Cumulative forces, such as the location of office buildings and deluxe apartments in an area, and the actions of real estate promoters, in directing growth along certain arteries.

Geographers refer to such elements as *site factors,* since they pertain to locational considerations within a place. The purpose of the following two sections is to look at San Antonio's external linkages and internal spatial structure in these terms. The implicit hypotheses are (1) that San Antonio has reached out farther into Texas and into the United States between the mid-1950s and the present, and (2) that San Antonio's internal growth has followed spatial sectors radiating outward from the city center. It needs to be emphasized that support of the first hypothesis is only circumstantial evidence that San Antonio's economic base is expanding. Nevertheless, an expanding export base and a larger areal field of influence frequently go hand-in-hand.

Changing External Linkages for San Antonio: Selected Indices

Richard Andrews classified basic economic activities into two categories: the movement of services, goods, or capital to the consumer or purchaser; and the movement of the consumer or purchaser to services, goods, or capital.[12] This flow can take many forms, each of which is economically basic for a city. For example:

1. *Services:* the inflow of consumers taking advantage of a city's educational and health services; the inflow of tourists in response to the attractions in a city; the inflow of consumers taking advantage of various personal services provided by the city.

2. *Goods:* the outflow of finished manufactured goods to an external market; the inflow of consumers purchasing goods in retail establishments.
3. *Capital:* the inflow of transfer payments (e.g., retirement, welfare) from outside the community.

Table 2.A1 (at the end of this chapter) lists several indices of San Antonio's external spatial linkages over time and ties them to the theoretical concepts above. Because of difficulties in getting truly representative and comprehensive data, the indices are only imperfect reflections of the concepts. Nevertheless, analysis of the indices, in the following tables and maps, reveals some striking changes in San Antonio's role as a national and regional center.

Consider first the example of an educational service sought by "customers" traveling to San Antonio—Trinity University. This private school, whose enrollment had increased to 3,400 by the fall of 1979, is not necessarily representative of all universities in San Antonio, but no single school in the city would fulfill this criterion. Between 1957 and 1978, the major portion of the increase which occurred in out-of-state enrollments was concentrated in the Southeast and South Central regions of the country. Less significant increases derived from the states of the manufacturing belt and the Southwest. An explanation for the relatively lesser attraction for students in the farther states may be that Trinity has gone from a Presbyterian-affiliated school drawing a special cohort of students from all across the country to a quality liberal arts school competing with similar schools in the other parts of the country. Thus, Trinity's attraction in 1978 was more regional (as opposed to nationwide) than it was in 1957. Conversely, however, within Texas the growth in Trinity enrollments has chiefly derived from metropolitan areas—particularly Dallas–Fort Worth, Houston, Austin, El Paso—while enrollment from counties within a hundred miles or so of San Antonio declined. An explanation for this trend is that along with quality, tuition at Trinity has increased in the face of proliferating low-tuition public colleges and universities in the South Texas region; thus, only better-off families (who tend to reside in the metropolitan areas of the state) can easily afford to send their offspring to Trinity.

To summarize, Trinity University has, over approximately the past twenty years, expanded its drawing power by reaching out to enroll students from neighboring states and from metropolitan areas within Texas, even though its drawing power in the Northeast and Midwest has declined. Table 2.3 verifies that over the period, Bexar County's proportion of en-

Table 2.3: Origin of Students of Three San Antonio Universities, Selected Years (Percentages)

	Bexar County (San Antonio)	Rest of Texas	Rest of U.S.	Foreign Countries
Trinity University				
Fall 1957	65.4	21.5	11.3	1.8
Fall 1974	49.8	30.6	18.3	1.3
Fall 1978	49.5	25.6	21.8	3.1
St. Mary's University				
Fall 1974	58.6	18.4	18.7	4.3
Fall 1979	55.4	24.7	16.9	3.0
Univ. of Texas at S.A.				
Fall 1975	90.0	8.0	1.7	0.3
Fall 1979	89.8	7.8	1.7	0.7

SOURCES: Offices of Admissions at the respective universities.

rollees dropped more than 15 percentage points, an indication that Trinity has decreased its dependence upon local financial support, at least in the form of tuition and fees. As the same table shows, however, from the mid- to the late seventies, local enrollment in Trinity, St. Mary's University (a private Catholic school enrolling some 3,300 in 1978), and the University of Texas at San Antonio (a member of the UT system, opened in 1973 and enrolling 9,450 by fall 1979) decreased only marginally. At Trinity, for example, an expansion in the percentage of out-of-state students was almost exactly offset by a contraction in the percentage of students from Texas outside Bexar County. St. Mary's showed a significant increase in the percentage of students from the rest of Texas, but a contraction in percentages for the rest of the United States and for foreign students. The University of Texas at San Antonio, which (unlike the other two schools) had substantial enrollment increases over the period 1975–79, exhibited practically no change in its percentage distribution of student origin, with the exception of a doubling of the percentage of foreign students—who were still only 0.7 percent of the total in the fall of 1979. These short-term trends may well continue, owing to a decline in college enrollments nationwide expected after 1980; however, UTSA, allowing for its size, growth rate, and the maturation of its programs, will probably begin to draw a greater proportion of its students from outside Bexar County.

San Antonio is undergoing a tourist boom; visitors increased some 45 percent between 1976 and 1978, pumping some $150 million into the economy per year.[13] San Antonio has been the mecca of tourists to Texas, accounting for more yearly person-visits than any other city (and some 22% of the total for Texas).[14] As Figure 2.1 indicates, the city is increasing its drawing power in the Midwest, Northeast, and California, while its drawing power in the Southeast and near Southwest has decreased. The data on which this map is based cover only two years and doubtless reflect the exceptionally severe winters of 1976–77 and 1977–78 in the East. Nevertheless, other evidence suggests that the trend implied in Figure 2.1 may be more than just a passing phase. Climatic data show a pronounced decline in average annual temperatures in the northern United States since about 1940, and long-run climate trends (180- and 20-year cycles) promise colder and wetter weather in the Northeast and Midwest in the 1980s. Recent surveys of interest in touring Texas[15] indicate that Texas is highly preferred by residents of many of the same states which show increases in Figure 2.1. Such preferences probably indicate future visitation and retirement in Texas.

Table 2.4 indicates that the post-1955 period brought to San Antonio a relatively high proportion of capital-intensive industrial plants. Such plants tend to have a large engineering and research and development component, hire a high proportion of skilled labor, and produce little in the way of air and water pollutants. Furthermore, while the industrial firms established before 1955 tend to produce for a local market, post-1955 firms tend to produce for a national or regional market. To mention a few examples, among the pre-1955 firms are Finesilver Manufacturing Company (est. 1897), which produces military wear and work clothes for a local and state market; Roeglein Provision Company (est. 1936), involved in meat processing and packing largely for a south Texas market; and the Lone Star Brewing Company (est. 1940), manufacturing beer for a predominantly (90%–95%) Texas market. Among the firms established since 1955 are Chromalloy-American, Turbine Support Division (est. 1966), which repairs and re-finishes jet engine parts for the U.S. Air Force as well as for major U.S. airlines; the Datapoint Corporation (est. 1968), which produces and leases electronic data processing systems for a national and international market; and Bakerline, a division of Baker International (est. 1975), producing oil-field tools and machine parts for most of the western United States. These data emphasize that San Antonio's economy is maturing. Because these latter industries are more footloose in their locational decisions, they tend to be independent both of local raw materials and of local markets for their goods. Such industries generally add significantly to the value of their

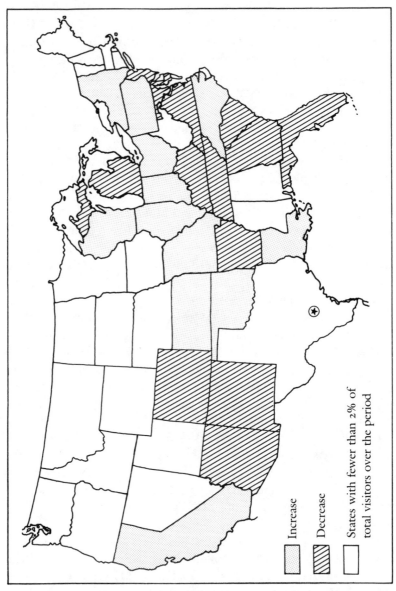

Figure 2.1: Change in origin of visitors registering at the San Antonio Convention and Visitors' Bureau, Visitor Information Center, October 1978 compared to October 1976 (ave. change = +45%).

Table 2.4: Standard Industrial Classification (SIC) Categorization
of Large Manufacturing Plants, by Date of Establishment in San Antonio

SIC Category	Number of Plants Established		
	Before 1955	1955 and After	Totals
20–25 (labor-intensive)a	35	8	43
34–38 (capital-intensive)b	14	14	28
Totals	49	22	71

SOURCES: Data from San Antonio Economic Development Foundation, *Manufacturers Directory* (1976); Greater San Antonio Chamber of Commerce, *Directory of Largest Employers* (1977).

NOTE: Large plants are those with 100 or more employees in 1977.

aComponent sectors are as follows: 20 = food and kindred products; 21 = tobacco manufacturers; 22 = textile mill products; 23 = apparel and other textile products; 24 = lumber and wood products; 25 = furniture and fixtures.

bComponent sectors are as follows: 34 = fabricated metal products; 35 = nonelectrical machinery; 36 = electric and electronic equipment; 37 = transportation equipment; 38 = instruments and related products.

product within the manufacturing process, and thus channel income into the city at a high rate.

Geographers are always on the lookout for overall indices of a place's area of influence within its region and nationally. One commonly used index of a city's national and regional ties is its air-passenger hinterland.[16] This measure, recording the inflow and outflow of people in a given year, jointly indexes the business, professional, tourist, and other ties between one city and other cities—as well as a city's inmigration and outmigration connections (places to which migrants have gone or from which they have come), inasmuch as visits to relatives often reflect previous migration. Figure 2.2 shows those cities with above-average and those with below-average growth in passenger flows to and from San Antonio over the period 1963–77. Most notable is the above-average growth from cities in the West, compared with below-average growth from cities in the East. This trend is to be expected, because the western cities had higher population growth rates over the period, thus generating more passengers. It has been shown that air passenger flows between major U.S. cities may be predicted largely by the sizes of the cities and the distances separating them,[17] and this appears to be the case with San Antonio. For example, the growth in

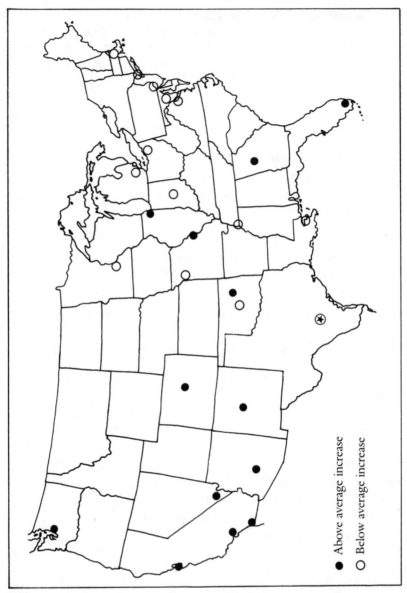

Figure 2.2: Change in total inbound plus outbound airline passengers for San Antonio, 1977 compared to 1963. Cities shown are non-Texas cities with 1% or more of total passengers in either year.

passengers to and from San Antonio and such western cities as Phoenix, San Diego, Denver, and Albuquerque is generally proportional to the population growth of the latter cities, with the exception that closer cities (Albuquerque and Denver) have passenger growth somewhat greater than the growth of population, and farther cities (Phoenix and San Diego) have somewhat slower than average growth. These trends are interesting, but more important is the fact that the number of passengers in and out of San Antonio grew 229 percent over a period when the overall metropolitan population in the United States grew by only about 20 percent, and San Antonio's population, by about 30 percent. Thus, San Antonio's national connections were forged much more rapidly than either its own, or national, metropolitan growth would have suggested.

A commonly employed index of a place's area of influence at the regional and local levels is the subscription area of its major daily newspapers.[18] Such an index indirectly reflects the inflow of consumers to a city's retail and service offerings, because an important part of newspaper revenues is advertising receipts from retail and service businesses, and such businesses will pay only for advertising which increases their consumer patronage from the city's trade area. In Figure 2.3, the Texas counties indicated by one of the two patterns had at least twenty-five weekly subscribers to the San Antonio *Light, Express,* and *News* in both 1957 and 1977. In the pattern of change revealed by these counties, it is notable that circulation has decreased at the periphery of San Antonio's trade area while it has increased at the center of the area (with the exception of Bexar County itself) over the twenty-year period. Assuming that a newspaper circulation area reflects a city's basic retail and service connections with its hinterland we might conclude that suburban and exurban counties immediately tributary to San Antonio have become more strongly oriented to the city, and that peripheral counties in the larger hinterland have become more independent of San Antonio's influence. The explanation is more complicated than this, however. The loss of circulation in San Antonio's periphery may be explained by (1) competition to the north and east, from dailies not only in Austin, Dallas, Fort Worth, and Houston, but also in smaller cities such as San Marcos; (2) the development of new daily newspapers in small cities to the south and west; and (3) changes in family composition and preferences—especially the increasing preference for newspapers with a more national focus.[19] On this last point, it is surprising that between 1957 and 1977, combined circulations of the three San Antonio dailies grew by only 17 percent, even though San Antonio SMSA population grew by close to 45 percent.[20] These results undoubtedly indicate a certain disenchantment with the San Antonio

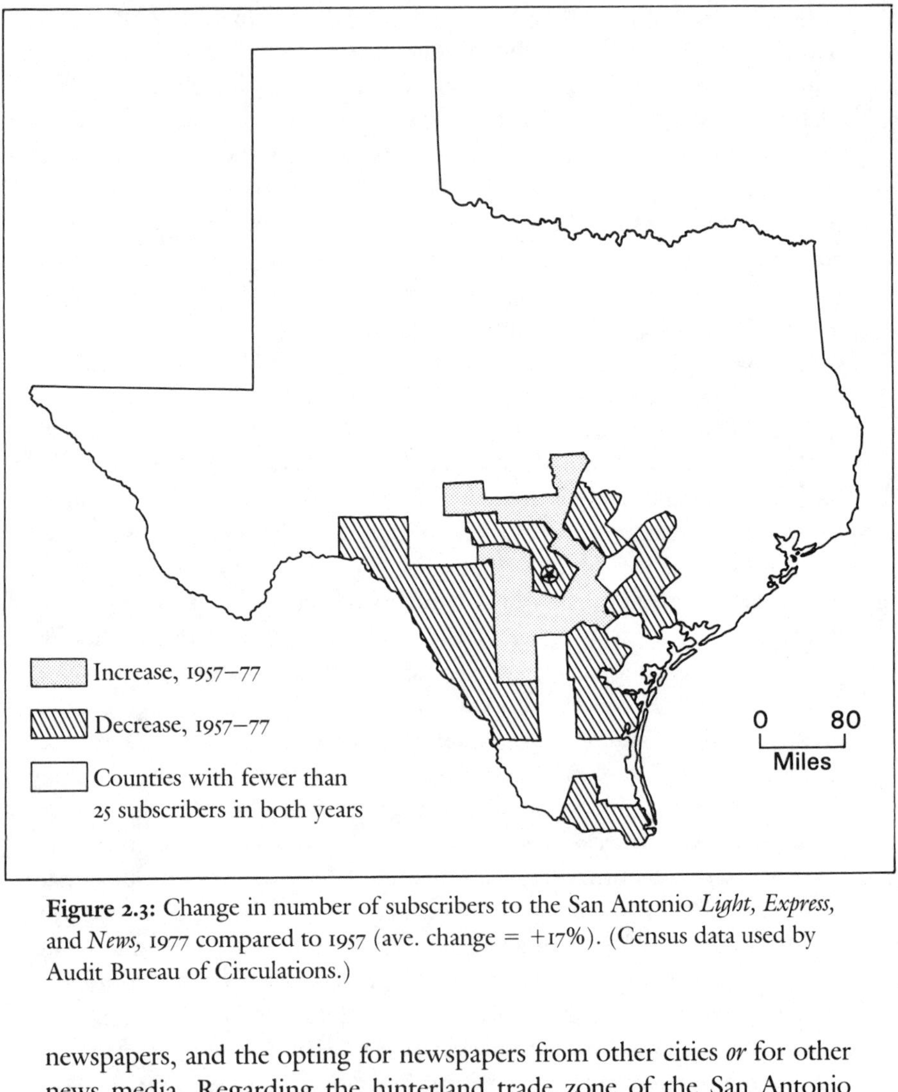

Figure 2.3: Change in number of subscribers to the San Antonio *Light, Express,* and *News,* 1977 compared to 1957 (ave. change = +17%). (Census data used by Audit Bureau of Circulations.)

newspapers, and the opting for newspapers from other cities *or* for other news media. Regarding the hinterland trade zone of the San Antonio papers (the circulation area outside of San Antonio) we find a decline from 25 percent of total circulation in 1957 to 18 percent in 1977, and an actual growth rate in circulations of only 2 percent.[21] A partial explanation for such slow growth in circulation is the low population growth in the south-western and southeastern portions of the retail trade zone; another reason may be found in the decline in popularity of San Antonio's newspapers; and the rest of the explanation may lie in a loss of San Antonio's economic influence, owing to independent growth of smaller cities in San Antonio's hinterland. One could not necessarily conclude, from these data, that San Antonio's influence has declined within its retail trade zone, since this would be consistent only with the last of these explanations.

The expansion of San Antonio's regional, national, and international ties may be indexed by still another type of flow—that of investment capital entering the city. Such capital is basic to the city because payment to local persons for land, buildings, and combinations of these by outsiders creates jobs within the local economy. In the absence of hard data, a few examples will serve. First, a substantial number of San Antonio banks (about 40% in mid-1979) are affiliated with bank holding companies; such affiliation gives them access to large pools of loan funds, expertise in certain specialized types of loans and investments, and savings in accounting costs. Although some two-thirds of affiliated San Antonio banks are associated with locally based holding companies (notably, Cullen-Frost Bankers, Inc., and National Bancshares Corporation of Texas), the other one-third are affiliated with holding companies in Dallas or in Houston. These latter banks are thus capitalizing on funds generated elsewhere. Furthermore, only one of these banks could be considered a small bank (less than $30 million deposits); thus, according to at least one study,[22] they were in all likelihood gaining more from their affiliation than it cost them in management fees paid to the holding companies for services performed. Second, groups from Dallas and Houston, as well as large eastern corporations, are investing in San Antonio at an accelerated rate. Witness the investment in land around UTSA in the early 1970s by Dallas and Houston syndicates and the prevalence of outside investors in the proposed "new town," San Antonio Ranch, as well as in several large malls recently built or proposed in the city. Third, and finally, one must note the burgeoning foreign investment in San Antonio, including considerable Mexican investment in downtown office buildings, restaurants, and small shopping centers and European investments such as the purchase of Colonies North by a Liechtenstein corporation, the purchase of Wonderland Shopping City by a German group, the leasing of McCreless Shopping City by a British firm, and the purchase of office buildings and apartments by Canadians.[23] Inasmuch as such foreign investors pay premium prices and support certain developments that would otherwise go undeveloped, they are responsible for pumping millions of dollars into the San Antonio economy in the form of wages and rent, even if profits accrue to foreign stockholders.

The preceding indices of economically basic connections for San Antonio—in the form of goods, services, and capital flows—point to San Antonio's expanding regional and national, though not necessarily local, role. On the one hand, nationwide student growth at Trinity University, national and regional market areas for goods manufactured in the city, and growing airline passenger hinterlands indicate an increasing role in the western and central portions of the country. On the other hand, the in-state enrollment at local universities and the trade area of the city's daily newspapers suggest relatively little expansion of San Antonio's influence in South Texas. Since 1976 there is evidence for increasing ties between San Antonio and the Northeast and Midwest. We have noted that tourists are being drawn increasingly from the Frostbelt. There is also evidence from other sources. Maria Pisano's article "The New Carpetbaggers" catalogs the inmigration of skilled professionals from New York, Boston, Chicago, and elsewhere in the north and east.[24] The University of Texas at San Antonio has drawn an unusually large population of its faculty from these regions, and within various public agencies, local and state planners increasingly hail from there.

Recent Internal Growth Patterns in San Antonio

The external linkages just documented have led to an unequal internal expansion and development in the city, with the northern sectors strongly favored. Such expansion fits well into Hoyt's sector model, in that growth has followed high-quality residential corridors northward and has avoided low-income "ethnic" sectors in the west, southwest, and east portions of the city. Hoyt's model cannot, however, fully explain the motive forces behind such spatially unequal growth. For this, we must look into a few major projects in the north which were magnets for growth and into San Antonio's political structure.

The northern part of San Antonio has led the metropolitan area in recent population and commercial growth to an astounding degree. The data in Table 2.5 demonstrate that between 1960 and 1976, population grew at above-average rates in only three of nine census tract series: the northeast, northwest, and north central. Furthermore, when the city's population growth slowed in the early 1970s the differential between northern growth and growth elsewhere in the city increased, with the south central, southwest, and west central series actually recording population losses while the northeast and northwest sustained only slight declines in their high growth rates. The dominance of growth in northern San Antonio is apparent from the following fact: between 1970 and 1976, the three northern series of census tracts, with 33 percent of Bexar County's population (in 1970), accounted for no less than 96 percent of net population growth in the

Table 2.5: Population Change by Census Tract Series, Bexar County

Series	Designation	Average Annual Compound Population Change (%) 1960–70	1970–76	1976 Population
1100	CBD	−4.02	−2.73	31,687
1200	Northeast	5.12	4.78	139,621
1300	East Central	1.19	0.48	81,567
1400	Southeast	0.04	0.48	67,661
1500	South Central	1.27	−0.10	100,126
1600	Southwest	1.92	−0.87	115,649
1700	West Central	1.63	−0.25	132,612
1800	Northwest	5.52	4.68	117,833
1900	North Central	2.49	0.70	99.845
1100–1900	Bexar County	1.92	1.34	899,388

SOURCES: Data from U.S. Bureau of the Census, *Census of Population,* 1960 and 1970; and Comprehensive Planning Department, City of San Antonio, 1976.

county—meaning that of every twenty persons added (net) to the population of the county between 1970 and 1976, from migration as well as from natural increase, nineteen of them were residing in the northern parts of the city in 1976. Inside Loop 410, closer to the city center, growth was very slow or negative, except along its edge; north of the Loop, growth was very rapid while south of it, growth was only moderate. Relative to commercial growth in the city, the north dominated once again, With some 10–20 percent of the employment in commercial establishments in the city, the north has accounted for between 60 percent and 70 percent of the growth in commercial employment in recent years.[25] This commercial growth reproduces the spatial pattern of population growth, except that in the northwest just outside Loop 410 (the city's fastest growing area), commercial growth is just beginning to catch up with population growth.[26] One surprising component of recent northern commercial growth has been that capital-intensive manufacturing has more and more tended to locate in northern San Antonio (especially, in the north central region around the airport and in the northeast in newly created industrial zones). Of San Antonio manufacturing firms in SIC categories 34–38 (the more capital-intensive types; see Table 2.4), only 21 percent of those established before

1955 are located in the north, but 50 percent of those established after 1955 are in the north.[27] This marks a significant move of industry away from its traditional locations in central San Antonio.

San Antonio's spatial patterns of population and commercial growth fit well into Hoyt's sectoral growth model. Land-use maps for the city show that in 1956, residential land in San Antonio was distributed equidistantly from the central business district, whereas by 1969 it had spread amoebalike northward of Loop 410, but little to the south.[28] Such residential land use was accompanied by the proliferation of parks and schools and by new commercial districts in the north. The fact that new northern residential land was priced for high-income consumers simply reflects the demand for its locational and geographic features: higher elevation (scenic, flood-free), accessibility to the early pioneering establishment of such fashionable suburban communities as Alamo Heights, Laurel Heights, Tobin Hill, and Beacon Hill, even before the turn of this century.[29] Given its price, it is not surprising that such northern land was populated by higher-income Anglos, leaving behind ethnically distinct wedges which served to accentuate San Antonio's sectoral patterns of income and land use. Inside Loop 410, five tract series have above 68 percent of their population in a single ethnic group. These are the west central (79% Hispanic); the east central (72% black); and the northeast, north central, and northwest (respectively, 84%, 68%, and 73% Anglo).[30] The other four tract series (the central business district, southwest, south central, and southeast) are too ethnically mixed to be categorized simply. Despite this apparent ethnic segregation, San Antonio's *level* of white–nonwhite segregation is actually considerably lower than the levels of Houston, Dallas, Fort Worth, and a number of smaller Texas cities.[31]

San Antonio's political structure under the Good Government League (1955–c. 1975) provided the trigger mechanism for explosive northern growth in the late 1950s and the 1960s. Booth and Johnson (Chapter 1) have already pointed out that the GGL's promotion of overall urban growth, regardless of partisan interests associated with certain ethnic groups, resulted in an effective favoritism of northern San Antonio. This was simply a case of the dilemma of "growth and imbalance" versus "welfare and balance" models of urban development, here decided by the GGL in favor of growth. Whether by explicit design or not, developers, brokers, bankers, insurance men, and physicians from northern San Antonio were nominated in predominant numbers for city council and city government positions (many of them, because of their wealth, could afford to serve for free). Because of their backgrounds in free enterprise, such persons favored allowing growth to occur where the market forces suggested—that is, a continuation of northern growth. In their support of projects such as UTSA, the University of Texas Health Science Center, and utilities for northern residential developments, they were aided by the fact that all council members served at large, thus effectively preventing opposition from the neglected southern parts of the city. At any rate, several landmark projects were shepherded through, under GGL auspices. The approval of major accessways in the north (especially the construction of Loop 410 and the widening of San Pedro, Fredericksburg, and Bandera Roads) encouraged development in the form of major malls (beginning with North Star in 1960 and Wonderland in 1961), more distant residential suburbs, and such entities as the United States Automobile Association and the Koger Executive Center. Further decisions—to build the South Texas Medical Center (completed in 1968) one mile north of Loop 410 and UTSA (completed in 1973) some five miles farther north—began a second round of residential and commercial expansion in the northwest. A capstone to the prodevelopment sentiments of the GGL was the decision of Datapoint (currently San Antonio's largest manufacturer) to locate along IH10 in northwest San Antonio in 1969.

Despite the GGL's importance as a developmental force in San Antonio over the period of study, we should not overemphasize its role. The residential trends favoring northern growth are rooted in geographic and historical factors which predate the GGL, and the expressway system which brought such rapid growth to the north was inaugurated in 1947. It is also significant that although Hemisfair '68, a GGL-promoted international exposition, refocused the city on its downtown and resulted in substantial building there afterwards, northern economic growth after Hemisfair accelerated rapidly. Finally, despite the demise of the GGL and the burgeoning of the aquifer issue with the Ranchtown litigation beginning in 1972, northern growth has continued apace. Indeed, the whole history of the aquifer issue is one of moral and civil-rights victories for the proponents of environmental protection and ethnic representation, followed by economic and frequently legal victories for prodevelopment interests (see Chapter 8). Northern growth emerges out of this history as an inexorable force which manages to spring forth regardless of the odds against it.

Conclusions

The main findings of this chapter may be summarized as follows. First, recent population and economic growth in San Antonio has been about average for a Sunbelt city of its size, and much of this growth can be explained in terms of Texas's special attractions for business, industry, and tourism, *vis-à-vis* deteriorating conditions in the Northeast. Second, San Antonio's growth sectors over the period 1956–76 have included medical and health services, membership organizations and business services, contract construction, and metals and machinery manufacturing. These sectors were also leading ones for the state. San Antonio's economic structure has in fact become more like Texas's over the last twenty years. Third, San Antonio's spatial economic connections have, in general, expanded over the past twenty years: its tourist-drawing area has expanded significantly into the Northeast and Midwest; its industrial structure has progressed from raw-materials processing for a largely local market to machinery and electronics for a regional and national market; and it is increasingly drawing investment funds from larger Texas cities, from the Northeast, and from overseas. Regarding its South Texas connections, however, the evidence suggests a relatively static or even declining role—partly a function of the reorientation of the city to the "outside world," which has come almost full cycle from San Antonio's days as a cattle, cotton, and military outpost for South and West Texas. Fourth, within San Antonio, population and economic growth in recent years have been predominantly concentrated in the north; in fact, some 96 percent of the city's net population growth has been there. Such spatial imbalance may be partially explained by the higher elevation of northern land and the early growth of high-status residential neighborhoods there, both of which encouraged cumulative high-status growth. Part of the explanation also lies in the pronorthern policies of the GGL, which held political power in San Antonio between 1955 and 1975, and which promoted major expressways, residential utility connections, and public institutions along and north of the present Loop 410. However, there is a certain inexorable feature about northern growth, as evidenced by its continuation even after the demise of the GGL and the onset of the aquifer protection issue. The growth setbacks that resulted from these two events appear to be temporary.

Regarding San Antonio's external ties, the city's growth has come to be dominated by the same forces that dominate the state as a whole. This has both favorable and unfavorable dimensions for future growth—favorable in that traditional slow-growth sectors are being supplanted by rapid-growth sectors, unfavorable in that San Antonio will find itself less insulated than before against national economic setbacks. Regarding San Antonio's internal pattern of growth, the perpetuation of northern growth again has positive and negative implications. Northern growth, spontaneous and laissez faire, has attracted investments from across the country and internationally; on the other hand, such growth is partly at the expense of growth in the southern part of the city. Spatial growth imbalances correspond to ethnic imbalances, presaging confrontation at some point in the future.

Table 2.A1: Theoretical Concepts and Empirical Indices for Changes in San Antonio's Spatial Economic Ties in Recent Years

Theoretical Concept	Empirical Index	Explanation
Services		
1. Inflow of consumers attracted to city's higher-order professional services	Trinity University students' county and state of residence, 1957 vs. 1978 (*Source:* Trinity University Office of Admissions)	Indexes degree to which students are drawn from farther away or closer in
2. Inflow of tourists in response to scenic/historical/recreational attractions	State of residence of tourists visiting San Antonio's Visitor Center downtown, October 1978 (*Source:* S.A. Convention & Visitors Bureau)	Indexes degree of expansion or contraction in San Antonio's tourist hinterland
Goods		
3. Outflow of finished manufactured goods	Number of large (≥ 100 employees) manufacturing plants in San Antonio, by SIC category, pre-1955 vs. post-1955 establishments (*Sources:* San Antonio Economic Development Foundation, *Manufacturers' Directory* [1976]; Greater S.A. Chamber of Commerce, *Directory of Largest Employers* [1977]	Indexes degree of change toward capital-intensive and away from labor-intensive industries

(*continued*)

Table 2.A1: (*Continued*)

Theoretical Concept	Empirical Index	Explanation
Services and Goods		
4. Inflow and outflow of people, particularly businessmen, tourists, professionals, with ties outside the city	Outbound plus inbound airline passenger flows for San Antonio, 1963 vs. 1977 (*Source:* Air Transport Assn. of America, CAB, *Origin-Destination Survey of Airline Passenger Traffic,* 10% sample survey)	Indexes the city's national sphere of influence; an aggregate index of various types of economic connections
5. Inflow of retail and service consumers from outside a city	Number of San Antonio *Light* and *Express-News* subscribers, by county of residence, 1957 vs. 1977 (*Source: ABC Audit Report: Newspaper* [Audit Bureau of Circulations])	Indexes the city's informational sphere of influence, indirectly reflecting its retail/personal service/entertainment trade area

Richard J. Harris

Chapter Three

Mexican-American Occupational Attainments in San Antonio: Comparative Assessments

This chapter provides an overview of the socioeconomic characteristics of the population of San Antonio and a detailed examination of the occupational characteristics and mobility experiences of Mexican Americans compared to others. Hispanics comprise over half of the total population, with blacks constituting only a small proportion (6 percent). This large concentration of Mexican Americans[1] in San Antonio is one of the city's unique features. In fact, among the ten cities in the United States with the greatest proportion of Mexican Americans, San Antonio has by far the largest metropolitan area.[2] Furthermore, the numbers of Mexican Americans continue to grow relative to others groups, both as a result of continued immigration and their comparatively higher fertility.

Socioeconomic Status in San Antonio

Table 3.1 provides occupational, educational, and income data on San Antonio's racial and ethnic groups for 1970, and reveals tremendous economic divisions in the population. The median family income of blacks ($5,374) is only 57 percent as large as that of Anglos ($9,458), while the median family income of Mexican Americans ($6,438) is only 68 percent as large. The incidence of poverty corresponds closely to the pattern for median income, with blacks and those with Spanish surnames much more likely to be poor.

The income differences may be partly related to differences in education. As revealed by the median years of school completed, the percentage of high school graduates, and the percentage of college graduates, Anglos have substantially higher levels of formal education. Mexican Americans have the

Table 3.1: Occupation, Education, and Income in San Antonio for the Anglo, Black, and Spanish Populations, 1970

	All Groups		Anglos[b]	
Occupation[a]	No.	%	No.	%
Professional, technical, and kindred	16,126	11.91	11,061	18.37
Managers and administrators, except farm	14,603	10.78	10,178	16.91
Sales workers	11,629	8.59	7,889	13.10
Clerical and kindred workers	14,008	10.34	6,451	10.72
Craftsmen, foremen, and kindred workers	33,298	24.59	13,197	21.92
Operatives, including transport	22,989	16.98	6,174	10.25
Laborers, except farm	8,680	6.41	1,353	2.25
Farm workers	724	0.53	367	0.61
Service workers, except private household	13,229	9.77	3,532	5.87
Private household workers	125	0.09	3	0.00
All occupations	135,411	99.99	60,205	100.00
Percentage of total population	(100.0)		(44.5)	

Education[c]	All Groups	Anglos
Median no. of years completed	10.8	13.5
Percentage of high school graduates	42.7%	59.4%
Percentage of college graduates	8.7%	14.6%
No. of people (%)	324,856 (99.9%)	156,726 (48.2%)

Family Income	All Groups	Anglos
Median	$7,734	$9,458
Percentage below poverty	17.5%	7.2%
No. of families (%)	156,218 (99.9%)	71,290 (45.6%)

[a]Employed males 16 and over.

[b]A residual category of nonblack and non-Spanish-surname population consisting primarily of whites, or "Anglos."

[c]Persons 25 and over.

lowest level of education, substantially below even that of blacks.[3] Only 25 percent of adult Mexican Americans had graduated from high school in 1970.

Distribution in the occupational structure of a community is partly a function of levels of educational attainment and is an important determinant of economic well-being. Based on the descriptions of educational and

Table 3.1: Continued

	Blacks		Mexican Americans	
Occupation[a]	No.	%	No.	%
Professional, technical, and kindred	551	6.62	4,514	6.75
Managers and administrators, except farm	327	3.93	4,098	6.13
Sales workers	158	1.90	3,582	5.36
Clerical and kindred workers	905	10.88	6,652	9.94
Craftsmen, foremen, and kindred workers	1,602	19.26	18,499	27.66
Operatives, including transport	1,827	21.97	14,988	22.41
Laborers, except farm	811	9.75	6,516	9.74
Farm workers	48	0.58	309	0.46
Service workers, except private household	2,038	24.50	7,659	11.45
Private household workers	50	0.60	72	0.11
All occupations	8,317	99.99	66,889	100.01
Percentage of total population	(6.1)		(49.4)	

Education[c]	Blacks	Mexican Americans
Median no. of years completed	10.8	7.8
Percentage of high school graduates	39.5%	25.0%
Percentage of college graduates	5.3%	2.8%
No. of people (%)	24,815 (7.6%)	143,315 (44.1%)

Family Income	Blacks	Mexican Americans
Median	$5,374	$6,438
Percentage below poverty	31.2%	25.3%
No. of families (%)	12,076 (7.7%)	72,852 (46.6%)

SOURCE: U.S. Bureau of the Census, *Census of Population and Housing: 1970 Census Tracts,* Final Report PHC (1)-186 San Antonio, Texas SMSA (Washington, D.C.: U.S. Government Printing Office, 1972).

income differences, it is not surprising that there are substantial differences in the occupational distributions of Mexican Americans, blacks, and Anglos. Anglos are much more likely to be in the high-status professional or managerial occupations and also substantially more likely to be in clerical or sales positions. Over 59 percent of the Anglos are in these white-collar jobs compared to about 23 percent of blacks and 28 percent of Mexican Americans. Conversely, blacks and Mexican Americans are much more likely to be in skilled and unskilled blue-collar jobs. Blacks have the highest percentages in lower-status service and labor occupations, followed by the Mexican Americans and Anglos, respectively.[4] Nevertheless, the outstanding feature of the percentages in Table 3.1 is the similarity of the positions of the blacks and Mexican Americans. Both are concentrated in lower-status occupations in comparison to the Anglos.

Aside from the census data summarized in Table 3.1, there are no available data to provide details on the experiences of blacks in San Antonio. There are resources, however, to examine the occupational experiences and to seek an explanation for the relatively lower status of the Mexican-American majority of San Antonio.

Theoretical Perspectives on Ethnic and Racial Inequality

The findings in Table 3.1 are consistent with results from other studies of ethnic and racial socioeconomic differences in Texas, the Southwest, and the United States as a whole.[5] Sociological and historical perspectives on the experience of immigrants to the United States are useful in attempting to understand these socioeconomic differences.[6] There has been much discussion of the experience of Mexican Americans in terms of whether they represent an oppressed, colonized ethnic group or a group of voluntary immigrants assimilating into American society in the same manner as that described for European immigrants.[7] Edward Murguia summarizes these two points of view: "The assimilationist explanations for the low socioeconomic condition of the Mexican American people center on the 'traditional culture' of the Mexican American people, the recency of their immigration and their lack of commitment to the United States. Colonial explanations focus on Anglo American economic exploitation and the conditions of poverty and powerlessness in which the Mexican American people have been placed."[8]

The main ideas behind these perspectives can also be expressed in terms of the models of status attainment developed in sociology.[9] Basically, individual socioeconomic success is considered to be a function of achieved and ascribed characteristics. The relative importance of these different factors indicated the "openness" or "closedness" of the attainment process. From the assimilationist perspective, achieved characteristics would include such factors as customs, dress, fluency in English, educational levels, and types of vocational skills. With a decline in cultural differences, structural assimilation is expected to occur, and socioeconomic differences should decline over time or in succeeding generations.[10] Therefore, these "achieved" variables should be very important in explaining the socioeconomic position of Mexican Americans. From the colonial perspective, the ascriptive identifiers of race or ethnicity are central to the explanation of the socioeconomic status of Mexican Americans owing to discrimination and exploitation. Essentially, the assimilation perspective assumes a model of equality of opportunity where inequality is largely a result of unequal qualifications. The colonial model, on the other hand, emphasizes discrimination and exploitation, suggests that equal qualifications do not produce equal rewards, and argues that achieved variables will be less important than the ascribed variables for the oppressed group.

Other chapters in this volume refer to the long history of poverty among Mexican Americans and blacks in San Antonio. Booth and Johnson, in Chapter 1, argue that the "much poorer occupational status, educational attainment, income, public services, school systems, political participation, and representation in public office" are largely the result of "deliberate policy decisions" and the "systematic subversion of their interests . . . to the class interests of the elites." Gambitta, Milne, and Davis, in Chapter 7, document the unequal provision of educational resources in different school districts, with disproportionately adverse effects for Mexican Americans and blacks. Unequal access to quality education is particularly problematic because education is one of the most important variables in the process of occupational attainment.

These chapters suggest an historical and political context in San Antonio most consistent with a discrimination and exploitation interpretation of socioeconomic differences. Yet the large concentration of Mexican Americans in both absolute and relative terms and the close proximity of San Antonio to Mexico may make it possible for Mexican Americans to retain traditional language and cultural identity, which would also inhibit occupational integration. Furthermore, affirmative action, recent political changes, and a greater political mobilization of Mexican Americans in San Antonio may have enhanced opportunities for occupational attainment in the 1970s.[11]

This study provides an empirical basis for evaluating these conflicting perspectives by assessing the occupational mobility and the determinants of occupational attainment for Mexican Americans compared to Anglos. Murguia and Gordon both observe that occupational mobility is very important in evaluating assimilation and the experiences of an ethnic or racial group.[12] Occupational integration is an important indicator of the level of structural assimilation between minority and majority segments of society. Trends in occupational attainment, therefore, both reflect the past and may influence the future political environment of the community.

Previous Studies of Mexican-American Mobility

The literature on the mobility patterns of Mexican Americans is limited, but a few published studies provide valuable background. Mexican Americans in San Antonio between 1870 and 1900, a period just prior to the large-scale immigration of the twentieth century, were overrepresented in the un-skilled jobs. In 1876, while Mexican Americans were only 22 percent of the total population, 90 percent were classified as manual laborers.[13] There was, however, a certain amount of occupational mobility. In the manual labor class, over the thirty-year period 11 percent of the Mexican Americans experienced upward occupational mobility. The same was true for 14 per-cent of the native whites, 19 percent of European immigrants, and 5 percent of black Americans. Downward mobility ranged from 4 to 7 percent of all manual laborers.[14] San Antonio Mexican Americans, therefore, were more than twice as upwardly mobile as blacks but experienced considerably less upward mobility than the city's European immigrants.

The situation of San Antonio Mexican Americans resembles that found elsewhere in the Southwest. A study in Los Angeles, based on marriage records from 1917 and 1918, also found Mexican Americans heavily concen-trated in the unskilled positions. Substantial upward movement was evi-dent over three generations, but there were few class gains from blue-collar to white-collar job status.[15] A 1960–61 study of occupational mobility in a Mexican-American community in Southern California found evidence of even greater movement, especially among the more highly educated second generation that had also achieved greater fluency in the English language.[16]

Overall, then, these studies suggest that historically Mexican Americans have experienced some upward occupational mobility—more than that experienced by blacks, though less than that experienced by European immigrants. Furthermore, their mobility appears greater more recently, suggesting possible improvements in opportunity over time. Against this background, we will now turn our attention to the study of occupational mobility in San Antonio.

Data and Methods of Analysis

Data for this study are drawn from a variety of sources. First, published census data are employed to compare occupational distribution by race and ethnicity, and to provide a "snapshot" of the San Antonio population in 1970. Second, a 1977 survey of a sample of 132 Mexican Americans in San Antonio is used extensively. This survey, conducted by Dr. Crandall A. Shifflett under a Department of Labor grant to the University of Texas at San Antonio, provides information on the characteristics of the respondents, their parents, and their grandparents.[17] Third, in order to establish a roughly comparable "Anglo" sample with information similar to that contained in the Shifflett sample, data were drawn from the National Opinion Research Center (NORC) General Social Surveys from 1977 and 1978.[18] For this purpose, non–Spanish origin white males in Standard Metropolitan Statistical Areas (SMSAs) of the South Atlantic, East South Central and West South Central states were selected, providing a total of 167 cases. Although the Shifflett and the NORC samples are small, they permit a comparison of the intergenerational occupational mobility of San Antonio Mexican Americans with Southern Anglos and an evaluation of the determinants of occupational position for the two groups.[19] Finally, additional analyses are presented from a sample of men drawn from the 1968 *Polk City Directory of San Antonio*.[20] The sample members were classified as Hispanic and non-Hispanic on the basis of surnames. The vast majority of the Hispanics are Mexican Americans and the vast majority of the non-Hispanics are Anglos, though the latter group also include blacks, and will be referred to with these more general labels. The sample members were traced forward from the 1968 to the 1978 city directory, providing information on *intra*generational occupational mobility over the ten-year period for 717 Mexican Americans and 1,006 Anglos.[21]

The occupational distributions in the Shifflett sample of Mexican Americans, the NORC sample of Anglos, and the city directory sample have been carefully compared with the appropriate distributions from the 1970 census for San Antonio and the Southwest.[22] In general, the sample distributions are very similar to the census distributions. The only major exception is that the Shifflett sample overrepresents the higher-status occupations and underrepresents the skilled labor positions. For the following analysis, therefore, this sample is weighted to reflect the occupational distribution of the Spanish-surname population of San Antonio from the 1970 census, enhancing our ability to generalize about the total population.[23]

Intergenerational occupational mobility is assessed directly through a comparison of father's occupational position and son's occupational position. Then intragenerational occupational mobility is studied by comparing occupational positions in 1968 with those held by the same individuals in 1978. Finally, there is an examination of the principal determinants of the respondent's current occupational position, employing correlation and regression analysis to evaluate the relative impact of a number of the potentially important factors identified in the earlier theoretical discussion.[24]

Results

Descriptive Comparisons

Table 3.2 summarizes some of the comparable descriptive data from the Shifflett sample of Mexican Americans in San Antonio and the NORC sample of Anglos in the South. Included are variables whose potential impact on occupational mobility will be examined in greater detail: age, family size, and both the father's and the respondent's education and occupational status. Age, which is closely related to career progression and job seniority, has similar distributions for both the Mexican Americans and the Anglos. A striking difference exists, however, in terms of family size. It is evident that the Mexican Americans in San Antonio have substantially larger families than the Anglos, and family size may have some impact on the prospects for occupational mobility.[25]

Substantial increases in educational attainment have marked the most recent generations, especially among the Mexican Americans. Sons of Mexican Americans gained four years of education beyond that of their fathers

Table 3.2: Descriptive Profiles of Mexican-American and Anglo Samples

	Mexican Americans in San Antonio			
	Median	_Mean_	_Standard Deviation_	_No. of Cases_
Respondent's occupation[a]	2.06	2.19	0.93	132
Respondent's education	12.15	11.59	3.51	128
Father's occupation[a,b]	1.80	2.02	1.07	118
Father's education	7.78	7.77	4.65	95
Age of respondent	38.38	40.17	14.08	132
Respondent's family size	3.74	3.91	1.81	118

[a]Occupational position is ranked as follows: 1—unskilled labor, 2—skilled labor, 3—clerical or sales, 4—professional or managerial. Therefore, a higher median or mean indicates greater numbers of people in higher-status occupations.

[b]Father's occupation refers to the father's last occupation in the San Antonio data, and to the father's occupation at age 16 in the NORC data.

Table 3.2: Continued

	Anglos in Southern SMSAs			
	Median	Mean	Standard Deviation	No. of Cases
Respondent's occupation[a]	2.35	2.61	1.09	162
Respondent's education	12.29	12.65	3.62	167
Father's occupation[a,b]	2.08	2.34	1.14	143
Father's education	10.07	10.07	4.61	122
Age of respondent	37.25	41.14	16.06	167
Respondent's family size	2.44	2.70	1.41	166

SOURCES: Data on Mexican Americans from a random sample of Mexican-American male heads of household in San Antonio, 1977, weighted according to occupational distribution of San Antonio in 1970. See Crandall A. Shifflett with Richard J. Harris, *Occupational Mobility and the Process of Assimilation of Mexican Immigrants to San Antonio, Texas*, DOL 21-48-78-06 (Springfield, Va.: National Technical Information Service, 1979), PB-299 862.

Data on Anglos from the General Social Survey, NORC, 1977 and 1978, including non-Spanish white males in the South Atlantic, East Central, and West Central states. See James A. Davis, *General Social Surveys, 1972–1978* (Chicago: National Opinion Research Center; New Haven: Roper Public Opinion Research Center, 1979).

(the median for fathers was 7.78 years; for sons, 12.15 years). Anglo fathers, who started with a higher average level of education than Mexican-American fathers (a median of 10.07 years), were also surpassed by their sons, who acquired over two additional years on average (median of 12.29 years). Education is generally acknowledged to have an important effect upon ultimate occupational status.

The current occupational status of the Mexican Americans in San Antonio is substantially lower than that of the Anglos, as illustrated by the median and mean occupational scores.[26] Among Mexican Americans, occupational mobility is indicated by the shift from a median occupational score for the fathers of 1.80 to a median of 2.06 for the sons. This compares to a shift of 2.08 to 2.35 for the Anglos. Based on these figures, both groups have experienced upward intergenerational occupational mobility on average, and roughly to the same extent.[27] These averages, however, conceal considerable upward and downward mobility that warrant more detailed consideration.

Intergenerational Mobility

Table 3.3 presents information on intergenerational occupational mobility for the two samples. The entries on the main diagonal represent no occupational mobility, with the sons employed in the same broad occupational category as their fathers. For example, among the Mexican Americans 13.3 percent of those whose fathers were professionals or managers are themselves professionals or managers, and 32.1 percent of those whose fathers were clerical workers are themselves clerical workers. Comparable percentages for skilled and unskilled labor are 70.8 and 33.1 percent respectively. The

Table 3.3: Intergenerational Mobility of Mexican Americans and Anglos

	Son's Occupation					
Father's Occupation	*Professional, Manager*	*Clerical, Sales*	*Skilled Labor*[a]	*Unskilled Labor*[b]	*Total*	*N*
	Mexican Americans in San Antonio[c]					
Professional, manager	13.3	13.7	60.2	12.8	100.0	18
Clerical, sales	27.9	32.1	28.1	11.9	100.0	13
Skilled labor[a]	6.3	12.9	70.8	10.0	100.0	39
Unskilled labor[b]	15.5	12.5	39.0	33.1	100.1	47
All occupations	13.5	15.0	51.6	19.9	100.0	
N	16	18	61	23		118
	Anglos in Southern SMSAs[d]					
Professional, manager	50.0	7.9	36.8	5.3	100.0	38
Clerical, sales	25.0	25.0	50.0	0.0	100.0	8
Skilled labor[a]	29.8	12.3	45.6	12.3	100.0	57
Unskilled labor[b]	15.8	44.7	18.4	21.1	100.0	38
All occupations	32.6	13.5	43.3	10.6	100.0	
N	46	19	61	15		141

SOURCE: See Table 3.2.

[a]Includes craftsmen and operatives.

[b]Includes laborers, service workers, farm laborers, and farmers.

[c]Chi square = 19.38, $p < .05$; Pearson's $r = 0.13$, $p = .086$; Kendall's tau $b = 0.14$, $p < .05$.

[d]Chi square = 11.29, $p = .25$; Pearson's $r = 0.21$, $p < .01$; Kendall's tau $b = 0.18$, $p < .01$.

entries below the main diagonal designate upward mobility, while the entries above the diagonal indicate downward mobility. The row totals indicate the current occupational distribution for each of the samples.

Consistent with the occupational distribution throughout the United States, the largest category of employment for males is the skilled labor position, containing about 52 percent of the Mexican Americans and 43 percent of the Anglos (see the rows with percentages for all occupations). The Anglos are slightly less likely to be employed in clerical positions and are less likely to be in the unskilled labor category. San Antonio Mexican Americans are much less likely to be employed in professional or managerial positions (13.5 percent) than the Anglos in southern SMSAs (32.6 percent).

The patterns of occupational movement revealed in Table 3.3 are striking. Mexican-American sons whose fathers were unskilled were more likely to remain unskilled themselves than were Anglo sons. Yet, in both samples at least two out of every three sons whose fathers were unskilled workers managed to move beyond this lowest occupational position during their careers. Nevertheless, occupational advances across what might be called social class lines—from skilled labor to clerical or professional ranks—was much more limited and was especially difficult for the Mexican Americans. Over 70 percent of the Mexican-American sons whose fathers were skilled remained skilled workers themselves, while the same was true for less than half of the Anglos. The attainment of a skilled occupation by fathers was important to sons of Anglos and Mexican Americans in different ways. For Anglos it was an important avenue of mobility to the nonmanual ranks. Nearly 30 percent of Anglo sons of skilled fathers became professionals. The same was true for only 6 percent of the Mexican Americans. For the latter group, it was insurance against skidding. Only 10 percent of the Mexican American sons of skilled fathers dropped to the unskilled ranks. Most striking of all was the failure of Mexican Americans in San Antonio to retain high-status gains beyond a single generation. Only 13.3 percent of Mexican-American sons of professionals or managers ever became professionals themselves, yet 50 percent of the Anglo sons whose fathers had been professionals or managers achieved a similar status.

Both Mexican Americans and Anglos display substantial occupational mobility. Southern Anglos, however, were more likely to either attain upward occupational mobility or retain professional or managerial status, while the Mexican Americans of San Antonio were more likely to be downwardly mobile or to preserve skilled blue-collar status. This can be summarized by focusing on movement across the blue collar/white collar social class line. Of those whose fathers were in blue-collar (skilled or unskilled) occupations, 41.1 percent of the Anglos moved into white-collar (professional or clerical) occupations, compared to 23.3 percent of the Mexican Americans. Of those originating in white-collar statuses, 43.5 percent of the Anglos became blue-collar workers compared to 61.3 percent of the Mexican Americans. Yet another way to make the comparison is to consider the index of occupational dissimilarity.[28] Focusing on the fathers, the index of dissimilarity between the Mexican Americans and the Anglos is 18.6. The comparable index for the respondents is 19.1. This suggests, at best, no change in the occupational dissimilarity of Anglos and Mexican Americans in the most recent generation.

Intragenerational Mobility

Because of the sizes of the samples and the comparability problems in the previous analysis, it is worth focusing more precisely on comparative occupational mobility in San Antonio. Data collected from Polk city directories in San Antonio permit a comparison of intragenerational occupational mobility between 1968 and 1978 for Hispanics (predominantly Mexican Americans) and non-Hispanics (predominantly Anglos). These results are presented in Table 3.4.

The rows with percentages for all occupations in Table 3.4 indicate that San Antonio Mexican Americans are again much more likely to be in the lower-status occupations, and possibly as a result, the city's non-Hispanics were much more likely to be in professional or managerial positions as of 1978. Considerable mobility, however, is evident for both groups. About 21 percent of the Mexican Americans attained upward occupational mobility, with 10 percent encountering downward mobility. The comparable figures for the Anglos are 14 percent and 8 percent respectively. The Hispanic population, therefore, is more likely to encounter both upward and downward intragenerational mobility in this recent time period. In terms of upward mobility, however, Mexican Americans were less likely than Anglos to move to professional or managerial jobs. And in terms of downward mobility, Mexican Americans were more likely to move to lower positions. Nearly 10 percent of all Mexican-American professionals or managers from 1968 moved to skilled or unskilled blue-collar positions by 1978. This compares to only 2.3 percent for non-Hispanics. Furthermore, Mexican Americans were less likely to preserve high status. Only 80.9 percent of Hispanic professionals or managers were still in this category by 1978, compared to 89.7 percent of the Anglos. The lower measures of statistical association

Table 3.4: Occupational Mobility, 1968 to 1978, by Ethnicity

Major Occupation, 1968	Major Occupation, 1978					
	Professional, Manager	Clerical, Sales	Skilled Labor	Unskilled Labor	Total	N
	Hispanic[a]					
Professional, manager	80.9	9.6	7.0	2.6	100.1	115
Clerical, sales	14.0	77.2	7.3	1.6	100.1	193
Skilled labor[a]	8.4	13.6	67.6	10.5	100.1	287
Unskilled labor[b]	13.1	11.5	27.0	48.4	100.0	122
All occupations	22.3	29.7	34.7	13.2	99.9	
N	160	213	249	95		717
	Non-Hispanic[b]					
Professional, manager	89.7	7.9	1.7	0.6	99.9	466
Clerical, sales	21.7	67.5	8.8	2.1	100.1	240
Skilled labor[a]	19.8	7.7	69.6	2.8	99.9	247
Unskilled labor[b]	15.1	9.4	13.2	62.3	100.0	53
All occupations	52.4	22.2	20.7	4.8	100.1	
N	527	223	208	48		1,006

[a]Chi square = 717.15, $p < .01$; Pearson's $r = 0.63$, $p = .01$; Kendall's tau $b = 0.59$, $p < .01$.

[b]Chi square = 1298.07, $p < .01$; Pearson's $r = 0.72$, $p < .01$; Kendall's tau $b = 0.69$, $p < .01$.

between fathers' and sons' occupational status for the Mexican Americans appear to reflect this lower ability to preserve status.

Focusing again on movement between blue-collar and white-collar positions, 27.0 percent of Anglos in blue-collar positions in 1968 moved to white-collar positions by 1978. This compares to 22.7 percent for Mexican Americans. Of the Anglos in white-collar jobs in 1968, only 5.2 percent moved to blue-collar positions in 1978, compared to 9.1 percent of the Mexican Americans. The index of occupational dissimilarity between San Antonio non-Hispanics and Mexican Americans in 1968 is 30.2, very close to the results from the 1970 census data presented earlier in Table 3.1. As of 1978 the index is 30.0, again indicating essentially no change over time in the occupational dissimilarity of these groups.

The occupational experiences of Mexican Americans in San Antonio as reflected in these samples is complex. On the one hand, the attainments of Mexican Americans seem substantial. Based on the Shifflett sample, 36 percent of the Mexican Americans had moved up the occupational ladder from the status of their fathers, while only 23 percent of their fathers had been upwardly mobile.[29] Furthermore, according to the city directory sample, 21 percent of Mexican Americans had been upwardly mobile in their own careers between 1968 and 1978. This picture of achievement must be tempered, however, by an understanding of the nature and extent of their occupational gains. Movement into nonmanual positions has been much more difficult for Mexican Americans than for Anglos. Additionally, downward mobility has been much more prevalent for them. Furthermore, even with all of this mobility, there has been no decline in the extent of occupational dissimilarity between Mexican Americans and Anglos. A more rigorous analysis of the determinants of occupational status is needed in order to understand these trends.

Multiple Determinants of Occupational Mobility and Attainment

The greater educational gains for Mexican Americans documented in Table 3.2 would be expected to have contributed to greater occupational gains than those actually made. This paradox may be partially clarified by an examination of the medians and the means. There is more than a one-year difference in the mean years of education between Mexican Americans in San Antonio and Anglos in southern SMSAs (see Table 3.2). This difference is explained by the larger numbers of Anglos completing college levels of education. The medians, however, do not reflect such a difference. Discrepancies might be expected, therefore, in the relative proportions employed in professional or managerial jobs, where a college education is essential. Much larger proportions of Anglos have completed some college (see Table 3.1). Yet if education actually explains the differences in occupational attainment, one would expect equal access to positions below the professional or managerial level, where the educational attainments of Mexican Americans have equalled those of Anglos. This does not appear to be the case. Clearly, other factors are operating to influence the process.

Traditionally, number of years of formal schooling has been considered the most important determinant of occupational status.[30] Additionally, characteristics of the family of origin, facility with the language of the host country (English), and the adoption of its cultural and behavioral patterns are thought to play a role in occupational attainment.[31] In Table 3.5 the

Table 3.5: Correlations between Selected Variables for Mexican Americans in San Antonio (above the diagonal) and Anglos in Southern SMSAs (below the diagonal)

				Mexican Americans					
Anglos	*Curr. Occup.*	*Resp. Educ.*	*Father's Occup.*	*Father's Educ.*	*Resp. Age*	*Family Size*	*Gen. in U.S.*	*Visit Mexico*	*Lang. Prob.*
Curr. occup.	—	0.29	0.13[a]	0.11[a]	−0.01[a]	−0.12	0.21	−0.15	−0.33
Resp. educ.	0.55	—	0.20	0.42	−0.32	0.04	0.46	−0.18	−0.71
Father's occup.	0.21	0.36	—	0.29	−0.19	−0.25	0.21	0.03[a]	−0.18
Father's educ.	0.25	0.45	0.51	—	−0.38	−0.03[a]	0.22	−0.02[a]	−0.36
Resp. age	0.16	−0.19	−0.04[a]	−0.16	—	−0.03[a]	−0.42	−0.11	0.20
Family size	−0.08[a]	−0.05[a]	0.05[a]	−0.14[a]	−0.13	—	−0.14[a]	0.23	0.06[a]
Gen. in U.S.							—	−0.30	−0.52
Visit Mexico								—	−0.24
Lang. prob.									—

NOTE: Correlations are based on varying numbers of cases, depending on missing data.

[a] Not significant at $p < 0.05$.

interrelationships among several variables in the attainment process are presented. Where appropriate, information is provided from both the Shifflett sample of Mexican Americans in San Antonio and the NORC sample of Anglos in the Southwest.

Among Mexican Americans, lack of fluency in English appears to be the single most important deterrent to high occupational position, with a correlation of −0.33. This is closely followed by level of education, with a correlation of 0.29. Education and language ability, as would be expected, are closely related (−0.71). The number of generations that the respondents' families have lived in the United States is positively related to current occupational position (0.21), and, as a further measure of acculturation, respondents who visit Mexico frequently are less likely to be in higher status occupations (−0.15). These are among the most important variables in the assimilationist model that might be used to explain the occupational differences observed earlier.

Comparing the Mexican American and Anglo samples, education is the most important of the variables common to both groups. But the relationship between education and occupation is much stronger in the Anglo sample (0.55 versus 0.29), suggesting that education may actually have less of a payoff in terms of occupational attainment for the Mexican Americans. Evaluating this possibility would require a multivariate framework. Father's occupation and father's education are also more strongly related to son's occupation for the Anglos. This is consistent with the results from Tables 3.3 and 3.4, which show that Mexican Americans in San Antonio are less likely to retain high-status positions and more likely to encounter downward occupational mobility.

Age is generally positively related to occupational attainment through a process of cumulative career development, although younger people often attain higher levels of education than older people. For the Anglo sample, age is positively related to occupational position as expected, but for the Mexican Americans age has an insignificant negative relationship. This may be due to the stronger negative relationship between age and education for the Mexican Americans, again suggesting the need for a multivariate framework. Current family size appears unrelated to current occupational position in the absence of other controls. There is an insignificant negative relationship between family size and occupation position for Mexican Americans (−0.12) and for Anglos (−0.08).

Cumulatively, the results to this point suggest the need to examine several explanatory variables simultaneously. Tables 3.6 and 3.7 present the results of multiple regression analyses for each of the samples. Table 3.6 examines

Table 3.6: Determinants of Current Occupational
Status for Mexican Americans and Anglos

	Mexican Americans in San Antonio		Anglos in Southern SMSAs	
	Unstand. Coeff.	Stand. Coeff.	Unstand. Coeff.	Stand. Coeff.
Education	0.11[a]	0.38	0.16[a]	0.53
Father's occupation	0.08	0.09	0.01	0.01
Father's education	0.04	0.02	0.01	0.03
Family size	−0.08	−0.15	−0.04	−0.06
Age	0.01	0.16	0.02[a]	0.27
Constant	0.60		−0.11	
R^2	0.18		0.37	
Adjusted R^2	0.13		0.34	
(N)	(77)		(119)	

[a]Significant at $p < 0.01$.

the variables common to both the San Antonio Mexican-American and the southern Anglo samples. Education is the only variable that is statistically significant in both samples. The coefficients indicate, however, that education has a smaller impact for the Mexican Americans than for the Anglos, confirming the evidence from the correlations discussed earlier. Father's occupation and education are not significant in either of the samples, suggesting that the effects of these two variables is primarily mediated by the educational attainments of the sons. Controlling for age and education, family size is consistently negatively related to current occupation, although the results are not statistically significant. Nevertheless, it can be safely concluded that family size is not significantly more important for the Mexican Americans than for the Anglos.

These variables account for 37 percent of the variance in occupational position for the Anglos, but for only 18 percent for the Mexican Americans. This is largely attributable to the greater impact of both education and age for the Anglos. These findings reinforce the earlier suggestion that the traditional determinants of occupational attainment are less predictive of the experience of Mexican Americans. Clearly, other factors operate to influence occupational attainment for Mexican Americans in San Antonio.

Finally, Table 3.7 presents results for the Mexican Americans in San

Table 3.7: Determinants of Current Occupational Status
for Mexican Americans in San Antonio

	Unstandardized Coefficient	*Standardized Coefficient*
Education	0.13[a]	0.46
Father's occupation	0.08	0.10
Father's education	0.01	0.06
Family size	−0.08	−0.15
Age	0.02	0.18
Generation in U.S.	−0.11	−0.08
Visit Mexico	0.09	0.09
Language problem	0.10	0.10
Constant	−0.01	
R^2	0.20	
Adjusted R^2	0.11	
(N)	(76)	

[a]Significant at $p < 0.01$.

Antonio, introducing generation in the United States, frequency of visits to Mexico, and whether or not the respondents indicated that they have problems with the English language. Generation has a small negative coefficient, and language has a small positive coefficient; both of these results may be due to multicollinearity.[32] Visiting Mexico has a small effect in the expected direction. None of these measures suggested from the assimilationist perspective, however, is statistically significant in predicting occupational attainment.

Again, these results suggest that education is the only significant determinant of occupational position for Mexican Americans in San Antonio, but that education does not seem to have as great an effect for the Mexican Americans as it does for the Anglos. Furthermore, traditional measures of assimilation do not explain the differential effects of education and do not contribute significantly to the explanation of occupational attainments.

Conclusion

Given the large concentration of Mexican Americans in San Antonio, their chances for attaining higher occupational statuses may actually be greater than those of Mexican Americans elsewhere. Furthermore, given the political participation of Mexican Americans in recent years, their attainments relative to Anglos may improve in the future. Nevertheless, at present it must be concluded that San Antonio Mexican Americans have not attained equal chances for occupational success even in the city's relatively favorable environment.

The patterns of occupational mobility documented here appear to be largely due to the changing occupational structure of San Antonio rather than to any trend toward increasing integration of Mexican Americans and Anglos. This kind of structural mobility has done little to reduce the social and economic segregation associated with unequal distribution in the occupational structure of the community. This is clearly illustrated by the stagnant levels of occupational dissimilarity evident in both the intergenerational and the intragenerational analyses.

Judging from the evidence of this analysis, no progress has been made toward greater occupational integration. Furthermore, traditional assimilation variables do not appear to be very important in explaining the lower occupational attainments of Mexican Americans, and education appears to have a smaller effect on later occupational success. These findings are consistent with arguments presented in other chapters of this volume, displaying an historical and political context in which the interests of community elites have been advanced, often at the expense of minorities. The inequality of educational opportunity and the differential quality of education documented by Gambitta, Milne, and Davis (Chapter 7) may play an important role in the interpretation of the results presented here. Specifically, the evidence of a smaller payoff from education for Mexican Americans in San Antonio is consistent with their argument about the long-term repercussions of unequal access to quality education.

In the absence of other evidence, the themes of discrimination and exploitation appear to be the most relevant for interpreting the occupational inequality observed in San Antonio. The patterns of occupational cleavage documented here will undoubtedly be important in defining the context of political action in San Antonio throughout the 1980s.

Part II: Contemporary Political Forces

Robert Brischetto,
Charles L. Cotrell, and
R. Michael Stevens

Chapter Four

Conflict and Change in the Political Culture of San Antonio in the 1970s

It is conventional wisdom among social scientists that the legal framework of a democratic government must be consistent with the values of a society. When the formal rules of a political system do not reflect the social, economic and cultural environment,[1] the rules will be questioned, the basis of political representation challenged, and popular pressure brought to bear to change the political structure and its elected officials.

San Antonio provides a case example of just such political upheaval. During the 1970s, the city was transformed from an oligarchic political system dominated by an "Anglo" business elite to a system with elected representatives roughly approximating the ethnic, geographic, and class divisions in the city's population.

While changes in the city's social and economic character can be attributed to forces operating within the region popularly known as the Sunbelt,[2] the political transformation of San Antonio is more nearly due to major policy changes in the formal rules of local political representation. In altering its legal framework from a council elected at large to one elected from single-member districts in 1977, the city opened its politics to a public significantly different from that which participated in the past. Moreover, these new participants have demanded a redefinition of the agenda of public debate and policy making in city government.

The most striking characteristic of San Antonio is that, demographically, it is a Mexican city. Over half of the city's residents are of Mexican descent. Having been founded as a colonial outpost of Mexico, San Antonio has long been a Mexican city culturally, although Anglo political and economic domination has been a settled fact since 1847.

San Antonio's Mexican-American majority is largely concentrated in thirty-five contiguous census tracts located on the west and south sides of the city. (See Figure 4.1.) These thirty-five tracts, each with 70 percent or more Hispanic residents, contain some 55 percent of the city's Mexican-American community. Many of the residential neighborhoods surrounding this area had ethnically and racially restrictive covenants in the deeds to their properties in earlier decades.[3] The pattern of *de facto* ethnic segregation persists even today. In addition to being ethnically segregated, Mexican Americans are notably poorer, less educated, and worse housed than their Anglo counterparts.

Blacks constitute a relatively smaller proportion of the city's population—approximately 7 percent. They too are highly segregated, with 59 percent of their numbers in eight census tracts of 50 percent or more black residents on the city's near east side. On the average, family income in these tracts is less than half that of the predominantly Anglo areas, the median education level 2.5 years lower, and housing considerably less adequate than housing in Anglo areas. (See Table 4.1.)

A recent series of studies of city service delivery shows patterns of inequities in which Mexican-American west side and black east side neighborhoods consistently received lower levels of some services than Anglo North side neighborhoods. The services measured and found to be less available to the city's minority neighborhoods included services supported by federal revenue sharing funds, responsiveness of the Zoning Commission to neighborhood requests, street paving and repairing, the drainage system, and public libraries.[4]

Historically, discrimination has typified the electoral politics of city government. During the modern charter era in San Antonio (1952–76), before the change in the representation system, only about one-fourth of the city council members were Spanish surnamed, even though the group was a majority of the population. Moreover, only 13 of the 117 council members for the same period lived in the predominantly (70%–100%) Mexican-American west side. The city council appointees to boards and commissions reflected the same pattern of ethnic underrepresentation. A survey of members of six important boards and commissions from 1952 to 1974 found that only 10 percent of 314 appointees lived on the west side.[5] Representation of the predominantly black east side census tracts on the city council began as an established pattern in 1965 when the ruling political party fielded a black candidate for the first time on its ticket. Since blacks constituted only about

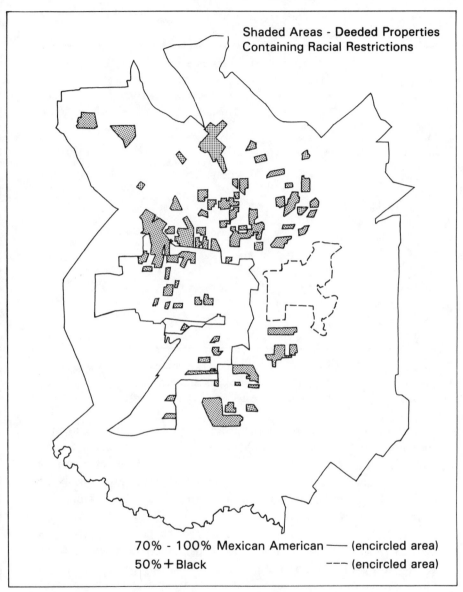

Shaded Areas - Deeded Properties Containing Racial Restrictions

70% - 100% Mexican American ——— (encircled area)

50% + Black   --- (encircled area)

Figure 4.1: Deeded properties with racial or ethnic restrictions before 1950 and ethnic group concentrations in 1970, San Antonio.

Table 4.1: Select Socioeconomic Characteristics
of Anglo, Hispanic, and Black Neighborhoods, 1970

	Anglo (25 census tracts; 70%+ Anglo)	Mexican-American (35 census tracts; 70%+ Mexican-American)	Black (8 census tracts; 50%+ black)	San Antonio
Median income	$11,958	$5,803	$5,617	$6,563
Families below poverty line	4.8%	22.1%	29.4%	17.5%
Median year of school completed	12.8	6.8	10.3	10.8
Houses without any or some plumbing	1.7%	13.5%	6.0%	6.0%

SOURCE: U.S. Bureau of the Census, *Census of Population and Housing: 1970 Census Tracts*, Final Report PHC (1)-186 San Antonio, Texas SMSA (Washington, D.C.: U.S. Government Printing Office, 1972).

8 percent of the city's population, a victory for a black candidate in an at-large numbered place system would have been next to impossible without endorsement from the ruling party at that time. East side representation on city boards and commissions was also low from 1952 to 1974: only about 3 percent of the appointments to the six selected boards and commissions were east side residents.

Although nonpartisan politics characterized the modern charter period in theory, access to San Antonio municipal government was in reality controlled by a ruling political party, the Good Government League, or GGL. The GGL in turn was controlled by a group of Anglo businessmen who established and maintained their power through such devices of municipal reform politics as nonpartisan elections, council-manager government, at-large elections, single-place competition, and majority election.[6] The GGL's control of public policy shaped the city's development patterns and furthered the economic interests of its supporters.[7] By astute strategy and superior campaign resources, the GGL monopolized municipal elections from 1955 to 1973, winning seventy-three of the eighty-one council races. While this success was accomplished with support from all segments of the electorate, an examination of voting patterns by neighborhood shows unmistakable evidence of ethnic polarization in which voters in predominantly Mexican-American precincts voted for non-GGL candidates, particularly those with Spanish surnames.

The city elections of the 1970s illustrate well the politics of ethnic polarization. From 1971 to 1975, when the GGL was still alive politically, Mexican-American voters expressed their opposition to this ruling Anglo political elite by supporting Mexican-American candidates who were not slated by the GGL over Anglo and Mexican-American GGL candidates for city council. Table 4.2 illustrates this pattern by relating the percentage of votes cast for GGL candidates and for all Mexican-American candidates to a precinct's ethnic concentration in each at-large race during 1971–81. Table 4.3 presents the same election results in a different fashion with correlation coefficients and slopes of the regression lines relating percentage voting for GGL candidates and for Mexican-American candidates to a precinct's concentration of Spanish-surnamed voters. The Pearson correlation coefficient (r) indicates the extent to which there is a linear pattern in the relationships, and the slope (b) shows the severity of the polarization. For example, the patterns of ethnic polarization are illustrated by the relationship of the percentage of votes cast for the Mexican-American candidate for mayor in 1971 (Peter Torres) to the percentage Spanish-surnamed of registered voters in each precinct. The pattern is clearly a direct linear relationship (with an r of .94) and the degree of polarization is severe (with a slope of .72). See Figure 4.2 for a graphic display of this and other examples.

An examination of the patterns of voting presented in Tables 4.2 and 4.3 reveals that, with only four exceptions out of twenty-nine races during 1971–81, when at-large elections were held for council seats, candidates with Spanish surnames polled considerably greater percentages of the votes as the proportion of Mexican-American registered voters in the precincts increased. Conversely, precincts which were almost all Anglo (0%–30% Spanish-surnamed) cast a smaller percentage of their ballots for Mexican-American candidates than the city as a whole and considerably smaller percentages than those precincts with predominantly (70%–100%) Mexican-American populations. Each of the four exceptions to this pattern of voter support for candidates of one's own ethnic group occurred when a Mexican-American candidate was sponsored by the Good Government League.[8]

Support for GGL candidates in predominantly Mexican-American pre-

Table 4.2: Percentages Voting for Good Government League and Mexican-American Candidates by Ethnic Concentration of Precincts in San Antonio Municipal Elections, 1971–81

Election & Place	GGL Candidate	0%–29.9% Sp. Surnames		30%–69.9% Sp. Surnames		70%–100% Sp. Surnames		50%–100% Black		All Voters	
		GGL	M-A	GGL	M-A	GGL	M-A	GGL	M-A	GGL	M-A
1971											
Place 1	Haberman*	75%	15%	48%	40%	24%	65%	42%	30%	58%	31%
Place 2	Hill*	71	5	51	21	30	44	53	11	59	16
Place 3	Becker*	78	12	55	34	32	59	63	27	64	26
Place 4	Hilliard*	79	12	60	30	42	47	81	10	68	22
Place 5	Mendoza*	67	73	57	72	52	78	58	71	62	74
Place 6	G. Garza*	61	66	40	48	25	42	35	44	48	56
Place 7	Naylor*	75	13	49	40	25	67	41	32	59	30
Place 8	Trevino*	68	76	49	64	34	60	56	66	56	70
Place 9 (M)	Gatti*	79	19	52	46	28	71	58	40	62	36
No. of voters		58,565		26,670		22,661		4,395		112,271	
No. of precincts		76		48		35		11		170	
1973											
Place 1	Cockrell*	65	—	59	—	56	—	71	—	62	—
Place 2	San Martin*	58	66	60	75	67	87	69	81	61	72
Place 3 (M)	Barrera	8	39	51	53	69	72	51	52	47	49
Place 4	Black*	58	12	49	26	40	42	88	5	55	20
Place 5	Guess	44	7	41	22	40	39	62	11	43	16
Place 6	Morton*	42	16	30	40	23	61	59	20	37	29
Place 7	Beckman*	51	16	41	33	29	53	58	22	45	26
Place 8	—	—	64	—	68	—	77	—	66	—	67
Place 9	Dunn	39	44	29	57	20	72	40	48	34	52
No. of voters		45,044		18,989 ·		15,967		3,514		83,514	
No. of precincts		88		48		34		11		181	

1975										
Place 1	Pyndus*	54	27	35	52	14	79	25	63	42	42
Place 2	Montalvo	33	42	33	51	30	62	37	32	32	48
Place 3	Cisneros*	56	70	50	76	44	85	14	66	52	74
Place 4	McGowan	35	6	26	17	15	32	7	3	29	13
Place 5	Craig	31	9	21	25	9	50	17	15	24	20
Place 6	Beldon	44	6	29	22	16	43	16	7	35	16
Place 7	Mora	31	77	24	82	17	91	21	88	26	81
Place 8	O. Garza	49	49	47	47	48	48	21	21	48	48
Place 9 (M)	Cockrell*	59	10	43	26	22	47	36	11	48	21
No. of voters		—	56,593	—	21,287	—	21,935	—	3,549	—	103,364
No. of precincts		—	95	—	40	—	40	—	8	—	183
1977										
Mayor	—	—	14	—	34	—	57	—	12	—	28
No. of voters		—	53,621	—	24,339	—	23,430	—	3,930	—	105,320
No. of precincts		—	89	—	48	—	42	—	9	—	188
1979										
Mayor	—	—	3	—	11	—	22	—	4	—	9
No. of voters		—	41,186	—	22,083	—	18,664	—	3,052	—	84,985
No. of precincts		—	78	—	56	—	46	—	8	—	188
1981										
Mayor	—	—	45	—	73	—	94	—	78	—	65
No. of voters		—	65,426	—	35,281	—	34,570	—	3,594	—	138,871
No. of precincts		—	88	—	55	—	49	—	8	—	200

SOURCE: Official election returns are from City Clerk of San Antonio. Registration counts are from Bexar County registration tapes, County Elections Office.

NOTE: * = candidate won (M) = mayoral race — = no candidate fielded.

Table 4.3: Pearson Correlations (r) and Slopes (b) Relating Percentage
of Spanish-Surnamed Voters in Precinct to Percentages Voting
for Good Government League and Mexican American Candidates
in San Antonio City Council Regular Elections 1971–81

Election and Place	GGL Candidate	% Sp. Surnames Registered Voters with			
		% Voting for GGL Candidate		% Voting for M-A Candidates	
		r	b	r	b
1971					
Place 1	Haberman*	−.88	−.67	.95	.68
Place 2	Hill*	−.88	−.55	.96	.53
Place 3	Becker*	−.94	−.64	.96	.64
Place 4	Hilliard*	−.95	−.54	.97	.50
Place 5	Mendoza*	−.65	−.23	.22	.05
Place 6	Garza*	−.81	−.51	−.72	−.33
Place 7	Naylor*	−.89	−.67	.92	.74
Place 8	Trevino*	−.83	−.47	−.71	−.24
Place 9 (M)	Gatti*	−.94	−.70	.94	.72
1973					
Place 1	Cockrell*	−.48	−.15	—	—
Place 2	San Martin*	.26	.08	.66	.26
Place 3 (M)	Barrera	.84	.40	.85	.43
Place 4	Black*	−.65	−.31	.94	.43
Place 5	Guess	−.33	−.10	.95	.43
Place 6	Morton*	−.76	−.32	.90	.62
Place 7	Beckmann	−.72	−.32	.95	.51
Place 8	—	—	—	.58	.16
Place 9	Dunn	−.68	−.28	.84	.39
1975					
Place 1	Pyndus*	−.83	−.55	.91	.70
Place 2	Montalvo	−.18	−.42	.78	.27
Place 3	Cisneros*	−.47	−.16	.72	.20
Place 4	McGowan	.73	−.27	.98	.37
Place 5	Craig	−.68	−.31	.98	.57
Place 6	Beldon	−.04	−.50	.98	.51
Place 7	Mora	−.57	−.20	.62	.16
Place 8	O. Garza	−.00	−.00	−.01	−.00
Place 9 (M)	Cockrell*	−.38	−.57	.97	.52

Table 4.3 Continued

		% Sp. Surnames Registered Voters with			
		% Voting for GGL Candidate		% Voting for M-A Candidates	
Election and Place	GGL Candidate	r	b	r	b
1977 Mayor	—	—	—	.98	.57
1979 Mayor	—	—	—	.94	.27
1981 Mayor	—	—	—	.90	.66

SOURCE: Official election returns are from City Clerk of San Antonio. Registration counts are from Bexar County registration tapes, County Elections Office.

NOTE: * = candidate won   (M) = mayoral rate   — = no candidate fielded. The regression analyses were weighted by the number of persons voting in each race.

cincts was clearly lacking in all but two of the twenty-six races in which the GGL fielded candidates from 1971 through 1975. The most striking finding, however, is that this patterned opposition to the GGL occurred in most cases regardless of the candidate's ethnicity. Indeed, antipathy among Mexican-American voters to GGL leadership was so strong during this period that Mexican-American candidates nominated by the GGL risked outright rejection by voters in predominantly Mexican-American precincts in favor of non-GGL Anglos who had acquired unambiguous reputations as anti-establishment "reformers." In seven of the nine cases in which the GGL fielded Mexican-American candidates from 1971 to 1975, there was less support for the Mexican-American GGL candidate in the predominantly Spanish-surnamed precincts than in the predominantly Anglo precincts. This phenomenon is illustrated in 1971, when the GGL named Gilbert Garza and Felix Trevino to oppose the reform candidates D. Ford Nielsen and Merry Baker, respectively. The two reform candidates had joined former councilman Pete Torres (a candidate for mayor) in an effort to break the GGL's uninterrupted record of control over the city council. In both cases, the GGL's Mexican-American candidates received less than half as many

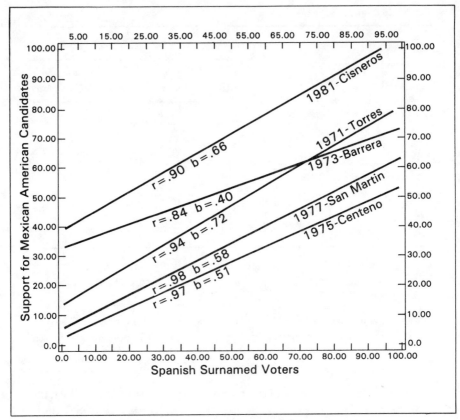

Figure 4.2: Regression lines relating percentage of support for Mexican-American mayoral candidate with percentage of Spanish-surnamed registered voters, San Antonio, 1971–81.

votes in the predominantly Mexican-American precincts as they did in the predominantly Anglo precincts (see Table 4.2).

The 1971 election challenge to the GGL's previously unquestioned hegemony is an important indicator of the changes that were taking place in the community's political culture during the 1970s. On the one hand, the historic opposition in the Mexican-American community was effectively exploited during the first half of the 1970s by independent candidates in municipal elections. The impact of this newly organized opposition to GGL domination is shown indirectly in the election statistics of this period. The 1971 election was remarkable not only because the GGL felt obligated to oppose two Anglo reformers with the two Mexican-American candidates in order to weaken the reform appeal in the Mexican-American population, but also for the extraordinary voter interest generated by Peter Torres' campaign for mayor against GGL nominee John Gatti. Voter turnout jumped from 33 percent in 1969 to 53 percent in 1971, a level of participation which has not been repeated since. The average turnout in the subsequent municipal elections of 1973–79 was 34 percent, ranging from 19 percent to 39 percent. Apparently the reformist approach of Torres, Nielsen, and Baker struck a responsive chord among Mexican Americans already dissatisfied with the Anglo oligarchy's ideals of good government. Higher voter registration and turnout among the Anglo electorate, however, assured victory for the GGL candidates.

The election of 1971 was the last time that San Antonio's council was totally composed of GGL-sponsored members. The two elections prior to the city's major charter change in 1977 marked a period of organizational unrest and decline within the GGL and the emergence of electoral competition on the part of former GGL supporters. It was also during this period that the city witnessed the advent and growth of a powerful citizen force in politics—Citizens Organized for Public Service (COPS). An Alinsky-styled neighborhood organization, COPS began in 1974 to press hard for greater equity in city services and for capital improvements in south and west side barrios.[9] Although as a matter of principle it refused to endorse candidates for political office, COPS worked through the Catholic parishes to conduct sweeping voter registration drives to improve the political clout of heretofore unenfranchised segments of the city's population. "Accountability nights" were staged to inform candidates of COPS's position on selected issues. COPS was soon to become the most influential mass-based organization in the city's history.

Ironically, however, the most dangerous threat to the establishment monopoly in municipal politics emerged from within the city's oligarchy. The 1973 council election provided an arena in which two groups of business leaders competed for control of the city government.

Shaken by the near success of the reformers in 1971, the GGL attempted to reestablish its dominance by coopting representatives of new interests as nominees on the party's slate for 1973. To appeal to female voters, Lila Cockrell was pitted against reformer Wanda Ford for council. To strengthen and rebuild the party's ties to the Mexican-American community, Dr. San Martin and Roy Barrera were nominated, with Barrera designated as the GGL's choice for mayor (see Chapter 6). To bridge growing divisions within the business community between the younger and older generation of developers, the GGL placed new developer Clifford Morton on their slate.

These well-laid plans came asunder, however, when Charles Becker, a prominent and successful businessman, decided to run as an independent against his former allies' choice for mayor. Becker's independent opposition to the GGL was strengthened by several other strong non-GGL candidates who abandoned the GGL slate just prior to filing as official candidates. The defection of significant members of the business community during this election—particularly the new developers of the Northside Chamber of Commerce—proved to be more costly to the GGL than the earlier opposition of the reformers. In 1973 the GGL lost five of the nine places on the city council and, having lost the majority, lost the mayoralty for the first time in its twenty-year history (see Table 4.2).[10]

The 1975 election saw a clarification of the division within the city's business elite and the final collapse of the GGL. Roughly, the two camps can be identified with the downtown Chamber of Commerce under the titular leadership of former mayor Walter McAllister and the other GGL influentials, on the one hand, and Northside Chamber of Commerce influentials under Becker's leadership unabashedly committed to developing the north side of the city, on the other hand. The dissident north side businessmen were joined in the effort to unseat the GGL once and for all by a loose coalition of disenchanted former GGL council members, south side businessmen, and reform-minded Anglos.[11] Calling themselves the Independent Team, this "overnight coalition"[12] succeeded in electing six of the nine council members (see Table 4.2). Since the city charter had recently been amended to provide for separate election of the mayor by popular vote, the GGL won that office.

During the demise of the GGL, Mexican-American representation on the council slipped from three members in 1971 and 1973 to two in 1975; the Mexican-American majority in the population lost representation on the city council despite the electoral success of the Independent Team. To understand the historical pattern of inadequate Mexican-American representation on the city council, we must examine the formal constitution of the city's political system. The political status of San Antonio's Mexican-American community has been defined to a large extent by the formal rules of political participation.

First, until recently Texas has had an extremely restrictive body of law regulating eligibility to vote. Texas retained the poll tax for state and local elections until 1966.[13] The influence of this economic cost of voting continues to discourage persons in lower-income groups whose ideas about politics were formed during the poll tax era. Until 1965 persons who had come to Texas as a result of military duty were denied the right to vote as long as they remained on active duty.[14] This peculiar restriction is especially relevant in a city whose largest employer is the U.S. Department of Defense. Property ownership was required to vote in bond elections until 1969[15] and in tax elections until 1975.[16]

But the most serious limitations on voter registration and participation were the general qualifications for registration. Until 1972 a person had to reside in the state for one year and the county for six months prior to registration.[17] Once the residency requirement was met, a prospective voter had to overcome the final hurdle of registration itself. Until 1972 Texas required annual registration of voters and cut off registration on January 31 or nine months before the general elections.[18] Equally important, it was not until 1975 that Texas law provided for the printing of registration and voting materials in Spanish, an omission which had the same effect as the infamous Southern literacy test for much of San Antonio's Spanish-speaking population.

The combined effect of these restrictions on participation was to severely limit political participation among low-income, poorly educated, non-English-speaking Texans, persons who have historically constituted a sizable portion of San Antonio's population.

Reforms of the Texas voting laws progressed slowly during the 1960s, but the principal source of change was the passage of the 1975 Voting Rights Act (VRA) amendments.[19] This revision of the 1965 VRA for blacks extended the federal standards of fair election procedures to Texas (in order to protect the voting rights of Mexican Americans). In response, the Texas legislature enacted a number of reforms in the state's election code which reduced registration requirements and simplified registration procedures to such an extent that nearly anyone over eighteen years of age who resides in Texas and is a U.S. citizen can register to vote (by postage-free post card, if necessary). These reforms have revolutionary potential in a major city whose population is characterized by exceptionally low per capita rates of literacy, education, and income—the chief socioeconomic correlates of low levels of political participation. In a stroke, the formal rules designed to discourage—if not prohibit—voting by the poor, the propertyless, and the immigrant were eliminated.[20]

The annexation of approximately sixty-six square miles of new territory in 1972 produced a second change in the formal framework of San Antonio politics. While the city council had viewed these new areas as sources of future population growth, the immediate effect was to bring into the city's political system 51,400 additional residents. As there was considerable opposition in those areas to annexation and to the city taxes that followed the change in city boundaries, these new precincts became additional sources of opposition to the GGL leadership which had approved and carried out the annexation policy. During the 1973 council election the average vote for GGL candidates in the annexed precincts was only 31.4 percent, compared to a 48.5 percent vote for the GGL in the remainder of the city. The total vote cast by the nine annexed precincts represented 5 percent of the total city vote in 1973, enough to make a difference in the close election.

The 1973 election was the first time the GGL lost its control of the office of mayor. The GGL candidate for mayor, Roy Barrera, lost the runoff election with 46.7 percent of the votes, or by 5,688 votes (see Table 4.2). A shift of only a little more than 3 percent of the votes, or 2,995 votes, would have translated into a Barrera victory. The newly annexed precincts opposed the GGL slate with approximately 70 percent of their votes. It is clear that the annexations brought about by the GGL-dominated council elected in 1971 contributed to the GGL's demise in the following election.

As it turned out, the secondary effects of the 1972 annexations were even more devastating to the political order and ideals of the Good Government League than their direct effects in the election of 1973. As a consequence of the 1975 VRA amendments, the San Antonio annexations were subject to review by the U.S. Department of Justice even though they had taken place prior to the extension of the VRA to Texas. In 1976 the Justice Department objected to the annexations on the ground that the proportions of Anglos to Mexican-American residents of the annexed territory (approximately 3:1 Anglo), when added to the rest of the city, diluted the majority status of the Mexican-American population. Such a diminution of the percentage of Mexican Americans was judged to be an official act having the effect of "denying or abridging the right to vote on account of race or color" because it reduced the opportunity for Mexican-American representation in the city government. The Justice Department indicated that unless the city altered its method of electing council members to provide more equitable representation of language and racial minorities, the nine precincts added in 1972 would have to be deannexed.[21] This was clearly an unrealistic alternative given the development of the city in those areas during the intervening years.

In spite of local opposition to submitting to the federal fiat, the city council proposed, and the voters of San Antonio adopted, changes in the city charter to replace the GGL-inspired electoral framework (at-large elections with a numbered place, majority vote requirement) with a council of ten persons elected from single-member districts and a mayor elected at large.[22] This change in the formal rules of the city's government has had a profound effect upon the informal rules of the community's politics. The electoral bias shifted away from the class which for so long has been out of power.

The at-large system of electing council persons used in San Antonio until 1977 rewards the majority of the persons who vote. In San Antonio, as is generally the case in this country, the likelihood that a person will vote is directly related to income and education. A clear majority of the city's participating electorate is Anglo (approximately 54% of registered voters), although a clear majority of the city's population is Mexican American.[23] At-large elections further exaggerated the influence of an Anglo electorate, since victory usually went to the candidates who were able to campaign successfully in the entire constituency. The size of the at-large district diluted the strength of candidates whose appeal was localized to geographic or neighborhood constituencies. Substantial resources were needed for a candidate to successfully appeal to a citywide electorate. These expenses added to the burden of an independent or minority group candidate seeking a seat on the city council.

The Good Government League capitalized upon those conditions which allowed them to monopolize the electoral process. The GGL offered potential candidates a vehicle by which their names would be advertised in a single citywide campaign effort at little or no personal cost. The economy of scale produced by a single campaign effort was also an inducement to major contributors, who could reduce the "costs" of local politics by supporting a single ticket of candidates. In the absence of a competing political party of comparable scope, the GGL was able to control city government by restricting access to the only citywide campaign organization. Nomination by the GGL meant virtual election to the City Council from 1955 to 1973.

The structure of competition in at-large elections, coupled with numbered places on the ballot, reinforced the advantages of a citywide organization. The organization was able to pit its most popular candidates and concentrate its efforts against the independent candidates most likely to make citywide appeals.[24] The city's poor, ethnic majority was always confronted with the double obstacle of not only organizing effective support for their most popular political spokespersons, but also of defeating the concentrated resources of the GGL. It was not sufficient to secure a place among the eight highest vote totals to win one of the eight city council seats: an independent candidate had to defeat the opponent handpicked by the GGL for a specific seat. The requirement that the winning candidate secure a majority of the votes cast in each contest only refined the advantage of the numbered place system for the GGL.[25] Candidates securing only a plurality in the election had to conduct a second citywide campaign in a runoff to secure a majority against their closest competitor. The resources of a well-financed organization were normally superior to those of an independent in meeting the expenses of a second campaign.

The effect of the formal rules in San Antonio on the outcome of elections is better understood if the conditions of ethnic polarization and the relatively low level of voter registration among Mexican Americans are kept in mind. While Mexican Americans may constitute slightly more than half the city's population, the percentage of Mexican Americans among those who register and vote is smaller than the percentage of Anglo registered voters.[26] Since both groups tend to support candidates of their own ethnic identity, Anglo candidates could attract more votes citywide than could Mexican-American candidates. By securing the loyalty and support of the Anglo electorate, the GGL was able to exploit the formal and informal rules of voting to its advantage for over twenty years. Mexican-American candidates, with few exceptions, were denied access to City Council unless they had the support of the Anglo elite as nominees of the GGL.

The change in the charter to district elections for city councils shifted the focus of the electoral process toward the number of city residents rather than the number of voters. In a single-member district system the council seats would be apportioned among geographic sections of the city that contained relatively equal numbers of residents. Therefore, neighborhoods were assured a representative regardless of whether their residents actually voted in the election. A fairly apportioned district system favored candidates who could appeal to a majority of the persons voting in a specific section of the community rather than a majority of the voters in the entire city. In a community divided between a distinctive ethnic majority and minority, each tending to live in relatively homogeneous neighborhoods, a system of single-member districts would tend to reflect the dominant group in each district.

Access to public office for Mexican-American and independent candidates would be increased when the size of the constituency was reduced, thereby lowering the cost of conducting a successful campaign.[27] Further, those districts containing a majority of Mexican-American residents possessed a greater likelihood of a majority of Mexican-American voters.

The 1977 elections produced the first city council with a majority of council persons being members of ethnic minorities. Five of the ten district seats were held by Mexican Americans representing the city's south and west sides, and one black council member was elected from an east side district. This shift in control of the council indicated a fundamental change in the distribution of political power in the community. Not only did the Anglo business elite lose its political arm, the GGL, as a result of the split in that elite in 1973, but it also lost control of the city council through an electoral system that reflects the city's Mexican-American majority.

The 1977 council responded to the change by altering a number of policies that earlier councils had adopted to support the goals of the Anglo elite. The new city council made efforts to check the city's uncontrolled geographic growth on the north side.[28] Related efforts were made to direct economic investment into the central business district and to improve the quality of city services delivered in the south, west, and east sides of the city. More-over, the 1977 council was careful to divide capital improvements equitably among the ten districts, revising the historic pattern of favoring the north side, predominately middle-class, Anglo neighborhoods.

The shift in political power from Anglo to Mexican-American sectors of the electorate was not complete, however. The changes in the formal struc-ture were not accompanied by comparable changes in voting behavior. Mexican-American voters still constituted a minority of the city's registered voters. Therefore, the Anglo voters still dominated conflicts resolved through citywide elections. These conflicts included the election of mayor, approval of city bonds, and charter revision. Elections in 1977 and 1978 illustrate the delicate balance within the city's political system between the supporters of further reform of city politics and the defenders of the status quo.

In 1977 the election to adopt the change in the city charter for single-member city council districts was approved by just 52.7 percent of the voters. While the support for the change was strongest in Mexican-American pre-cincts (89%, as shown in Table 4.4), some support of predominantly Anglo precincts was crucial to the success of the proposed revision. In districts where less than 30 percent of the voters had Spanish surnames, only one-third of the voters supported the change. In districts where 30–70 percent of the voters had Spanish surnames, more than 60 percent of the voters approved the district plan.

The significance of the Anglo support was made clear in a 1978 citywide election to approve a new bond for capital improvement. (See Table 4.4.) The proposed geographic allocation of these new capital improve-ments became the focus of the controversy during the bond election as Anglo council members voiced opposition to the decision of the non-Anglo majority to distribute the bulk of the city's total capital improvements among their south, west, and east side districts. By successfully mobilizing the Anglo electorate the proposed bonds were turned down by as much as

Table 4.4: Percentages Voting in Favor of Propositions in Special Elections by Ethnic Concentration of Voting Precincts, San Antonio, 1977–78

Election and Proposition	All Voters	By Ethnic Concentration of Precinct			
		0%–30% Sp.-Sur.	30%–70% Sp.-Sur.	70%–100% Sp.-Sur.	50%+ Black
1977 Charter Amendment					
10-1 Plan	52.7%	32.5%	61.4%	89.1%	69.0%
No. of voters	61,047	32,310	13,283	14,025	1,429
No. of precincts	186	87	48	42	9
1978 Bond Election					
Prop. 1: Police	44.0	21.9	52.8	84.8	80.0
Prop. 2: Fire	44.8	22.4	54.2	85.7	81.4
Prop. 3: Drain.	43.2	19.1	54.2	86.4	84.1
Prop. 4: Streets	43.2	18.8	53.5	87.5	83.8
Prop. 5: Parks	41.0	16.9	50.8	85.3	79.5
Prop. 6: Library	42.3	18.9	51.7	85.6	80.5
Prop. 7: Urban	40.8	16.4	51.1	85.3	81.7
No. of voters	93,712	50,183	20,487	20,384	2,658
No. of precincts	185	87	47	42	9

SOURCE: Official election returns, City of San Antonio, Office of City Clerk.

NOTE: Figures do not include absentee votes since these could not be classified by precinct.

60 percent of the city's voters (57,615 to 42,127). The 1978 bond election mirrors the voting divisions in the charter revision elections of 1974 and 1977. When the arena of electoral politics is the entire city and the conflict exacerbates the historic pattern of ethnic polarization, the Anglo voters can continue to poll majorities.

The ethnic balance created by the change to a council elected within single-member districts is a delicate one indeed. In 1979, at the end of a decade of great political upheaval and change, the balance of power shifted from a predominantly minority-group council (five Mexican Americans and one black) to one in which Anglos once again commanded a majority (with four Mexican Americans and one black). To understand just how precarious the ethnic balance is in such a pluralistic political culture, one need only examine the narrow margin of 84 voters by which incumbent

Rudy Ortiz was defeated by Bob Thompson in the 1979 election for city council in District 6.

The important political consequences of this shift in the ethnic balance of the council were clearly reflected in the policy changes adopted by the new council. No longer was there a clear majority in support of a master plan that would redirect growth from the north to the south and central sectors of the metropolitan area. A draft of the master plan setting out a philosophy fostering redevelopment in the central city and checking urban sprawl to the north, which had been hatched and supported by the 1977 council, was abandoned altogether by the 1979 council. New appointments to city boards and commissions under the 1979 council reflected the change in ethnic influence on the council. The two developers who spearheaded the opposition to the controversial draft of the master plan set forth during the 1977 council were appointed to the Planning Commission. The new council adopted a more liberal annexation policy allowing the city to annex additional property to the predominantly Anglo north side. Finally, the policy of spending bond monies in areas with the greatest need for capital improvements was abandoned by the 1979 council in favor of a policy of distributing dollars equally among the ten council districts, regardless of need.

But while the policy decisions of the 1979 council may seem more like those of the councils elected at large prior to 1977, there is one basic difference. Within a legal framework that creates a more pluralistic political system, the policy outcomes are no longer as predictable as they were under Anglo business elite rule. Instead, the winners of this new political game will be determined by the ability of the players to mobilize popular support.

The 1981 city council election was illustrative of the importance of popular support in a more open political system. For the first time anywhere in the country, a Mexican American was elected mayor of a large metropolitan community. Realizing the need for support from the Anglo community, Henry Cisneros campaigned on a platform based on the "politics of consensus." Last-minute attempts by his Anglo opponent, millionaire businessman John Steen, to polarize Anglo opposition to Cisneros by linking him to other, more militant Chicano members did not succeed. Cisneros received as much as 45 percent of the votes in predominantly Anglo precincts (Table 4.2). This is not to suggest that voter polarization did not occur along ethnic lines; indeed, the historic pattern of greater support for Mexican-American candidates by Mexican-American voters also emerged during the 1981 mayoral campaign. The all-important difference from previous races where Mexican Americans ran at large and lost was in the level of support received from the Anglo majority. Only if a crucial threshold of support from the Anglo precincts is reached does a Mexican-American candidate have a chance in an at-large election in which voters are polarized along ethnic lines. An examination of the patterns of relationships between support for Mexican-American mayoral candidates and the ethnic composition of precincts shown in the regression lines in Figure 4.2 illustrates this crucial point. Although the pattern of ethnic polarization is clearly evident in each race with only slight variations, the level of support for the Mexican-American candidate by predominantly Anglo precincts (left side of diagram) is the important determinant of the outcome.

For this situation to change, one of at least two conditions must develop. On the one hand a new political organization could emerge which, like the old GGL, will mediate the various interests within the city by building a citywide electoral coalition. Given the new importance of Mexican Americans in the city's electoral system, such a political organization would attempt to minimize the tendency toward ethnic polarization by supporting candidates and issues that represented compromises between these two groups of voters. The second and more likely condition is the growth of the Mexican-American electorate until its size approximates that of the Anglo electorate. This process requires a continued increase in the registration of Spanish-surnamed voters. Registration figures from 1972 to 1981 show a steady increase in the proportion of Mexican-Americans registered, from 35.1 percent to 41.6 percent.[29] But while efforts by reformers to register new voters among the Mexican-American population is a necessary condition to alter power relations in their favor, it is not sufficient. An increase in the level of turnout among Mexican Americans qualified to vote will also be required to complete the shift in ethnic balance of power in San Antonio.

Thomas A. Baylis

Chapter Five

Leadership Change in Contemporary San Antonio

The conditions under which the composition, outlook, and behavior of elites change is one of the oldest concerns of political analysis. What Pareto called the "circulation" and a contemporary writer characterizes as the "transformation" of leadership groups in a society[1] is central to the understanding of political change, whether as a cause, consequence, or intervening variable. Students of elites have often undertaken historical comparisons of the social composition and other characteristics of leadership groups at different periods in time;[2] they have less frequently examined elites in the very process of alteration during a relatively brief time span. San Antonio offers an unusual opportunity for undertaking such an analysis.

In this essay I wish to explore the possibility that, since the early 1970s, the accustomed dominance over San Antonio's affairs of an integrated, consensual "influential minority" may have been giving way to a more ambiguous, less stable, and more widely diffused structure of influence. In the long and somewhat wearying controversy between advocates of "elitist" and "pluralist" theories of community power, the two perspectives have usually been treated as irreconcilable analytic opposites; the possibility that in real cases a pyramidlike power structure dominated by a single group might gradually give way to a genuinely plural distribution of influence, or vice versa, was not usually entertained.[3] Certainly such a change does not come easily, or without pain, to those for whom political dominance has seemed a natural and just complement to their economic success. If, however, such a transformation can be shown to be under way in San Antonio, it may also tell us something about other cities facing comparable alterations in their environments. Thus I wish in this chapter to examine the history of the change which appears to be taking place, investigate its underlying causes, and examine its present status and possible consequences—particularly the question of whether the change is merely transitory and superficial or potentially enduring and structural.

"Elite" is defined here in terms of influence: that minority of San Antonians "whose judgments, decisions, and actions have important and determinable consequences" for many of their fellow citizens.[4] With this definition I seek to avoid the common errors of automatically linking elite membership to social prestige, wealth, or public visibility; such links frequently exist, but they must be demonstrated, not simply assumed. "Influence," of course, is not easily defined and measured. It may be attached to formal roles, but it may also depend upon the energies and skills of particular individuals largely apart from the positions they occupy. Thus, while any list of San Antonio elites would begin with the incumbents of important positions—city council, city manager, directors and managers of prominent banks and business firms, leaders of key pressure groups, and so on—these would have to be supplemented with the names of others whose influence is more personal than institutional. The "reputational" approach—the degree to which power is *attributed* to other individuals by competent observers—is one method of identifying such elite members, although it may mistake high visibility for actual influence. The "decisional" approach to identifying elites—who it is that appears most greatly to influence the most important decisions for the city, and who is most influential in setting the *agenda* determining which questions are considered at all and which are not—is probably the most appropriate one here, burdened with subjectivity though it necessarily is.[5] Here, I have used apparent influence over decisions and the agenda as a general guidepost for identifying leadership. I have not, however, adopted a formal procedure for the process of identification.

There is an additional difficulty in dealing with power in a political subsystem such as an American municipality: many critical decisions are made elsewhere, by forces over which local elites may have little influence. To put it slightly differently, San Antonio elites operate within a political, economic, and sociocultural *context;* this context includes federal and state law and the courts that interpret it, the economic institutions of a corporate capitalist society, and the complex cultural and ideological commitments of American society as a whole. To examine elites within an American city requires that we concentrate on the limited political space in which they actually have room to maneuver.

It is worth remarking, however, that San Antonio is less dependent on externally based business and banking giants than many other large cities;

its largest businesses tend to be headquartered locally (e.g., Tesoro Petroleum, Datapoint, Frost Bank, United Services Automobile Association). The city's largest employer—the U.S. military—is, of course, based externally, but rarely intervenes directly in local affairs. It is represented, however, on the Chamber of Commerce, and no San Antonio politician can afford to ignore its local needs. Also, civilian employees of the military and military retirees constitute important segments of the electorate, and the retirees provide a significant recruitment pool for both voluntary and paid civic positions.

In this chapter I will direct much of my attention to elective and appointive city officials, among whom changes have been particularly obvious and rapid. In the period under discussion here, 1973–81, an unusual number of both symbolically and substantively important issues have been brought into the governmental arena for decision, suggesting that formal political leadership is indeed deserving of close attention in San Antonio. More subtle changes have been taking place among the business elite, which has until recently dominated San Antonio politics. Moreover, it is arguable that other once powerless groups have begun to acquire influence in the city, suggesting more fundamental structural changes in the configuration of leadership.

Forces Underlying Leadership Change

To explore both the significant changes of personnel among existing elites and the rise to influence of new groups, it is necessary first to examine the shifting foundations of power in San Antonio. Many are discussed in detail elsewhere in this book; here it is necessary only to enumerate them.

Most apparent is the changing ethnic composition of San Antonio's population. Between 1960 and 1970 the proportion of Mexican Americans in the city grew from 41.15 percent to 52.17 percent of the total population; the Anglo population declined by almost the same percentage: from 51.19 percent to 39.19 percent. The proportion of blacks and other nonwhites grew slightly, from 7.35 percent to 8.63 percent.[6] After 1970 the population shift was slowed in part by the annexation of areas containing Anglo majorities. Anglos have retained a plurality in voting registration and in the work force, owing to the much lower average age of Mexican Americans and the lower levels of electoral participation and employment which are normal among low-income groups (see Chapter 4).

The shift in San Antonio's ethnic composition has been accompanied by a growing ethnic consciousness and even militancy among Mexican Americans—in part undoubtedly a reflection of national trends among this group, but also a product of the familiar clash between rising education and material expectations on one hand, and the persistence of widespread poverty and discrimination on the other. Mexican-American organizations, some of them quite venerable, have become more numerous and more demanding.[7] Although political factionalism and clientelism persist, the growing perception among many Mexican Americans of both the need for and political attainability of concrete local objectives—for example, the extension of drainage and other services, a more equitable allocation of city resources, job creation, and the planning and redirection of economic growth—has welded them together into a more effective political force than they have been in the past. The most publicized and effective of these organizations, and the one which has largely forged this degree of issue consciousness, is Communities Organized for Public Service, or COPS, a community group created under the guidance of organizers trained by Saul Alinsky's Woodlawn Organization and supported by the Catholic Church.[8] COPS' extraordinary political success—in placing the issues it wants at the center of the political agenda, in getting out voters, in electing sympathetic candidates and defeating unsympathetic ones,[9] and in earning attention and, in many cases, respect from powerful figures in the business community—has served as a catalyst for political change in many ways.

Changes in occupational patterns have affected the character of the city's leadership in more subtle and gradual ways. One of the editors of this volume once described San Antonio as a "pre-industrial city," heavily dependent on government employment, lacking large or sophisticated industry, and burdened with a large underclass of poor Mexican Americans and blacks, many of them unemployed and many, unregistered and exploited immigrants (see Chapters 2 and 3). It is arguable, however, that San Antonio is leaping over the industrial stage to become something of a postindustrial city, with a growing and relatively affluent class of professionals and managers. These occupations are concentrated highly disproportionately among Anglos, but the size of the Mexican-American middle class (especially in the service occupations said to be characteristic of a postindustrial society) is also growing, and may indeed be one source of the sense of greater political efficacy mentioned above.[10] To be sure, there has recently been some growth in the manufacturing sector in response to the city's recruitment efforts, but as of 1979 that sector employed less than 12 percent of the labor force.[11]

The fourth factor underlying elite change is the successful intervention of the Justice Department under the federal Voting Rights Act to force the city to adopt a district system for electing its city council.[12] The Justice Department by its action did not impose a political revolution from above; it merely accelerated a process already well under way. But it did, with astonishing swiftness, bring a majority of Mexican Americans and blacks to the council, make possible the election of councilmen from sections of the city that had not in anyone's memory been represented before,[13] and change the major component of electoral success from heavy campaign spending to constituency organization and effort. The 1977 mayoral-council election confirmed that the Justice Department's pressures had profoundly altered the framework of San Antonio politics.

The Good Government League and Its Demise

The transformation of political leadership in San Antonio began with the decay of the political organization that dominated city council elections for the two decades between 1955 and 1975. The Good Government League may fairly be characterized as the political arm of the San Antonio economic and social elite during this period.[14] Presenting itself as a nonpartisan reform organization promoting the civic welfare of all San Antonians, the GGL enjoyed astonishing electoral success until 1973, losing only three of eighty candidacies for council seats.[15] The GGL served as a highly effective instrument of elite integration in San Antonio, bringing together leading bankers, developers, manufacturers, and other businessmen with a scattering of other community leaders on its board of directors, finance committee, and especially its crucial nominating committee. The work of this committee— meeting privately, screening potential candidates, and putting together carefully balanced slates of "responsible" citizens drawn from strategic sectors of the community—was critical to the league's success.[16] Responding astutely to the more successful challenges of its opponents, the GGL presented the voters with Mexican-American, black, and female candidates, along with a majority of Anglos; most were businessmen, and all agreed upon the need for economic development and growth in San Antonio and on the importance of avoiding narrow ethnic or interest group appeals. In spite of its evident economic bias, the GGL saw itself as a nonpolitical civic organization; it is noteworthy that, in keeping with the organization's intentions, no GGL Council member ever went on to higher elective office.[17]

The GGL's demise may be attributed to four not unrelated factors: (1) the retirement from active leadership of the GGL's dominant figure (and San Antonio mayor from 1961 to 1971), W. W. McAllister, and his closest political advisers;[18] (2) the growing differences within the business elite, especially those between north side developers and their supporters and the more traditional downtown elite;[19] (3) the political fallout from a prodigious leap in utilities rates, following the failure of the city's natural gas suppliers to fulfill the contracts negotiated with a city-owned public utility;[20] and (4) the always fragile nature of GGL support in the Mexican-American community. The GGL selected its Mexican-American candidates on the basis of recommendations from the West Side Coalition, a league affiliate made up of Mexican-American businessmen; while its candidates did well among the GGL's Anglo clientele, the coalition was never very successful in delivering the Mexican-American vote itself.

The split among the GGL's business supporters was most dramatically reflected in the defection of Charles Becker, a GGL councilman who chose to run as an independent in the 1973 election. Becker, president of a large grocery chain, had never fit the rather bland and agreeable prototype of most successful GGL candidates. Feisty and controversial, he clashed sharply with Mayor John Gatti during his council term, very often over questions of interest to developers and builders.[21] As Becker explained it himself, he sympathized strongly with the dynamism and the expansionary ambitions of these men, and was close friends with several; he regarded the traditional business elite as stodgy and fearful of the changes which rapid economic expansion might bring.[22]

Denied renomination by the GGL (partly because of the conditions he demanded), Becker forged a loose alliance with two defecting Mexican-American councilmen and an independent Anglo candidate, spent heavily on his campaign,[23] and swept to a runoff victory. Undoubtedly one element in Becker's success was the fact that he was running against the GGL's first Mexican-American ticket leader (and thus mayoral candidate) Roy Barrera, at a time when Anglo voters continued to enjoy a solid registration majority. But Becker also drew some Mexican-American and liberal support from opponents of the GGL.[24] It is also worth noting that the GGL's nomination process came under closer public scrutiny in 1973 than it had before; disappointed candidates began to reveal some of its inner workings, and the names of members of the nominating committee were made public.[25] Moreover, the GGL found itself obliged to nominate a slate made up almost entirely of newcomers. It also found itself increasingly vulnerable to charges of being a "machine" serving the interests of only the more affluent parts of the city.

In 1975 the GGL was again opposed by an independent candidate for mayor with the personal resources to outspend the GGL in the campaign, and also faced a rather disparate rival council slate (the "Independent Team") made up largely of former GGL figures or disappointed aspirants for GGL nominations, supported by retiring Mayor Becker and generously bankrolled by developer and builder interests. Once again the GGL had to rely on newcomers; only the mayoral candidate, Lila Cockrell, had served on the retiring council. While the campaign was almost empty of well-defined issues or visible ideological differences, both the independent mayoral candidate and the Independent Team, aiming their attacks against high utility rates and GGL autocracy, did well, especially in the Mexican-American and black precincts. The GGL mayoral candidate won narrowly; only two other GGL councilmen were elected. By the end of 1976 the GGL had quietly disbanded—an astonishingly rapid demise for an organization that had so thoroughly dominated municipal politics for so many years.

The Transformation of Political Leadership

The real estate interests that had financed the Independent Team, however, found they had little time for self-congratulation. In order to put together a sufficiently attractive slate to win the votes of a variety of dissatisfied San Antonians, they had not publicized their own role, and had nominated and subsequently elected at least three councilmen who quickly showed that they were, indeed, "independent." One, the Reverend Claude Black, had been a GGL councilman and enjoyed his own firm basis of support in the black community; the second, Glen Hartman, a retired intelligence planner with the Defense Department, proved himself to be a strong advocate of planning in municipal affairs, including land use, as well. The third, Al Rohde, a real estate broker who had attracted publicity by dressing in an Uncle Sam costume on festive occasions, turned out to be outspoken and unpredictable in his performance on the council. So quickly and decisively did the developers' "majority" evaporate that by August 1976 some of the same men who had financed the Independent Team's victory were calling for a recall of five of the nine council members, including Hartman and Rohde.[26]

The chain of events leading to this singularly maladroit initiative cannot be fully recounted here. But the highly symbolic event that adumbrated a fundamental shift in the balance of political power in the city was unquestionably the January 1976 referendum over rezoning a tract above the Edwards Aquifer recharge zone for a giant shopping mall. An Anglo environmental protection group joined with COPS in gathering the necessary signatures to force the vote. In spite of heavy spending by business and the strong support of many prominent elite figures, rezoning was beaten by a citywide margin of 4–1, losing in north side as well as south side precincts (see Chapter 8). The size of the vote seems to have persuaded a council majority, no longer dominated by the GGL, to move toward a more consistent advocacy of planning for growth and of efforts to revive the inner city. The vote demonstrated a continuing distrust of developer and builder interests among San Antonio voters—even northside ones—in spite of the transient Becker and Independent Team successes. And, above all, it established the reputation of COPS as a force to be reckoned with in San Antonio politics, as an organization capable of delivering a relatively heavy and nearly unanimous Mexican-American vote.

The transformation of San Antonio's political leadership was given additional impetus by the intervention of the Justice Department under the expanded federal Voting Rights Act. Using as a lever the threat to nullify recent city annexations, the Justice Department pressured San Antonio to move from an at-large system of council elections to a district system, which presumably would protect the Mexican-American vote from being submerged in the larger Anglo vote. The issue was put to San Antonio voters in a referendum at the beginning of 1977. A new political group, the "Alliance for a Better City," had emerged from the 1975 elections; it included many old GGL figures but was dominated by builder and developer interests. The ABC sought the defeat of redistricting, hoping to capitalize on citizen resentment against the alleged federal *Diktat*. But with the support of most city councilmen and moderate Anglo leaders, the districting plan won approval by some 2,000 votes of nearly 42,000 cast. The ABC, which had spent $42,000 opposing the scheme,[27] immediately all but disappeared from public view, except as a pejorative label attached by rival candidates to those the ABC was believed to support; the latter, even when they denied any ABC affiliation, all went down to defeat in the subsequent election. No more was heard of the ABC, and since then no new formal business- or developer-oriented electoral organization has surfaced.

The first city elections held under the district plan gave a majority of council seats to minority candidates from the six lower-income districts on the west, south, and east sides of San Antonio. Five of these candidates were Mexican-American (one of them part Chinese), and the sixth was black. Each had been unopposed by COPS, which amounted to tacit support, insofar as the organization worked against potentially strong opponents whom it suspected of links to north side business interests. Each successful candidate appeared to be a relatively independent spokesman for his own district and had no obvious organizational links to the other five.

Only one had previously sat on the council or had otherwise been politically prominent. While differing in their levels of militancy, all seemed determined to secure a larger share of city benefits for lower-income areas, to resist unrestricted north side expansion, and to support measures for reviving the central city.

Several early council votes divided sharply along ethnic lines, and talk of growing ethnic polarization became frequent in the media and elsewhere. Anglo council members, including moderates, became indignant at what they perceived to be an attempt by the new majority to force through, without deliberation or concessions, its own version of a large bond issue favoring low-income districts. The Anglos, who had favored the original bond proposal, opposed the revision, presumably in order to teach their new colleagues a salutory lesson in political manners. After a bitter campaign, the bonds were voted down on a nearly straight north side–south side split (see Chapter 4), in spite of the efforts of COPS to save them. The bond issue seemed to illustrate the limits of the powers of COPS and the council majority; so long as Anglos retained a voting advantage, no city-wide candidate or issue could be successful without at least some support from moderate Anglo leaders. The election of a moderate Mexican-American candidate, Albert Bustamante, as county judge with such support later in 1978 served to underscore this lesson.

The defeat of the bonds seemed to have a sobering effect not only on the council majority but also on the Anglo moderates who had helped bring it about. Many council votes continued to divide along ethnic lines, but on others the council factions showed internal fissures.[28] The level of overall interethnic acrimony diminished, while individual rivalries and resentments among the Mexican-American and black members became more visible. The outlines of a pattern of working cooperation between moderate Anglo businessmen, city officials, and council members on the one side, and COPS members and several minority councilmen on the other, centering on a common concern for economic development, seemed to begin to emerge; it took symbolic form in the invitation accepted by COPS to participate in the deliberations of the business-dominated Economic Development Foundation.

These hopeful signs of greater harmony threatened to be lost in the growing controversy over a master plan proposed for future urban development by the city Planning Department; the plan sought to impose modest limitations on north side growth in order to redirect development back toward the central city. The city's Chamber of Commerce, consistently the voice of more conservative business interests, and many individual businessmen and developers publicly expressed their determination to kill "anti-growth" sections of the plan, while COPS sought to accelerate its approval. The possibility that the plan might become the object of new ethnic polarization was enhanced by the resignation of the council's leading Anglo moderate and advocate of planned development (Hartman). North side developers and other business interests, recognizing that their loss of a council majority was at the root of their political difficulties, began to talk of seeking to revise the existing district election plan to reestablish a number of at-large seats.

The 1979 election, however, returned one "minority" seat to an Anglo whose campaign enjoyed business support,[29] Robert Thompson, in a disputed vote. Thompson, representing a district split between Anglo and Mexican-American voters, did not prove to be an automatic supporter of Anglo business interests, but his victory appeared to tip the balance on the master plan and quieted talk of restoring at-large seats. Shortly after the election, the plan was returned to the Planning Commission and Planning Department for revision; the version finally passed was deprived of many of its teeth and even received the endorsement of the Greater San Antonio Chamber of Commerce.[30]

The pattern of cooperation between the San Antonio business elite, the city government (including all factions of the city council), and most of the major Mexican-American and black organizations of San Antonio was reaffirmed in early 1980 with the highly publicized formation of an organization called United San Antonio. USA was consciously designed to unite the diverse political and social elements of the city behind its economic development, and in particular to lure new and, it was hoped, high-technology and high-wage industry. COPS remained formally outside USA, but appeared to give the organization its qualified informal blessing. USA proved to be more than a mere symbol of urban unity; together with the Economic Development Foundation it helped attract several important firms to San Antonio, most notably in the electronics sector, and helped win state approval for the city's first engineering program at the University of Texas at San Antonio.

Prior to the mayoral election of 1981, Henry Cisneros, a young, photogenic Mexican-American city councilman with advanced degrees in public administration from Harvard's Kennedy School and from George Washington University, mended his fences with many of the north side business interests who had once vowed to frustrate his political ambitions.[31] With a sizeable campaign chest coming largely from his new business allies, Cisneros swept to an easy electoral victory over a wealthy Anglo councilman, John Steen. Cisneros was the first Mexican-American to become mayor of San Antonio since 1842; he carried eight of the ten city council districts, including two of the four with large Anglo registration majorities. Cisneros and Steen were succeeded on the city council by new Mexican-American and Anglo members, respectively, while all other incumbent council members were reelected, once again (with the mayor) shifting the council's ethnic balance in favor of the minorities. Cisneros' victory earned him nationwide media attention, which he sought to use to the city's advantage; San Antonio had become the largest American city with a Mexican-American mayor. At the end of 1981, after eight months in office, Cisneros appeared to have retained his popularity with nearly all segments of the city, in spite of some grumbling by COPS. As mayor he had acted both as an effective symbolic leader and a skilled broker among the concerns of different city groups. Cisneros' success as an advocate for the city before external audiences, his well-organized, systematic approach to raising, researching, and analyzing city issues and generating proposals for dealing with them, and simply the economic success of San Antonio in a period of national economic travail, served for the time being to muffle controversy. A development that may be equally significant for the future shape of political power in the city, however, was the emergence of Bernardo Eureste—perhaps the most feisty and controversial figure in city politics—as quite possibly the most effective member of the city council, able to mobilize its minority majority on behalf of his own budget revisions and other proposals.[32]

Power in San Antonio Today

Elective Officials

There is little political organization behind elective officials in San Antonio today. Since the dissolution of the GGL and the brief and unsuccessful episode of the ABC, no comparable surrogate party has arisen to succeed them. It is arguable that the district election system and the high degree of ethnic polarization in city voting patterns present severe obstacles to the formation of coherent citywide political organizations (see Chapter 4). County elections are contested on a partisan basis, and the Republican party has experienced a modest rejuvenation on that level; county officeholders are no longer all but automatically selected in the Democratic primary. Nevertheless, county offices receive much less attention and carry much less weight than city ones;[33] Texas counties lack ordinance-making and zoning powers.

The intervention in San Antonio politics by the city's state legislators (such as Representatives Matt Garcia, Frank Tejeda, and Lou Nelle Sutton) appears to be based more on personal and factional ties than on ideology or formal organization. Other individual power brokers continue to have some importance, particularly in the Mexican-American community. Congressman Henry B. Gonzalez makes occasional forays into city politics, and has thereby earned the bitter enmity of Mayor Becker and his erstwhile developer allies. Gonzalez's interventions, while they must be taken seriously in the light of his great local popularity, tend to be idosyncratic and independent of any organizational links; also, he rarely endorses local candidates.[34] His sporadic attacks upon other Mexican-American politicians— including his one-time disciple Bustamante—have also not facilitated political organization.

COPS, whose influence and support was vital to the success of several incumbent councilmen, professes distrust for all politicians and prefers to stress its key issues rather than individual personalities. COPS can be a formidable opponent to those who do not endorse its program; it can also be counted upon to act as a vigilant watchdog over incumbents who might be inclined to deviate from its wishes. It is not likely, however, to provide any individual officeholder with positive, reliable, and continuing organizational support.

All this tends to leave council members thrown largely upon their own political and financial resources. Their weak financial base is especially significant, since San Antonio councilmen receive only a token salary for what has become nearly a full-time occupation. Of the seven ethnic-minority council members since 1977, three work for local universities and colleges (Cisneros, Ortiz, Eureste), a fourth (Wing) is a civil servant employed at Kelly Air Force Base, a fifth (Webb) is a grocery store owner, the sixth (Alderete) is an insurance broker, and the newest member (Berriozabal) was formerly head of the 1980 census in San Antonio and is now described as a "management and public relations consultant." Eleven Anglos have served on the council in the same period. They include a retired Air Force planner (Hartman), the co-owner of a sales firm (Dutmer), a small publisher (McDaniel), and the owners of a small steel firm (Pyndus) and a prosperous insurance agency (Steen). The former mayor Lila Cockrell had been president of the League of Women Voters and is married to the (recently retired) executive director of the Bexar County Medical Society. Robert Thompson is an attorney, Gene Canavan an insurance executive, Van Archer a wealthy stockbroker and state Republican committeeman,

James Hasslocher the owner of a restaurant chain, and Ed Harrington a prominent builder. The minority council members, then, have come from modest middle-class occupations, and some must make a considerable financial sacrifice in order to serve; the Anglo members are somewhat more prosperous as a group, and a few can be described as wealthy. None, however, appear to represent directly either traditional San Antonio wealth or the city's major business and financial institutions.[35]

The power of the council is significant in several areas—perhaps most of all as a distributor of and channel of access to federal monies. It allocates federal funds made available through such programs as Revenue Sharing and Community Development. It makes appointments to major city boards and commissions dealing with planning, zoning, public transit, and water, and of course appoints the professional city manager.[36] Through its influence over zoning, but still more through its provision of infrastructural (e.g., water lines, roads) and other forms of assistance and subsidy, it can influence economic development (see Chapter 8). The significance of the master plan, particularly in its earlier, stronger version, was that it reflected an effort to use these powers in a coordinated way. Yet the council's authority in this area is limited by state law and by a court system inclined to be friendly to the rights of individual property owners; in spite of the council's extraterritorial jurisdiction, its ability to redirect growth from the north side to the inner city rests more on incentives and persuasion than on raw power. City government can, however, facilitate the development of civic amenities—recreational and cultural facilities, parks, and protection of historic neighborhoods—and thus have a substantial impact on the attractiveness of the city to tourists, new residents, and new businesses. It can also use its zoning and condemnation powers, the offer of city-owned property, subsidies, and requests for federal grants as a means to stimulate development, particularly in the inner city.

Do council members exercise these significant powers with genuine independence, or are they merely the instruments of more powerful social and economic interests? Given their modest financial resources, one would expect them to be particularly vulnerable to such external influences, as past city officials undoubtedly often have been (see Chapter 1). Thus far, however, there is little evidence of such dependence in the present council, perhaps because the district system has kept campaign costs low and because of the continuing scrutiny of COPS.[37] Mayoral elections, on the other hand, are expensive, and COPS has raised questions about the "price" Mayor Cisneros was required to pay for his business support.

Appointive Officials

Appointive city boards and commissions enjoy substantial influence over important municipal services in some cases, and have significant advisory functions in others; among these bodies are the City Public Service Board, City Water Board, San Antonio Development Agency Board, City Planning Commission, City Zoning Commission, and the VIA Metropolitan Transit Authority. While their members are generally appointed by the city council (except for the City Public Service Board, which is self-perpetuating) they have often acted with considerable independence. In the days of GGL dominance, these boards tended to be dominated by businessmen and to reflect their outlooks; appointees often did not live within the city limits and would not have been eligible for elective office. Thus the president of the Greater San Antonio Builders' Association (Ed Harrington, now a city councilman) for a time simultaneously headed the (then combined) Planning and Zoning Commission; the Water Board was until recently headed by a prominent developer; and the five-member City Public Service Board included at one time the board chairman of the First National Bank, another director of the bank, and the chairman of Tesoro Petroleum.

With the change in city council composition, the makeup of the boards began to change as well. Both the City Public Service Board and the Water Board acquired Mexican-American/black majorities, although the former is still not subject to direct city council appointment and the latter has harbored serious differences with the council majority over water development policy. The City Planning Commission has changed its character substantially from the old Planning and Zoning Commission and worked closely with the City Planning Department in its preparation of the controversial master plan.

Full-time appointive city officials are headed by the city manager. During most of the period in question, the manager was an able, conservative professional whose previous assignment was in California; prior to 1976, city managers had generally come from the GGL. The heads of city departments are not well paid by comparison with those employed by municipalities of comparable size elsewhere, and in the past were often local people who had been in their jobs for many years. The overall level of professionalization of city staff, however, appears to have been raised substantially in recent years. The generation of significant policy initiatives from within the city bureaucracy (apart from the manager himself) appears to be relatively rare, although the role of the City Planning Department in drawing up the master plan suggests that a change here, too, may be underway.

The Business Elite

San Antonio has few businesses that rank high in assets or employment on a national scale. Two corporations, Datapoint and Harte-Hanks (communications), belong to the *Fortune* "second 500," and the largest bank (Frost), with assets of about $1.3 billion, ranks below the top 100 in the country. The largest private employer is an insurance company, United Services Automobile Association, which serves active and retired military officers. As in many communities, real estate developers and builders are among the most visible of those businessmen active in politics, along with automobile dealers, small manufacturers, retailers, and the like. Until the collapse of the GGL, men like these dominated the organization's board of directors and candidate selection committee.

The prominence of developers and builders in particular can be explained in part by the degree to which they see themselves as having a direct stake in a variety of municipal decisions—those, for instance, having to do with zoning and utility extension and, more generally, with environmental regulation and overall economic development. A number of developers and other businessmen closely associated with them have run for or been appointed to public office themselves,[38] while others are frequent and heavy contributors to political campaigns and are often active behind the scenes in promoting the candidacies of others.[39] As we have seen, it was the disaffection of a number of developers and their allies with what they viewed as the inertia of the traditional business leadership that led to a split within the politically active portion of the business community and finally to the dissolution of the GGL. Today the division is less clearcut, but the largest contributors distribute their political support among a surprisingly broad range of candidates for both local and state office, suggesting that these contributions are viewed as much as investments as expressions of ideological preference.

Bankers have played an important role in city politics, although many prefer to maintain a relatively low public profile.[40] In the 1973 city council elections, the heads of the two largest banks were strong supporters of the GGL and of Charles Becker, respectively. The chairman of another large bank apparently provided crucial financing for the Independent Team in 1975. Other bankers have also been major contributors and have served on important city boards and other bodies; one banker, along with his family, has been prominent in his financial support of and personal involvement in liberal causes. There is necessarily a close relationship between bankers and the developers whose projects they finance, and these relationships have sometimes led to political alliances of diverse kinds. As might be expected, there is fairly extensive interlocking between bank directorships and those of other large businesses, which also presumably facilitates such alliances.[41] Bankers also tend to be prominent in public service positions: they are said to have dominated the board of the Hemisfair exposition in 1967, for example.[42] Finally, the head of the largest savings and loan association in San Antonio was Walter McAllister, the long-time GGL mayor; even at the age of ninety (in 1979), he, along with his son and grandson, continued to be active in supporting conservative but established candidates and causes.

The complexion of the city council elected in 1977 and the visible influence of COPS forced business leaders into something of a defensive posture. The sharply etched division of the earlier part of the decade appeared to have become blurred; in early 1979, two of former mayor Becker's most prominent one-time developer supporters worked actively for the reelection of Mayor Cockrell and thus against his forlorn effort to recapture his old position. Opposition to the master plan appeared to bring most business figures together once again, but no well-organized or sustained effort to recapture a City Hall majority in the 1979 elections was apparent. In 1981 much of the business support that once would have been expected to go to the conservative Steen was captured by Henry Cisneros.[43] The general air of optimism concerning San Antonio's economic future appears to override the discomfiture at the changing balance of political power in the minds of many of the most important business leaders, who continue to fill important service roles in agencies and committees concerned with industrial development, urban projects, the fostering of trade arrangements with Mexico, and the like.

Others

There are other elements in the changing power equation in San Antonio which can only be mentioned here. The old Anglo social elite, most visible in the annual rites of the Spring Fiesta and most frequently to be found at other times in the more exclusive private clubs of the city,[44] retains an overlapping relationship with the elites of economic and political power but appears to be in decline as a political force. The San Antonio Conservation Society, predominantly a women's organization, has in its fifty-five-year history contributed impressively to the saving, restoration, and nurture of some of San Antonio's most distinctive buildings and tourist attractions. In recent years it has found that its conservationist interests have brought it into the center of the political arena, beginning with the North Expressway controversy and extending today to concern over inner-city development and the master plan.[45] As yet it is not possible fully to assess the concrete political impact of the large new class of medical professionals associated with the burgeoning South Texas Medical Center or of the growing community of academics at the new University of Texas at San Antonio as well as at older institutions. A number of local political figures, including the mayor and several council members, have close links with the universities, however. A fourth element deserving of attention is the trade union movement, which, although traditionally embattled throughout Texas, would appear to have a considerable potential for influence, owing to the large number of public employees in San Antonio and the growing activity of public employee unions. Only about 10 percent of the city's nonmilitary work force is presently unionized, however, and until now the unions' overt political activities have borne little fruit.[46] Nevertheless, they came to enjoy greater access to city government under Mayor Cockrell, and their support of the Cisneros candidacy suggests that this access will continue.[47] Much of the unions' leadership has been shifting into the hands of Mexican Americans, but like the other groups discussed in this section, they do not fall clearly on either side of the old GGL business-civic elite/new rising ethnic elite dichotomy, and thus promise to contribute additional dimensions to the structure of power in San Antonio.

Conclusions

What has happened in San Antonio is no revolution. The politics of municipal elite pluralism, like the politics of pluralism elsewhere, is essentially conservative—oriented to sharing available resources more broadly and to obtaining more of them, not to assaulting established economic, social, or political structures. A wider spectrum of social groups has found the means, and with them the incentive, to express their interests in city affairs with some hope of success, or at least of a hearing. Business influence has by no means disappeared, but businessmen have discovered that this influence can no longer be taken for granted, and some have perceived that it is most successfully asserted when it is made to appear consonant with the interests of other sectors of the city's population. The emergence of a new and relatively ambiguous balance of forces in city politics has not been lost on city planners and other professionals as well as on environmental and preservationist groups, who sense new opportunities for achieving their own objectives.

The possibility exists, of course, that San Antonio's politics are only going through a brief transitional episode, and that, once having learned the new rules of the electoral system and having searched out the susceptibilities of south side voters and councilmen, the traditional Anglo business and civic elite will reassert its control, although perhaps this time from further behind the scenes. COPS might come to suffer the infirmities of many maturing organizations and decline as a consequence of its own success, and the Mexican-American community could once again become dominated by patron-client politics.[48] It is also plausible that the traditional elite will become more adept at using external authorities to frustrate municipal decisions it does not like; the successful use of the courts and of multicounty and state agencies in the Edwards Aquifer controversy is instructive here (see Chapter 8). It might also be contended that the important decisions affecting the future of San Antonio will be private economic ones over which city government will have no influence. Alternatively, it might be suggested that San Antonio will become a Chicano-ruled city only at the price—the same price paid by blacks in other cities—of having its more affluent population and its tax base move beyond city government's reach. To be sure, San Antonio's annexation powers reduce this possibility, but numerous older enclaves and exclaves free from city control and city taxes continue to provide a refuge for many more prosperous Anglos.

While none of these prospects can be entirely dismissed, the forces that I argued at the outset to have been fundamentally responsible for leadership change—the shift in the population's ethnic composition, rising ethnic consciousness and organization, changes in occupational patterns, and federal intervention—appear to be essentially irreversible. Thus it seems likely that, in spite of the rhetoric of conflict and ethnic polarization, the old and the new San Antonio elites will ultimately learn to live with one another. Tied for the most part to local businesses and other investments, psychic as well as material, the old elite will find it can neither dislodge nor entirely co-opt the new but surprisingly well-entrenched black and Mexican-American representatives of south, east, and west districts. (The one exception, as I noted, is a district with nearly even Anglo and Mexican-American registration.) The new council members, in their turn, will have to temper any putative inclinations toward radical change with considerations of the economic dependence of most of their constituents on Anglo business interests and of the middle-class aspirations of most of these constituents. Elite conflict will center on the distribution of governmental and government-influenced resources; because the resources are scarce and are not likely to become less so in the next years, the conflict will be intense, at least verbally, but not irreconcilable. The vocal, disorderly, but ultimately limited nature of that conflict will reflect what San Antonio's leadership structure has become—a disparate set of elites who have little in common in terms of social background, wealth, ethnicity, or political sophistication, but who share enough common or complementary interests and objectives to remain together in a marriage of both convenience and necessity.

Chapter Six

Mayoralty Politics in
San Antonio, 1955–79

Mayoralty politics changed significantly in San Antonio during the 1970s. The mayor came to be elected directly by the voters rather than indirectly by the city council. From 1955 to 1973, the city's politics were dominated by the Good Government League, but this organization vanished in 1976. Other organizations, including ones which represent minority groups, surfaced and began to play a major role in elections and policy making. The emergence of these groups reflected the increased politicization of the minority populations in the city. Single-member districts replaced the at-large elections of the city council, and under the present apportionment formula, it became possible for the minority populations to elect a majority of the members of the city council. Mayoralty elections remained costly, but there were a number of changes in campaign financing and campaign expenditures.

While changes occurred in the 1970s, many older patterns also persisted. There was still considerable support for the principles of the council-manager form of government, and there was little evidence of widespread support for reviving partisan politics in local elections. People still tended to resist increasing the salaries or support for the city council to create a more professional governing body: the council and mayor were still regarded as part-time policy makers, and in a referendum, the voters rejected a proposal to increase the salaries of the mayor and council. A pattern of bloc voting for the mayor and city council members on the basis of ethnic and economic factors continued in the 1970s. Given the ethnic composition of the city, the big question for mayoralty politics for the 1980s was whether this pattern would persist or whether the various recent institutional changes would initiate other patterns of voting.

The Institutional Setting

San Antonio operated under a commission form of government from 1914 to 1951. There were several efforts to revise the city charter during this period, but it was not until 1951 that the reformers were able to develop sufficient support for the adoption of the council-manager form of government.[1]

The 1951 charter provided for a city council comprised of nine council members. These individuals were elected in a nonpartisan, at-large election held in April of odd years. To be elected, the council member had to obtain a majority of the votes cast for that office. If any candidate failed to obtain a majority, a run-off election was to be held two weeks after the first election. Council members took office on the first day of May. They were to be paid $20 per meeting of the council attended, but the total compensation of a council member could not exceed $1,040 per year.

This city charter clearly reflected the theories of nonpartisanship and council-manager municipal government. Municipal office-seekers could not run under a partisan banner. Policy making performed by the council was perceived as a part-time function requiring a limited amount of time on the part of the mayor and the members of the council. The charter was quite explicit in its distinction between policy making and management. Under the charter, "members of the council shall not direct or request the City Manager or any of his subordinates to appoint or remove from office or employment. . . . The Council and its members shall deal with the administrative service solely through the City Manager."[2]

Under the 1951 charter, the mayor of San Antonio and the mayor pro tem were selected by the council members from their membership. The mayor was, in fact, a member of the city council, subject to the same provisions of power and restrictions as were all of the other council members. The charter identified the mayor's primary function as that of presiding over the city council, and with few exceptions, the mayor had only limited responsibilities beyond that of the other members of the city council. The charter did provide for an additional $3,000 salary to be paid to the mayor above that of the regular $20 a meeting paid to the other council members.[3]

From 1955 to 1973 the institutional restrictions imposed on the mayor by the charter were offset by the monopoly that the Good Government

League, a citizens' association, exercised in the recruitment of candidates to the city council. During this period of time, seventy-seven of the eighty-one council members were members of the Good Government League.[4] Since the council elected the mayor, the mayors were GGL members. City managers served at the discretion of the city council, and with the unquestioned control of the GGL in the council, public policy initiated by the city managers reflected, in general, the majority opinion within the council as well as the opinion of the mayor. As a result of its political dominance, the Good Government League mayors of San Antonio were able to exercise considerable political leadership in the policy-making processes despite the institutional limitations.

Changes in the Charter

The indirect election of the mayor came under attack after the election of 1973. In this election, Charles Becker, a GGL council member who had served on the council from 1971 to 1973, bolted the organization after being refused the nomination as the league's mayoralty candidate. Capitalizing on some internal problems within the league as well as the breakdown of elite consensus on the questions of economic development and policy making, Becker was successful in his bid for a position on the city council. By the time the council was seated, Becker was able to convince additional GGL members as well as the independents on the council to elect him mayor.

As a result of Becker's election and the election of several independent candidates, there developed after the election of 1973 a charter revision movement. A commission was appointed, and from the commission's recommendations, three major changes in the charter were presented to the voters in the general election in November of 1974. These proposals were the direct election of the mayor, single-member districting, and provisions enabling the council to increase salaries for the council members. Of these three propositions, the only one to pass was the provision for the direct election of the mayor. This proposition passed by a margin of two to one, while single-member districting received 48 percent of the vote, and the proposal for a salary increase for the council received only 44 percent of the vote.[5]

Beginning with the election of 1975, the mayor of San Antonio was elected citywide directly by the voters. At the same time, members of the council were also elected citywide in the at-large elections. In the mayoralty and council elections of this year the Good Government League mounted a slate of candidates including the mayoralty candidate. After a highly contested race, the league was able to win only two council seats and the mayoralty election. Under the original charter, the six independent council members would have elected the mayor, and their choice would not have been a candidate slated by the Good Government League. Because of charter revision the GGL mayoralty candidate was elected despite the failure of the organization to win a council majority.

This election anticipated a subsequent pattern of council elections in which the mayoralty election was detached from that of the members of the city council. The direct election of the mayor was one reason for the separation of the mayoralty election from that of the members of the city council. The other reason was the adoption of single-member districting. The interest expressed in the 1974 special election in single-member districting continued after the city council election of 1975. The council's six independents were publicly committed to single-member districting, and soon after the new council was organized in 1975, efforts were once again initiated to amend the charter.

The movement toward single-member districting was given further impetus by the fact that the state of Texas was included under the Voting Rights Act when it was amended in 1975. A lawsuit had been filed challenging the at-large elections, and the provisions of this law provided the various interested minority groups with significant legal resources. Within a relatively short time after the law was passed, the Department of Justice began to use the law to force the city to modify its at-large election system. (See Chapter 4 for details.)

A charter revision commission was appointed in 1976, and by the summer, the commission reported back to the council with a plan providing for the election of ten council members in single-member districts. Submitted to the voters in January of 1977, the plan was approved by a margin of 51 percent to 49 percent.

The city of San Antonio still operates under the council-manager form of government, but the continued pressures to change the city's charter indicate that various factions and groups have found some parts of the charter to be incompatible with their interests. The direct election of the mayor reflects the desire on the part of many individuals to focus responsibility for policy initiatives with a single individual. Even during the Good Government League era, it was evident that the mayors performed more than a symbolic function. The charter separated the political functions from that of the administrative functions, but as the demands have increased for the city to respond to a range of problems through a variety of new programs, it has become more difficult for the mayor to stay aloof from the administrative decisions, especially when the mayor is politically accountable for the decisions and the performance of the city's government.

Single-member districting is also a reflection of the increased demands by minority groups for more adequate representation in the city council. The high cost of the at-large elections and the general class bias of the nonpartisan elections were argued to be particularly detrimental to the black and Mexican-American communities. After council members began to be elected by single-member districts, there was a noticeable change in the ethnic composition of the city council.

At the same time, council members were confronted with greater constituency demands and an increased demand to perform casework for their respective constituencies. Council meetings became longer and more frequent, and committee activities increased.

The mayor of the city is still not involved in the day-to-day details of managing the city's government, and in this sense, the organizational principles of the council-manager form of government still characterize the general structure of city government. At the same time, the increased range of policy questions that now confront the city have required more and more attention by the mayor. This increased policy workload has required more planning and policy initiatives on the part of the council, and to a considerable measure, the mayor plays a predominant role in policy initiatives. With the decline of the Good Government League, which provided permanent coalitions within the city council, and with the adoption of single-member districts, which has produced a constituency orientation on the part of the council members, the mayor is required to give more attention and time to the political details of coalition-building and conflict resolution. Constituency, racial, and ideological divisions surface with more regularity in the deliberations of the council, and the mayor is required to play a greater political leadership role in the policy-making processes.

While there are increased expectations of the mayor to exercise leadership and to commit the necessary time to carry out this leadership, there has been a general reluctance on the part of the electorate to give the mayor greater compensation for the jobs performed or to increase his or her formal powers. For example, the mayor still receives the same salary that was enacted in the charter of 1951, and there has been no general support for increasing this salary in recent years. There have been private conversations regarding the changed status of the mayor and the relationship to the city manager, but there has been no public movement to amend the charter and increase the powers of the mayor.

The Recruitment of Candidates

The three mayors elected between 1955 and 1971 were members of the Good Government League and part of the successful slates of candidates recruited and nominated by the league. During this period the Good Government League dominated the electoral processes, and it was impossible for any candidate who aspired to the office of mayor to be elected without an alternative slate of candidates. It took five votes of the council to be elected mayor, but the at-large election system greatly reduced the prospects of the election of a majority of non-GGL candidates. There were partial slates of candidates who opposed the GGL slates, but these slates were never able to develop a broad base of support transcending all three ethnic groups. Furthermore, the non-GGL slates that emerged in any given election represented temporary coalitions; there was no sustained organizational effort to create alternatives to the GGL.

One clue to the electoral domination of the Good Government League is to be found in its recruiting and nominating procedures.[6] Candidates were nominated by a committee appointed by the board of directors of the GGL. When this nominating committee was appointed, ethnic, economic, social, and geographical considerations were made as to the membership. The membership of this committee was kept anonymous, and its activities were kept secret. Its final decision regarding the slate of candidates was announced either by the chairman of the nominating committee or by the chairman of the Good Government League. Names of potential candidates were submitted to these nominating committees from several sources, and after an initial screening and review of the nominations, the committee would interview specific candidates. Considerations were given to the professional competence of the candidates, personal attitudes toward politics and the role of the councilman in city politics, and balancing a ticket with persons "representing" the dominant groups and interests within the city.

The nominating procedures were highly successful in arranging preelection coalitions among dominant interests within the city. The process was kept from public view; and even the participating interests could not be sure as to what factors had led to the inclusion of a group's nominee on the slate. If a group's candidate was not accepted, the procedures used by the GGL tended to neutralize the potential organizational activities of this group once it had learned that its choice of nominees was not included in the slate. Elections in San Antonio are held in the first week of April. The decisions of the nominating committee were often not made until February. By that time, the GGL had already begun to organize its campaign, and disappointed groups had little time to organize themselves for alternative political activity.

Moreover, the GGL candidates ran as a ticket or a slate under a platform prepared by the GGL. The speaking activities of the candidates were coordinated, and the media campaign was centralized. The problems of fundraising were left to the organization and seldom depended on one of the specific candidates. In terms of campaign propaganda, campaign slogans and rhetoric were usually directed toward economy, efficiency, management, growth and stability. It was most difficult for an independent candidate to match either the organizational or the financial resources that were available to a slated ticket of the GGL.

The indirect election of the mayor resulted in electoral emphasis being placed on the slate of candidates rather than on the nominee designated as the mayoralty candidate. It was generally known who the mayoralty candidate of the Good Government League was, but the team or slate was presented to the public to suggest the necessity of electing a cohesive and stable group of like-minded citizens to the city council. Campaign propaganda emphasized the team of which the mayor was part rather than the mayor's team.

The nominating procedures that the Good Government League developed did not eliminate self-recruitment of candidates, but they did have the effect of minimizing the city council as a stepping-stone to other elected offices and placing limitations on political ambitions. While past council members have been appointed to numerous boards and commissions after their terms of office, only one council member elected under the nonpartisan election system has been successful in a bid to a higher office. The recruitment process used by the GGL did appear to identify persons who were committed to the principles of nonpartisanship, and it minimized political ambitions that could have threatened the organizational theory on which the city's charter was based, since it required a potential candidate to subordinate his or her personal ambitions to the objectives of the league. (This is not to suggest, however, that ambition was absent as a person presented himself for candidacy.) By 1971, the system had considerable credibility, given the series of successes that the Good Government League had experienced from 1955 to 1971. This was perhaps even more true after the election of 1971, when the Good Government League turned back a serious challenge by three independent candidates.

Such a system is very delicate, however, because only continued electoral successes will guarantee that potential candidates comply with its values and procedures. The system broke down rapidly after the election of 1973, when Charles Becker successfully challenged the Good Government League. This challenge was followed by changes in the charter allowing for the direct election of the mayor, and council elections now come to be dominated by the center stage position of the mayoralty candidates. As might be expected, media coverage of council races became subordinated to the coverage of mayoralty races.

There are no longer any citywide political organizations to recruit candidates, and mayoralty candidates are now self recruited. Potential candidates are now hinting at their intentions much earlier than in the past. A potential mayoralty candidate with limited finances needs longer to put together a campaign organization than would a well-financed candidate who could hire many of the technical personnel necessary to run a campaign. A mayoralty candidate must recruit much of his or her own campaign organization, and of course, such organizations are candidate-oriented. Furthermore, mayoralty candidates have to assume a greater role in campaign financing.

Ethnicity and Mayoralty Elections

Ethnic voting has been prominent in mayoralty elections in San Antonio since the 1960s and persisted through the 1970s. Under the GGL, slates were clearly constructed in terms of coalescing the three ethnic groups.

In 1960, Mexican Americans comprised 41 percent of the city's population, while the black population comprised 7.4 percent of the city's population, and whites or Anglos comprised 51.6 percent.[7] By 1975, Mexican Americans comprised 51.8 percent of the city's population, but of the registered voters, 37.1 percent were Mexican Americans. The black population comprised 8.2 percent of the city's population and approximately 7 percent of the registered voters. Though Anglos made up a smaller percentage—39 percent—of the city's population in 1975 than did Mexican Americans, they made up 55.8 percent of the registered voters.[8] At no time for which there are data has the percentage of the voting population which was Mexican American approximated the percentage of the total population which was Mexican American. On the other hand, the Anglo voting population has always been a much higher proportion of the registered voters than the proportion of Anglos in the total population.

There are explanations for these disparities. For one thing, in the past the restrictive registration laws in Texas reduced voter registration and participation.[9] One-partyism and the consequent absence of party competition are related to the lower rates of political participation among the minority population. The lower overall educational and economic status among the minority populations are related to the lower rates of political participation. Finally, the minority populations have much lower median ages than the Anglo populations; consequently, a larger proportion of the Mexican-American and black populations are simply too young to vote.

The city is residentially segregated among the three major ethnic groups. The Mexican-American population is located in the central city, the southwestern quadrant, and the near northwestern part of the city. Since 1970, the Mexican-American population has expanded further into the southeastern and northwestern regions of the city. With the increased upward mobility of some Mexican-American families, there has been some diffusion of the Mexican-American population into the previously all-Anglo precincts in high-income areas. The city's black population is located primarily on the east side of the city. Some dispersion of the black population has also taken place since 1970, but this pattern does not match the shifts in residency for the Mexican-American population either in terms of size or proportion. The Anglo population is found primarily in the northern half of the city, the southeast, and the western fringe of the city. (see Figure 6.1.)

The Good Government League ran Anglo mayoralty candidates from 1955 to 1971, but from the organization's inception, Mexican-American candidates were placed with the Anglo majorities on the slate for the city council; and in the mid-1960s, a black was also added to the organization's slate. The presence of minority candidates on the GGL's slates was part of the coalitional strategy of the organization and was perceived to be beneficial in obtaining some support in the minority precincts. Nevertheless, opposition to the GGL came predominantly from the Mexican-American neighborhoods. While producing much lower rates of support for the GGL slates than did the Anglo precincts, black precincts tended to give higher proportions of their votes to the GGL than did the Mexican-American precincts.

Until 1971, mayoralty candidates who opposed the GGL can be considered as token opposition. Running as independents or as a mini-slate, these candidates were not in a position to match the financial or organizational resources of the GGL.[10] Even with the apparent hopelessness of such mayoralty candidates, the Mexican-American precincts would demonstrate a clear and persistent pattern of opposition to the Good Government League. This was true whether the opposition candidate was Anglo or Mexican-American. (See Chapter 4 for more details.)

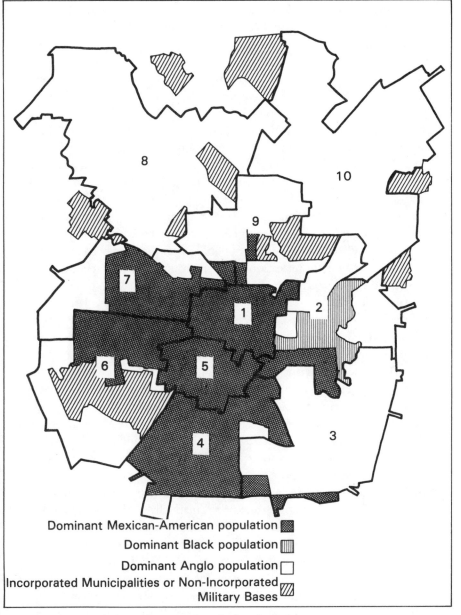

Figure 6.1: Ethnic residency patterns in San Antonio.

The success of the GGL mayoralty candidate depended, in part, on the consensus of the Anglo community elites, the higher rates of voter registration among Anglos as well as the higher rates of voter participation, the cohesion among Anglo voters, and the organizational and financial resources of the league. The city's pattern of ethnic voting developed early in the history of the council-manager form of government, and in general, the pattern persists today with some modifications.

The elections of the 1970s demonstrate the bloc voting patterns in the city and also reflect the potential for some realignments in the electoral coalitions. In 1971, Pete Torres, an incumbent on the city council and an ardent critic of the GGL, filed against John Gatti, the acknowledged mayoralty candidate of the GGL. Torres was perceived and portrayed by the GGL as representative of certain increasingly radical elements in the Mexican-American community, and in this particular election, an even more rigorous effort was made to "retire" him from public office than had been attempted in 1969 when he ran for reelection to the city council as an independent. His alleged radicalism was attacked extensively in the media, and by inference, he was compared with activists in other cities in which civil strife had emerged.

The GGL raised a hefty campaign war chest, hired campaign consultants, and ran a fairly effective media campaign reinforced by a precinct organization. The organization outspent Torres by ten to one, and GGL mayoralty candidate Gatti received 62 percent of the vote while Pete Torres received 36 percent. The other candidates received only a sprinkling of votes throughout the city. Torres' majorities were in the predominantly Mexican-American boxes, while Gatti's majorities were in the Anglo and black boxes. The cohesion within the Anglo voting precincts in these mayoralty elections was evident, but what was also clear was the support for the GGL that came from the black voting precincts. In subsequent elections, black support for an "establishment" candidate diminished markedly, and a shift toward an alliance with the Mexican-American community began to emerge.

As described earlier, the Good Government League was confronted with internal problems prior to the 1973 elections. Charles Becker bolted the organization, announced his candidacy for mayor, and took the executive director of the organization with him as well as some supporters within the organization. In response, the league slated Roy Barrera, a Mexican American and a former secretary of state, to head its ticket.

Becker carried the precincts that had traditionally been the base of support of the Good Government League—the north side Anglo precincts, the southeastern Anglo precincts, and a few black precincts. In sharp contrast to previous voting patterns, Barrera, the GGL candidate, carried the predominantly Mexican-American precincts and the remainder of the black voting precincts. In one sense, this election stood in marked contrast to previous elections in that a GGL candidate carried the predominantly Mexican-American boxes. On the other hand, the voting was along ethnic lines and consistent with earlier patterns.

The mayoralty race in 1975 was a three-way race between Lila Cockrell, the nominee of the GGL, Eloy Centeno, a Mexican-American businessman, and John Monfrey, a beer and liquor distributor. Cockrell received a majority or a plurality in the traditional GGL precincts; Centeno received a majority or a plurality in the Mexican-American precincts; and Monfrey received a majority or a plurality in the predominantly black precincts and a scattering of other precincts. Of the 103,000 votes cast in this first election, Cockrell received 47 percent of the vote; Monfrey, 26 percent; and Centeno, 18 percent. The remaining votes were spread among minor candidates.

The runoff campaign produced a high interest election with considerable resources allocated by both sides for an intense media campaign. This was the first election in which the mayor was elected directly, and unlike many of the previous elections in which voter turnout declined from the first to the second election, there were approximately the same number of persons in the turnout in this second election. Lila Cockrell received 54 percent of the runoff vote, while John Monfrey received 46 percent. Cockrell's majorities came from the GGL Anglo precincts. In addition to the black precincts that he had carried in the first race, Monfrey obtained majorities in most of the Mexican-American precincts. As an Anglo, Monfrey was able to build a voting coalition between Mexican-American and black precincts. This voting coalition has reappeared in several subsequent elections and was a departure of earlier alignments between Anglo and black voting precincts. Whether this coalition is permanent or not depends on several factors, including the specific campaign strategies developed by the leaders of all three ethnic groups.

In the 1975 race the Good Government League won only three council seats including that of the mayor. The other six members of the GGL were defeated by the slate of candidates called the "Independent Team." With its two successive defeats, the continued division among Anglo elites, and the decline in its internal organizational structure, the GGL was eventually to close out its organization in December 1976. There was a temporary effort in early 1977 to organize an alternative group to the GGL, but the efforts were soon terminated when it became evident that this new group had no broad base of support as had the GGL. As of 1983, there was still no alternative group or organization that has taken the GGL's place in the Anglo communities.

At the same time that the GGL was declining, Communities Organized for Public Services (COPS), an Alinsky-type organization, was developing and expanding its base in the Mexican-American communities (see Chapter 9). There is no evidence that there was a direct relationship between these two developments. The dynamics of each pattern was based on different sets of conditions within the respective communities. Since its inception, COPS has expanded its membership to include black communities within the city. In addition to COPS, other community organizations have begun to develop in the black communities—for example, Residents Organized for Better and More Beautiful Environmental Development (ROBBED).

The GGL's electoral victories and its control of city government were attributed, in part, to the coalitional nature of its slating of candidates from all three ethnic groups. Even with the demise of the GGL prior to the 1977 election, Lila Cockrell was still able to capitalize on the older GGL alliances. Twenty years of coalitional politics are not destroyed immediately at the point that an organization ceases to exist, but it is not clear at what point this pattern disintegrates and realignment in the city's political processes takes place.

COPS and similar community organizations are now faced with the problems of coalition building. These groups address the needs and interests of low-income ethnic populations. The tactics and strategies utilized by such community organizations as well as their ideological formulations of the nature of the problems that face the city are not conducive to building coalitions with the more affluent Anglo population. Such coalitions have been constructed, as was done in the 1977 referendum, when an environmental issue dealing with the city's water supply produced a coalition that included every ethnic and social group within the city.[11] In general terms, clean water solidifies a city, and as long as the issue is kept at an abstract level, such coalitions are manageable, but when this same issue raises questions about city planning, growth, and tax policy, the coalitions become temporary.

The 1977 election was a repeat of the 1975 election in that Lila Cockrell, the incumbent mayor, John Monfrey, and José San Martín, a popular Mexican-American optometrist who had served on the city council as a GGL candidate, were the three major contenders. As might be expected, the electorate split in patterns similar to those of the 1975 election. With the demise of the GGL and the general interest of COPS in the city council elections, there was no broad base of support any of these candidates could automatically mobilize. In a sense, this election demonstrated an emerging pattern in which a mayoralty candidate must build support around himself or herself. Reliance on media events and a campaign organization that is personally committed to the candidate appear to be key ingredients of contemporary mayoralty coalitions.

Cockrell received 39 percent of the vote; Monfrey received 31 percent, and San Martín received 26 percent. As had been true in the 1975 election, the Mexican-American candidate won either a majority or plurality in the Mexican-American precincts. John Monfrey carried the black precincts and a few Anglo precincts, while Cockrell carried the predominantly Anglo precincts in the city. Between the general election and the runoff election, John Monfrey's health deteriorated, and just prior to the election, he was committed to the hospital for an ailment, diagnosed as cancer, which soon took his life. Cockrell received 59 percent of the vote, carrying the Anglo precincts. Monfrey carried the black and Mexican-American boxes.

The 1979 election was a repeat of previous elections in which two fairly well-financed Anglo candidates ran against each other. In this instance, though, Lila Cockrell, the incumbent mayor with earlier ties to the now-defunct GGL, reestablished the voting alliance between the Anglo and black precincts. Her opponent was the previous mayor, Charles Becker, whose support was primarily located in the Mexican-American precincts.

Bloc voting on the basis of ethnicity has been a major determinant in the city's mayoralty elections. Through 1979, no candidate who relied predominantly on the Mexican-American vote had won. In 1981, however, Henry Cisneros was elected mayor of San Antonio by winning not only the Mexican-American vote but many Anglo votes as well. In the future, the proportion of voters who are Mexican American should increase as a result of the basic factors of demography, and this should continue to enhance the electoral possibilities of Mexican Americans. Cisneros' election resembled that of Albert Bustamante, who in 1978 was elected Bexar County judge; Bustamante, with considerable Anglo support, defeated an Anglo candidate in the Democratic primary. This suggests that Mexican-American candidates can continue to win by producing a coalition among ethnic groups, but such candidates will have to position themselves delicately among the competing demands of the three segments of the electorate.

Nonpartisanship, Institutional Changes, and Mayoralty Politics

Nonpartisanship has been an important movement in U.S. urban politics. From this movement came the concepts of the nonpartisan election system and the council-manager form of government. These theories of governance and structure were based on the business models of policy development, management, and expertise. Particular emphasis was given to the concepts of administrative efficiency. The goal was to create governments which minimized or reduced interest conflicts. A city council member's constituency in the at-large election system was the city itself rather than any specific interest group within the city. Furthermore, the indirect election of the mayor by the council and the separation of policy making from administration through the council-manager form of government was clearly intended to insulate the administrative processes of city government from interest group pressure or partisan politics.

The advocates of a council-manager form of government in San Antonio apparently accepted the basic premises of nonpartisanship. The Good Government League's origins in 1954 and 1955 were directly related to the view that the well-being of the city was threatened by the potential reestablishment of the commission form of government and the continued power confrontations that had transpired even after the charter was changed. Once the GGL had demonstrated electoral successes, its subsequent domination of city politics between 1955 and 1973 tended to reinforce attitudes based on the premises of nonpartisanship. The GGL stabilized city politics, minimized public political confrontation, and appeared to implement the efficient and businesslike operation of city government.

Nevertheless, the elections described in the previous section indicate that not all groups perceived this system to be advantageous to their interests. The greatest opposition to the GGL's mayoralty and city council candidates came from the Mexican-American community, with some additional opposition from black voters. Surprisingly, various Anglo residential areas also often alleged that they did not receive their fair share of city resources or expenditures. Yet this was not translated into electoral opposition to the Good Government League. Basic tensions resulting from varied interests existed, but it was not until Becker's election in 1973 that a serious challenge was initiated against the institutional forms of nonpartisanship as well as its basic premises.

Of the two charter revisions that came after Becker's election, single-member districting has appeared to be a greater challenge to the nonpartisan principle than has the direct election of the mayor. The single-member district more clearly identifies a council member's constituency, and the council member who is interested in reelection tends to be responsive to the interests and demands of his district. It becomes increasingly difficult for a council member operating under this system to express and respond to citywide concerns. Furthermore, the ethnic composition of the city council changed appreciably when single-member districts were adopted.

By the fact that single-member districts permit neighborhood interests to be represented on the city council, political controversy has increased appreciably in the deliberations of the city council. Among the minority groups of the city, single-member districting has been generally perceived as a beneficial change. On the other hand, certain Anglo groups particularly have viewed single-member districting with disfavor, and it is common to hear references to a return to "ward" or "machine" politics (see Chapter 10).

While there has been no systematic appraisal of all competing views and interests within the city and of the effects that they will have on institutional structures, it is quite clear that the businesslike style of council meetings and policy resolution that the GGL prided itself upon has been replaced since 1977 by intense interest conflicts within city council deliberations.

As noted earlier, mayoralty elections in the city are no longer directly linked to councilmanic elections. There is evidence to suggest the majorities represented on the ten single-member districts are different from the majorities compiled by a successful mayoralty candidate. The contrasts in registration and turnout data for the ten districts address this point. Although the districts are equal in population, the Anglo districts have a much larger voter registration than do the black and Mexican-American districts. If in the 1980s ethnicity should again become the primary determinant of voting and the shaping of expectations in city elections, the city council will more accurately reflect black and Mexican-American interests, while the mayor's constituency could revert to one disproportionately drawn from the Anglo population. These two constituencies would become institutionalized in the council and the mayor. Consequently, sharpened controversy and conflict between competing interests would become the normal pattern of council decision making and would more closely approximate the conflicts that are associated with cities with partisan election systems.

This is not to suggest that there is widespread support for partisan politics in the various political subcultures of the city, but it does point to the increasing inability of the nonpartisan election system to mute these controversies and follow the businesslike model of governance that has been associated with nonpartisanship.

Part III: Urban Policy Issues

Richard A. Gambitta,
Robert A. Milne,
and Carol R. Davis

Chapter Seven

The Politics of
Unequal Educational
Opportunity

An examination of a city's educational system reveals a great deal about the stratification of wealth, social status, and influence in that city. In San Antonio, governmental financing of public education has varied significantly among the neighborhoods. As a result, the quality of education delivered to the city's children has differed dramatically according to the neighborhoods in which they reside.

In 1973, the United States Supreme Court, in a landmark decision,[1] upheld the Texas school finance law which had established an expenditure system resulting in over twice the amount of state and local money being spent on the education of children residing in an affluent San Antonio neighborhood as was being spent on the education of children residing in the city's poor west side. Moreover, the property owners on the west side paid a higher tax rate than did the property owners in the rich San Antonio enclaves.

This chapter reviews the history and politics of public education in Texas in an attempt to illuminate both the reasons why unequal educational systems developed in San Antonio and the interests leading the Supreme Court to sustain a Texas law which seemingly perpetuates unequal educational opportunity in the public schools.

The Early Development and Financing of
Public Schools in Texas and San Antonio

Controversy concerning public school finance in Texas began with the creation of the first schools in the eighteenth century. With slight variations, the issues raised, the events that unfolded, and the political values that dominated early educational controversies reappeared in each subsequent era. The principal controversies over public school finance have been the source and availability of financial resources and the concept of local control.

Public school finance first became an issue when Spain governed Texas. In 1786, José de la Mata came to San Antonio from Saltillo and organized a school. In an attempt to establish a more permanent status and a more adequate financial base for the school, de la Mata requested that the Spanish authorities endorse the school and require that parents pay an annual sum towards its maintenance. This request was provisionally approved, resulting in the first formal relationship between government and education in Texas.[2] The de la Mata school, however, soon closed because of disagreements between de la Mata and the territorial governor.

Early in the nineteenth century, three other attempts were made to establish and maintain schools in San Antonio. Each of them failed because of inadequate financial resources. Although particular circumstances differed, a consistent pattern appeared in all four attempts.[3] In every case, the Spanish government supported the establishment of public schools in principle but failed to provide the necessary financial resources. Marked discrepancies between the promise and the performance of state and territorial governments in regard to education in San Antonio characterize the entire history of public schools in the area.

The role of state and local governments in the financing and control of education in San Antonio and Texas has been the subject of political debate from de la Mata's era to the present. The state's financial commitment to education has been particularly important because much of San Antonio did not and does not have sufficient wealth to support an adequate public school system. When state officials finally did offer financial support, they tied the funding to a policy dominated by the traditional commitment to local control. The state provided very minimal financial aid which local revenues could supplement. As a consequence, the children in the poorer sections of San Antonio have not enjoyed the educational support that others have. The history of public school finance in San Antonio and Texas demonstrates the reasons behind this deprivation.

After Mexican Independence in 1821, the state more aggressively promoted the local development of schools. The 1827 constitution of the state of Coahuila y Texas contains a good illustration: "In all the towns of the State a suitable number of primary schools shall be established wherein shall be taught reading, writing, arithmetic, the catechism of the Christian Religion, a brief and simple explanation of this Constitution and that of the Republic [of Mexico], the rights and duties of men in society, and whatever else may conduce the better education of youth."[4] Although the Mexican government required the development of local educational institutions, it, like Spain, provided little financial support. The responsibility for financing and developing schools remained with local government and private citizens.

The problem with this plan for San Antonio and other poor frontier towns became apparent to certain Mexican officials. In 1825, the state instructed José Antonio Saucedo, chief of the department of Texas, to encourage the San Antonio *ayuntamiento* (municipal government) to establish a primary school. After examining the resources of the penurious citizenry and town treasury, Saucedo reported, "I think it absolutely necessary that in this town should be established a primary school supported by state funds."[5] Saucedo's appeal fell upon deaf ears, for the Congress reported that its revenues were insufficient to help fund local schools. San Antonio's citizens, however, did raise revenues through subscriptions to pay a teacher in 1826, and the municipality instituted the first education tax—on livestock brought to slaughter.[6] These local efforts resulted in the opening of a school, but when Saucedo appealed again for state funds to preserve it, his request was again denied.

The most successful school in San Antonio under Mexican rule opened in 1828. The Mexican government contributed about twenty-six dollars worth of catechisms, cartoons, and charts to the school, constituting the first state aid to San Antonio's educational efforts. The government also forbade the frequent practice by school masters of selling seats or extracting other payments from students. Hence, equal access to education was a concern in San Antonio under Mexican rule, at this early stage of development. During good years, this school enrolled about 45 percent of the school-aged population, but it closed in 1834 as a result of diminished state and local funding, depressed economic conditions, poor attendance, and rising political instability.[7]

By the close of the Mexican era, the concept of local control over school development was firmly established. Repeatedly, the central government had committed itself symbolically, but not financially, to the development of Texas schools. This pattern would repeat itself after Texas Independence, even though central funding appeared to be necessary to sustain frontier schools.

Educational Funding and Organization, 1836–1900

In 1836, when Texas declared its independence from Mexico, it cited the failure of Mexico to provide schools as one of the major reasons for separation. The creation of the Republic of Texas, however, neither significantly altered the method of school finance nor increased the state's financial commitment to the development of schools in San Antonio. Although the Constitution of the Republic set forth that "It shall be the duty of Congress, as soon as circumstances permit, to provide by law, a general system of education," the legislature did not appropriate state funds for local schools.[8] Instead, when the legislature met, it accepted San Antonio's revised charter which made it "the special duty of the council to promote by every equitable means, the establishment of common schools."[9] Thus, the responsibility for financing education remained with the city.

In 1839, the Republic granted three leagues of land to each county. The counties were to use revenues generated from the leasing of this land for the development of local educational institutions. The following year, the congress adopted a decentralized school development plan, but local officials did little during the years of the Republic to implement it. As in much of the United States, the dominant ideology favored private rather than public schools. As a result, few Texas counties even bothered to select or survey the lands the state had awarded them. San Antonio's city council, in fact, rejected a plan to establish a primary school in 1844, and little else developed concerning public education in San Antonio or in Texas during the Republican era.

After annexation to the United States, the first Texas state constitution declared (Article X, § 1), "It shall be the duty of the legislature of this state to make suitable provisions for the support and maintenance of public schools," and (§ 2) "The legislature shall, as early as practicable, establish free schools throughout the state . . . [and] furnish means for their support by taxation of property." The constitution also reserved one-tenth of state annual revenues as a perpetual fund to support "free public schools, and no law shall ever be made, directing said funds to any other use."[10] Texas now had the constitutional mandate and the authorized means of taxing property to establish schools. But because property taxation was not imposed the annual revenues generated—less than $82,000 by 1853[11]—were insufficient to develop and maintain a statewide system of schools. Hence, in 1850, fewer than one-sixth of the school-aged children of Texas had received any formal education, and most of that was for relatively short periods in private schools.[12]

In 1853, however, San Antonio managed to open the first free public schools in Texas. The city opened four schools, one for boys and one for girls on each side of the San Antonio River. This distribution of the schools on both banks of the river reflected the already clear pattern of ethnic segregation among San Antonians—the Mexican population concentrated mainly on the west side, Anglos and Germans on the east. Ironically, the revenues for these schools came from the lands granted to localities by the Republic of Mexico when Texas, with Coahuila, formed a Mexican state. Thus, although Anglo claims about Mexican insensitivity toward education had provided a major rationale for Texas independence,[13] now, twenty years after independence, the gratuitous endowments by that Mexican government financed the only free schools in Texas.

In the 1850s Texans debated whether to pursue the development of transportation or of educational systems with the funds left after settling the state's boundary disputes with the U.S. government. Texas had received $10 million in indemnities and, after paying its debts, still had an abundant surplus in U.S. bonds. One political camp favored the investment of the capital in rail transportation projects, while others sought to use those funds for the development of public schools. In an innovative compromise, the Texas legislature set aside the $2 million surplus as a permanent school fund with the annual interest to be applied to the development and maintenance of a public school system. In turn, the state would lend the capital of the permanent fund, at that time yielding 5 percent interest as U.S. bonds, to private entrepreneurs, at 6 percent, to finance the development of railroads across Texas. Hence, the two great needs of the state would be financed using the same dollars.[14] Unfortunately, with the advent of the Civil War, the railroads defaulted on their loans, and the vast majority of the $2 million permanent educational fund, one of the largest in the nation, was lost. The fund's balance, appropriated to the Confederate war effort, was likewise lost forever. By the end of the war, the "permanent" fund for the education of Texas children had been totally depleted, leaving the state and San Antonio once again without schools or the funds to build them.[15]

The constitution of 1869, designed by the Reconstruction Republicans, established a radically different approach to public education. The Republicans launched an ambitious and aggressive program designed to open educational institutions for white, brown, and black children throughout Texas, under *centralized* Republican control. In 1870 and 1871 they passed legislation mandating an independent state school superintendent, uniform school districts (drawn up by the Republicans), compulsory school attendance, school board autonomy from popular control, and centralized funding from a 1 percent *ad valorem* tax upon property.[16] By December of its first year, over 1,300 schools were operating in Texas.[17] At last the state and San Antonio had established numerous public schools, and a statewide system of education began.

This centralized Republican school program, however, proved alien and threatening to most Texans. Violent opposition resulted, including the burning of schoolhouses and physical abuse for the teachers of minority children. Taxpayer conventions throughout the state publicly advocated resistance to the radical school program.[18] Ironically, the program most successful in opening schools induced the greatest public hostility. Racism, the tradition of local Democratic party control, and the tremendous opposition to the 1 percent tax overwhelmed the Republicans. In 1873, many Southern Democrats returned to power on a platform promising the destruction of the school program. The legislature soon returned the control and finance of education to the localities,[19] successfully demolishing the Republican centralized system and dismantling the schools it had established. The 1876 constitution eliminated the state education board, the powers of the state superintendent, compulsory attendance, and, in effect, any real possibility of local taxation. This reaction against centralized control and finance of public schools would have impact upon school policies until the present day.[20]

The Democrats also replaced formal state districting with a system of "community schools," allowing any group of parents to join and form school communities simply by petitioning the county judge, listing the children whom they desired to attend, and thereby qualifying for the per pupil revenues from the state's "available fund." Such radical local control allowed citizens to self-select and self-restrict their own school districts, thus encouraging both racial and economic segregation. Under this system, Texas experienced a proliferation of segregated community schools, many of which lacked credentials of any sort. Such community schools predominated in Texas until the mid-1880s, with vestiges remaining through 1909.[21]

The abuses and inadequacies of this community school policy grew increasingly apparent. The legislature reduced educational funding from one-fourth to one-sixth of the annual revenues and increased the powers of municipalities to control educational affairs within their boundaries. In 1879 the state ceded to the cities the power to levy educational taxes. Instituting a tax, however, required the approval of two-thirds of the property-tax-paying public. With private schools available for the children of the affluent, this two-thirds provision greatly frustrated efforts to raise revenues for public education. Furthermore, urban areas could subdivide into "independent" school districts, each empowered to tax for the maintenance of schools. This allowed wealthier neighborhoods to form independent school districts excluding poorer neighborhoods. As a result, the revenues generated from neighborhoods with relatively high property values contributed exclusively to the education of children residing within those affluent neighborhoods, while poorer urban neighborhoods faced reduced state financing and an inadequate property tax base for their schools.

Rural areas could neither form independent districts nor tax to support schools. A constitutional amendment ratified in 1883[22] relieved this problem somewhat by allowing counties to subdivide into districts. But rural property taxes generally proved too meager to support adequate school development. The policy of local control thus made it very difficult for rural and poor communities to create adequate educational systems.

Major school legislation, passed in 1884, increased the sources of revenue for the paltry permanent fund. It stipulated, however, that no portion of the fund could be allocated to "any school consisting partly of white and partly of colored children." Additionally, this legislation hatched another dual system, one between common and independent school districts (CSDs and ISDs). The legislature authorized county commissioner courts to divide each county into "convenient" common school districts. Hence, to the independent districts existing primarily in affluent sections of cities, commissioner courts added common school districts throughout the county. In pursuance of local control, the commissioners had total discretion in the drawing of boundary lines. Moreover, Section 29 of the law guaranteed the integrity of the boundaries drawn by these segregationist courts: "When districts are once established, they shall not be changed without the consent of a majority of the legal voters in all districts affected by such change." Therefore, residents in property-rich districts in San Antonio and other Texas cities could and did remain insulated educationally from those residing in property-poor districts, despite geographical proximity. By insuring local control over education, the state had limited its own role and provided both affluent areas and propertied citizens with checks upon the future direction and scope of educational development.[23]

Around 1890 schools began to proliferate both because of a new prosperity and because of the recognition by elites that education facilitated economic development. The perceived interests of business now coincided with the need for permanent schools. Yet the seeds of sustained inequality were inherent in the policy of local finance and control. From that time to the present, inequalities would arise among the schools of whites, blacks, and browns, of urbanites, suburbanites, and rurals, of independent and common districts, and of those residing in property-rich and property-poor districts.

The Movement to Consolidate Public
Education in Texas and Bexar County

After 1900, some permanent schools operated in Texas, but mostly in the affluent areas of larger cities, where independent districts had taxing authority. Because of the rapid economic change occurring as parts of Texas developed economically, disparities in access to both local revenues and educational opportunities became progressively more stark. Texas, increasingly prosperous, soon possessed the largest educational fund of any state in the union, and rural officials, intolerant of property taxes, insisted that this permanent fund was adequate to support education without local taxation. Despite these claims, Texas ranked thirty-seventh among the states in both per capita and per pupil educational expenditures.[24] The permanent fund provided a nice symbol, but many Texans were gradually recognizing that the state was not spending enough on education.

This awareness plus increasing demand for better educational facilities by business leaders led to the passage and ratification of a constitutional amendment in 1908 which increased the ceiling on tax rates and gave taxing authority to common school districts. The level of local taxation increased significantly after the ratification of this amendment.

Disparities in district financial resources also increased significantly as a result of the amendment. Generally the more affluent communities took advantage of the higher ceilings to raise additional revenue for their schools. Although taxation levels increased for the rural common districts after ratification, in most cases both the rural and the poorer city school districts operated on the minimal allocations from the permanent fund, contributing to radical differences between the funds available to the different districts.

Other changes after 1914 liberalized educational policy in the state somewhat. First, in 1915, a bill was passed establishing a very modest compulsory attendance policy. Secondly, in 1918 the voters ratified a constitutional amendment providing free textbooks to Texas students. This was financed by adding fifteen cents to the existing twenty cent *ad valorem* tax.

These and other reforms required that the state government significantly increase its educational appropriations. In reaction to this increase, fiscal conservatives, convinced that the state bore too great a portion of the cost of education, passed an amendment in 1920 raising the limit on local taxation levels, thus allowing the localities to assume greater responsibility for financing schools. Both conservatives and liberals promoted the amendment, arguing that local taxation increased freedom of choice and expanded educational opportunities so that the amendment won popular ratification.

Yet the inequalities that this policy would produce were barely discussed. Under the new system, the state would no longer increase its contributions to education; local enrichment funds would be required to meet local needs. As a consequence, the law aggravated the already tremendous disparities in financial resources between the school districts. If the state had maintained the primary responsibility for educational finance, the wealthier, propertied class would have paid a large share of every child's education in the state. Under the new policy, however, each local district chose how much to spend on itself. As a result, more affluent areas could employ their greater resources exclusively for their own children's education, leaving poorer districts to fend for themselves.

With virtually each schoolhouse constituting a separate school district, the number of districts in the state increased steadily. By the early 1920s, 7,369 common and 858 independent districts operated in the state.[25] Efforts to consolidate these districts proved frustrating to reformers because an 1884 law required the voters of each district affected by proposed consolidations to approve the merger by referendum. Thus, affluent districts with predominantly Anglo populations had veto power over proposed consolidations with districts having poorer or largely minority populations. (As will be explained in detail later, this provision had much to do with the failure of the Edgewood school district in San Antonio to consolidate with neighboring districts possessing greater resources.) Problems concerning transportation, racial and ethnic prejudices, and curriculum control also made consolidations difficult. By 1932, consolidation efforts had reduced the number of districts to 7,932, less than a 4 percent decrease.[26]

Immigration to Texas's urban areas increased during the Depression, and industrial development accelerated that pace during the 1940s. Ethnic populations clustered in particular neighborhoods within the larger cities, such as the Edgewood area of southwest San Antonio. While the affluent Anglo neighborhoods had maintained independent school districts since the early 1900s, the poorer ethnic communities, particularly the black and Mexican neighborhoods,[27] generally remained common school districts.[28] As was clearly the case in San Antonio, restrictive racial covenants in property deeds helped preserve the racial homogeneity of vast segments of the urban areas. Mexican Americans and Anglos were separated as a consequence of *de facto* segregated housing patterns reinforced by *de jure* restrictive covenants in property deeds. Blacks, of course, were prohibited by law from attending any white schools.

By 1947, statewide consolidation efforts had produced some further reduction in the number of districts statewide, from more than 8,000 in the 1920s to 5,145. But the consolidation movement had had less impact in San Antonio. At this time, Bexar County had forty-three common and six independent school districts.[29] These forty-nine districts displayed an extremely wide range of property and wealth. Of all the districts, none had greater financial problems than the Edgewood Common School District. The story of Edgewood demonstrates vividly the adverse effects of the Texas educational finance system and consolidation procedures on districts with few resources.

Edgewood and the Consolidation of Bexar County Districts

Edgewood had always had a relatively poor property-tax base. Originally, it had been a portion of the Mackey Common School District (CSD), but the two areas separated in 1919. Later, Mackey joined the predominantly Anglo, eventually prosperous, north side ISD. Financially poorer Edgewood, on the other hand, was never acceptable to any other Bexar County school district to which it sought attachment. Several restructurings of the Edgewood district after the First World War also proved disadvantageous to its financial position. For example, in 1922, a group of citizens in the area presently constituting the South San Antonio Independent School District (ISD) elected to break away from the Edgewood CSD. After county commissioners redrew its boundaries, Edgewood had lost a major factory, an oil company, and thirteen of its original fourteen miles of railway property.[30]

During the 1930s and even more so during the 1940s, massive immigration caused an explosion in Edgewood's school population. The district, unlike many others in the San Antonio area, had a very low percentage of residential property deeds with restrictive racial covenants prohibiting the sale of property to individuals of Mexican and black descent. In the richer areas, such as the north-side Alamo Heights, Olmos Park, and Terrell Hills zone, a majority of the deeds had such restrictive covenants.[31] These covenants remained legally enforceable until 1948[32] and had a great deal of practical impact long after that. Thus, while some school districts in the urban areas remained relatively immune to the extensive immigration of poor minority families, Edgewood attracted such newcomers to the city because of housing opportunities and newly created jobs at several military installations adjacent to the Edgewood CSD. Later, federally sponsored slum clearance projects along what became Interstate Highway 35 displaced hundreds of Mexican-American families from the San Antonio ISD into hastily built, poorly constructed houses with inadequate sanitation facilities in the Edgewood CSD.[33] Overall, from 1939 to 1949, Edgewood's school population increased from 1,586 to over 6,600 students.[34] These demographic changes, unaccompanied by proportional increases in the tax base, vastly magnified the economic pressures on the relatively poor school system.

The Edgewood district then, as a result of events quite beyond its "local control," found few remedies and little assistance in coping with its predicament. Alamo Heights ISD, San Antonio ISD (SAISD), and other contiguous districts remained solvent and stable because of local, not state, funds. For Edgewood, this possibility was not available. In the 1947 school year, for example, more than 700 additional pupils enrolled at a time when no additional classroom space was available. Faced with a lack of funds and a rapidly expanding student population, Edgewood placed 2,400 pupils and seventy classrooms on half-day sessions beginning in 1949. A congressional committee investigating the need for federal subsidies to school districts serving large numbers of children from military families characterized the Edgewood situation as "the worst we had encountered in any school district in this country."[35]

The problems confronting poorer districts such as Edgewood forced state officials to acknowledge that there was a crisis in the educational finance system. This belated recognition resulted in the passage of the highly publicized Gilmer-Aikin educational funding bill in 1949. The major reform contained in this law, the Foundation School Program, established the system of school finance which survives with some revisions to the present day. Under the minimum foundation program the state provided the revenue necessary to fund a minimal education for each child in the state. Local districts could then enrich the program with additional revenues raised through *ad valorem* taxes. The state now had changed its policy: it would guarantee a basic education to each child while preserving to a large degree the long-standing tradition of local control.[36]

Unquestionably, passage of the Gilmer-Aikin legislation had a positive impact on education throughout Texas. The minimum foundation program significantly increased state spending on education. Yet, as an *equaliz-*

ing reform the impact of the program was largely symbolic for three reasons. Foremost, from 1900–1950, inter-district disparities in property values grew tremendously. Property-poor districts such as Edgewood had to rely almost entirely on state revenue; their tax bases could not provide enough revenues to increase per pupil expenditures significantly. School districts with adequate tax bases and small enrollments, however, could generate revenues to raise per pupil expenditures far above the state's contribution. These local enrichment funds have allowed property-rich districts to provide educational advantages that children in districts like Edgewood have never had.[37]

Second, the minimum foundation program provided more state revenues for districts with such characteristics as more highly educated or experienced teachers, characteristics generally found in the more affluent districts that could afford to pay the higher salaries necessary to retain the teachers with better credentials. Third, in spite of the legislative struggle over Gilmer-Aikin, district consolidation procedures did not change.[38] This rejection of a new consolidation policy would have enormous implications for the school districts in San Antonio.

The push for consolidation of the forty-three common and six independent school districts in San Antonio and Bexar County began in 1947, an enormous task. After numerous town and local board meetings in 1947 and 1948, however, a master consolidation plan was set in motion. By 1951, this effort had reduced the number of districts to fourteen. Edgewood, however, was not a party to any of these consolidations.

Each quadrant of the rural, sparsely populated areas of the county conducted successful consolidation efforts. In the northwestern quadrant nine districts were combined to form the Northside Common School District.[39] Soon afterwards, the Northside CSD and three nearby common districts combined to form the Northside Independent School District. Of northeastern Bexar County's ten common school districts, seven consolidated in 1949 to form the Northeast RHSD, and the three others formed the Judson RHSD in 1958. Six southeastern districts formed the East Central RHSD. In 1949 East Central annexed four other common districts thereby completing efforts in that area. Five of the eleven southwestern common districts consolidated into the Southside Common School District in 1949, and four others combined in 1950 creating the Southwest RHSD. That same year Idlewild joined the Southwest RHSD. The remaining two districts consolidated to become the Somerset ISD.[40]

School districts were also consolidated within the urban center of the county. Five independent (San Antonio, Alamo Heights, Los Angeles

Heights, Harlandale, and South San Antonio) and three common school districts (Edgewood, W. W. White, and Hot Wells) existed within the central city area in 1947. The San Antonio Independent School District (SAISD) made a number of consolidation overtures to contiguous city districts. Alamo Heights ISD, more prosperous than the San Antonio ISD, consistently refused invitations to join the larger system, but Los Angeles Heights ISD took advantage of these overtures, petitioned for annexation to the SAISD, and was accepted in 1949.[41]

The Edgewood CSD also attempted to join San Antonio ISD, presenting a petition to the county superintendent asking for annexation.[42] Contrary to the quick, positive response to Los Angeles Heights, the SAISD board replied that a careful examination of the annexation proposal, Edgewood's physical plants, current and projected enrollments, tax resources, and operating costs had to be undertaken prior to any action. Shortly thereafter, the SAISD received annexation petitions from the Hot Wells and W. W. White CSDs, further delaying Edgewood's consolidation request. At a meeting held between the Edgewood and SAISD boards, a member of the San Antonio board bluntly stated that although a "moral obligation" might exist to share the city's tax resources among all the city's children, the law did not compel them to do so.[43] This statement accurately depicted the situation, for the state had designed that law precisely in a manner which protected the interests and integrity of the more affluent areas. Consequently, the SAISDs board actively discouraged and ultimately rejected Edgewood's annexation petition.[44] As a result, the wealth of the city as a whole would not contribute to the education of Edgewood's children.

Edgewood simply had too poor a tax base to adequately support education, and the SAISD had no desire to acquire responsibility for such a heavy burden. In 1949, when Edgewood was in such a desperate financial condition that it was forced to place 2,400 students on half-day sessions, the district possessed an assessed property value of only $300 per pupil, by far the lowest in the county. The average male head of household in the area worked as a day laborer earning a monthly income of $140. Seventy-five percent of the homes in an Edgewood elementary zone were substandard, many with dirt floors and outdoor privies. In the Carver Elementary School District, a majority of houses contained neither plumbing, fuel, nor electricity.[45] This was the property wealth that the Texas educational finance system directed Edgewood to use to enrich the education it offered. The concept of local control, which permits each district to choose the extent of enrichment it wishes to provide, became meaningless for the poverty-stricken Edgewood CSD. In practice then, the concept of local control served as a means for political elites, both statewide and locally, to rationalize and maintain a highly unequal system of educational finance which allowed an adequate education only in those neighborhoods that could afford it.

In the 1967–68 school year, a striking contrast appeared between the revenues available to the Edgewood and Alamo Heights ISDs. The Texas method of school finance resulted in the expenditure in Alamo Heights of over two and one-quarter times the amount of state and local revenues spent on the education of each child attending Edgewood. This occurred despite Edgewood's higher tax rate.

In a decision consistent with earlier actions, the SAISD board approved those pending petitions from Hot Wells and W. W. White in early 1950.[46] The isolation of Edgewood had become complete. Disparities in property values played the major role in the process of isolation. For example, in 1950, residential property values in Los Angeles Heights averaged approximately $11,000 and only $3,000 in Edgewood.[47] Undoubtedly, however, racial factors played a role in the series of decisions resulting in Edgewood's isolation because the district had a very high concentration of Mexican Americans relative to Hot Wells and W. W. White ISDs. Segregated schools for blacks and the extensive use of restrictive racial covenants in San Antonio, particularly in the wealthy communities, indicate that race was not ignored in public policy deliberations of the day.

Edgewood took advantage of the one remaining avenue open to improving the district's position by applying for and receiving state authorization to become an independent school district. By attaining independent status, Edgewood was allowed a higher tax ceiling. Yet the district continued to struggle with severe financial problems because no matter how high the district taxed, it could not raise adequate revenues. As a result, Edgewood children were not provided the minimum education Gilmer-Aikin purported to assure. It should be noted that Gilmer-Aikin did increase *state* funding and, as a result, heightened the quality of education offered in Edgewood and similar poor districts. This increase, however, was modest and did not alleviate the financial difficulties of districts with inadequate tax bases. Politically, the highly publicized increase in state funding and the language of the Gilmer-Aikin legislation, which guaranteed a minimum education for all Texas children, had an important negative impact on attempts to achieve more equitable educational funding in the state. The Gilmer-Aikin reforms effectively checked educational equalization efforts for almost three decades.

In 1954 and 1960, Edgewood again attempted without success to merge with the SAISD.[48] Subsequently, the fifty-seventh state legislature permanently blocked the petition route to merger by amending the state law to require that annexations be approved by every affected school board.[49] As a result of the failure of its numerous consolidation attempts, Edgewood remained isolated with very limited resources. In a striking contrast, during the early 1970s over two and one-quarter times more public funds were being expended on the education of each student in Alamo Heights than in Edgewood, less than five miles away, this despite the fact that Edgewood had the higher tax rate.

Rodriguez v. San Antonio Independent School District et al.

In 1968, plans to build tax-exempt public housing projects which would have large student populations threatened the Edgewood district with additional financial strain. With half-day sessions becoming a real possibility again, a group of Edgewood parents formed the Edgewood Concerned Parents Association and consulted Arthur Gochman, a San Antonio attorney. Demetrio Rodriguez, a member of the association, sought information on the necessary procedures to recall the Edgewood board of education because he believed that the problems of the Edgewood schools were the result of administrative mismanagement. Gochman knew few details about the school finance system in Texas, but as he began examining Rodriguez's complaints he realized that mismanagement was not the major problem confronting the district. In a subsequent meeting with Rodriguez, Gochman informed him that the real problem was the lack of adequate financial resources.[50]

Since previous efforts to solve Edgewood's problems either through consolidation or legislative relief had failed, the only forum left offering the possibility of relief was the judiciary. As a result, Gochman and Rodriguez decided to sue the state of Texas and numerous local school districts which they believed were contributing to their problem. Their action ultimately led to the landmark case of *San Antonio Independent School District v. Rodriguez*, decided by the U.S. Supreme Court on March 21, 1973.

Gochman filed the initial complaint in federal district court on July 30, 1968, naming SAISD, Alamo Heights ISD, and five other ISDs in the city of San Antonio, the Bexar County School Trustees, and the state of Texas as defendants.[51] Demetrio and Helen Rodriguez, along with five other parent-complainants, brought the suit as a class action on behalf of themselves, their school children, "all school children (and parents) similarly situated who live in the Edgewood Independent School District," and all other minority or poor school children and their parents residing in independent school districts with low property values. The suit contended that the Texas method of school finance violated the equal protection clause of the Fourteenth Amendment to the U.S. Constitution. The litigants alleged that education was a fundamental right and that classifications based on wealth were constitutionally suspect. Cases involving either "fundamental rights" or "suspect classifications" invoke the strictest judicial scrutiny; thus the highly unequal distribution of educational funds by the state government—based upon variations in the property wealth of the districts—violated the guarantees of the federal constitution.

The following year, after pretrial conference, the district court granted motions introduced by the ISDs dismissing them as defendants in the suit, with the consent of all parties.[52] Hence, SAISD and the others remained parties to the action in name only, with most districts subsequently filing *amicus curiae* briefs. The court joined the suit between the complainants and the state of Texas, since the latter had designed and enforced this system adversely affecting the poorer districts. In this same order, the court took notice that the legislature had authorized appointment of another committee in 1965, the Jaworski Committee, to study public school finance and to recommend "a special formulae to establish a fair and equitable basis for the division of the financial responsibility between the state and the various local school districts of Texas."[53] The district court held in abeyance the setting of a trial on the merits until possible legislative action on the committee's recommendations could be assessed. As a result of the committee findings, however, the legislatures of 1969 and 1971 chose not to alter the basic funding formula. Few in the legislature wanted to discuss such a controversial matter, especially in a period dominated by the notorious Sharpstown scandals, which involved corruption in the legislative leadership. It was also clear that the governor was not going to call a special session on the matter.

As was the case with previous blue ribbon committees[54] authorized by the legislature to study education and school finance in Texas, the Jaworski Committee's study was primarily symbolic. It ultimately had little impact on the redistribution of tangible resources along more equitable lines. More money came into the system, but it continued to be distributed inequitably. In fact, in the 1970–71 school year, the state foundation program alone contributed $492 to every child's education in Alamo Heights and only $356 to each of Edgewood's children. The disparity in state support had actually increased, with much greater inequalities in local enrichment exacerbating this growing disparity. The state's method of educational finance had become a "tax high, spend low" system for poor districts and a "tax low, spend high" system for property-rich districts. In 1971, within the 162 poorest districts in Texas, a $20,000 home was taxed, on the average, $130 a year in school taxes. These school districts, however, could generate only $529 per student from both local and state revenue sources. By contrast, in the 203 richest districts in the state, a $20,000 house averaged only $46 a year in school taxes; yet these districts spent $989 in state and local funds on each child's education.[55] Gochman and Rodriguez claimed that this system denied the residents in property-poor districts the equal protection of the law.

After extensive pretrial conferences, the federal district court, composed of a three-judge panel including native San Antonian Adrian Spears, unanimously ruled in favor of the plaintiffs on December 23, 1971. "Having determined that the current system of financing public education in Texas discriminated on the basis of wealth by permitting citizens of affluent districts to provide a higher quality education for their children, while paying lower taxes, this Court concludes, as a matter of law, that the plaintiffs have been denied equal protection of the laws under the Fourteenth Amendment to the United States Constitution."[56] The court rejected the traditional rationale of "local control" as an interest of the state so compelling as to legitimize its system of unequal educational finance. Moreover, the court dismissed the state's contention that the present system allowed each community to determine freely how much to spend on local education. Instead, the court noted that the state had actually, "in truth and in fact, limited the choice of financing by guaranteeing that some districts will spend low (with high taxes) while others will spend high (with low taxes)."[57] Under the current system, what choice was afforded Edgewood? How could Edgewood, or localities like it, control the extent of expenditures within its schools? If local control was the state's interest or goal, the means it employed were not rationally related to the achievement of that end. The district court concluded by ordering Texas to abandon the current method of educational finance and reallocate funds in a constitutional manner so that "the educational opportunities afforded the children attending Edgewood Independent School District, and the other children of the state of Texas, are not a function of wealth other than the wealth of the state as a whole."[58] The court stayed its order for two years to give the legislature time to comply with the mandate, but reserved authority to take further steps if the legislature failed to act within the specified time. These were the tidings delivered to the officials of Texas at Christmas eve 1971.

After the district court decision in *Rodriguez v. SAISD et al.*, many believed that the Texas legislature would initiate reform. Such was not the case, however, because most legislators felt that they should pass no legislation until the Supreme Court decided Rodriguez. Some even believed that they should pass no reform legislation even if the Supreme Court sustained the lower court decision.[59] Traditionally, when confronted with demands for equalization of expenditures, the Texas legislature responded by increasing expenditures across the board. A comparison of expenditures in Edgewood and Alamo Heights in 1968, the year *Rodriguez* originated, with expenditures for 1972 shows that equalization, as measured by the range, had not occurred among these districts. For example, comparison of these figures shows an increase from a $310 total per-pupil disparity in 1968 in state and local support between the districts to a $389 disparity in 1972. Overall, including federal funding, each Alamo Heights child in 1968 and 1972 received approximately two-thirds more money than did a child residing in Edgewood.[60]

When the legislature met in 1973, it was clear that the next move would come, not from the legislature, but from the Supreme Court. On March 21, 1973, the Burger Court reversed the district court's decision and sustained the validity of the Texas policy of public school finance by a 4–5 split. The nature of this split reflected the ideological change which had occurred in the court since Gochman had originally filed the Rodriguez suit in 1968. Had the 1968 Supreme Court remained intact, or had fewer of the justices retired, Gochman would surely have won his case. But consistent with Edgewood's lot in life, the court saw four relatively liberal and activist justices—Warren, Fortas, Black, and Harlan—resign between 1969 and 1971.[61] The retired justices were replaced by President Nixon's appointees—Burger, Blackmun, Powell, and Rhenquist. These more conservative justices were willing to defer to the policies of state legislatures and less willing to extend the equal protection clause.

Justice Powell, writing for the majority, refused to apply "strict scrutiny"—the test used in matters concerning racial discrimination—and instead employed the more traditional rational basis test. Powell found that Texas did have a legitimate state interest in the design of the program; that interest was to guarantee to each child a minimum education, and secondly, to encourage local participation in and control over the educational affairs of each community. The means adopted (the minimum foundation program supplemented by local enrichment) was rationally related to those legitimate state interests, and hence, the system, while not the most equitable, was constitutionally acceptable. The ringing dissent by Justice Marshall demonstrated the depth of the disagreement among the justices. "The majority's holding," Marshall wrote, "can only be seen as a retreat from our historic commitment to equality of educational opportunity and unsupportable acquiescence in a system which deprives children in their earliest years of the chance to reach their full potential as citizens."[62]

Whereas Powell noted several encouraging signs in the Texas legislature's activities in the area, Marshall found "that the state's purported concern with local control is offered primarily as an excuse rather than as a justification for interdistrict inequality," and concluded: "The quality of the educational opportunity offered any particular district is largely determined by the amount of taxable property located in the district—over which voters can exercise no control." Attempting to deal with the problem of inequity, Marshall displayed a more pessimistic view: "I, for one, am unsatisfied with the hope of an ultimate 'political' solution sometime in the indefinite future, while, in the meantime, countless children unjustifiably receive inferior education that 'may affect their hearts and minds in a way unlikely ever to be undone.'"[63]

In fairness, both sides were correct. Texas had invested much more money into poor school districts in recent years, undoubtedly raising the quality of educational offerings in the Edgewood ISD and in places like it that depended almost entirely on the state's foundation revenues. On the other hand, great disparities among often contiguous districts remained. These disparities had a disproportionately adverse impact upon racial and ethnic minorities. In Edgewood, for instance, 96 percent of the student enrollment was either Mexican American or black. In Alamo Heights, over 80 percent of the student population was Anglo.[64]

By one vote, the Texas system of public school finance and San Antonio's dramatic inequities had withstood constitutional scrutiny. Yet Rodriguez had brought unprecedented attention to the existence of substantial inequalities in the schools. The extensive data accumulated for the case and the publicity it received throughout five years of court proceedings stimulated extensive legislative debate about equalization. Although no significant reform arose from the 1973 legislature, the governor established an Office of Educational Research and Planning to conduct studies of state resources and to propose alternative plans of distributing aid. The major legislative reform came in 1975, when House Bill 1126, widely proclaimed as the "equalization" bill, became law. This bill increased state aid by approximately $650 million primarily for minimum salary schedule raises. It also introduced a state equalization aid component to assist in the enrichment of education in poorer school districts. This provision, however, was not as far-reaching as at first it might sound. Limited to $50 million, the formula for funding allowed districts containing 62.5 percent of the state's scholastic population to share directly in the appropriated money.[65] In other words, a large number helped divide a very modest pie. But it was a first step toward equalizing spending. Finally, the bill established that only the value of the district's taxable property would be used to establish the local contribution to the state program. The market values of each district's property varied greatly, especially when prorated among scholastic populations. House Bill 1126 formally acknowledged that, given the differential wealth of the districts, their abilities to support educational programs in the state varied tremendously. Therefore, the authors of the bill revised the system to increase the proportion of the state's local fund assignment carried by wealthier districts, while decreasing the proportion carried by the poorer districts. In a compromise necessary to insure passage, the sponsors attached "hold-harmless" provisions to the bill which guaranteed that no districts would receive less state revenues than they received in preceeding years.

According to a study supported by the National Institute of Education, the equalizing effect of this bill was very limited and did not significantly alter the basic statewide inequities.[66] School districts with the least resources, while exerting almost twice the tax effort, still generated less than 10 percent of the local revenue of the richest districts. Additionally, the local revenue gap between these school districts actually increased.[67] In Edgewood, reflects Dr. José Cardenas, a former superintendent of the Edgewood ISD, hopes ran high about the equalizing effects of HB 1126, "but when that next September rolled around, we found that things had actually gotten worse."[68] In general, the equalizing effects of the 1975 law were checked by countervailing increments in local enrichment revenues generated by the more affluent districts. So, although everyone got more money, the inequalities remained.

In Bexar County the market values of taxable property varied greatly across districts, and it is easy to see the difficulty for Edgewood and the relative ease for Alamo Heights in carrying the burden of financing education. (See Table 7.1.)

In 1977, the Texas legislature passed a second "equalization" bill which again did not fulfill the promises made by the state. Despite increases in state foundation support to local districts, the disparities remained rather constant owing to comparable increments in local enrichment revenues among the more affluent districts. Overall funding for the districts increased, but the dollar disparities continued. A look at the impact of the two equalization bills on selected districts in Bexar County illustrates the story.

Table 7.1: 1975–76 Bexar County Wealth Disparities per Pupil

District	GOER[a] Values	State Rank (lowest to highest)
Edgewood	$ 11,925	I
Harlandale	21,509	5
South San Antonio	25,057	13
Southwest	40,318	36
Southside	41,644	41
San Antonio	42,266	45
Northside	47,670	66
Judson	50,774	73
Somerset	59,002	116
North East	67,220	181
East Central	68,154	192
Alamo Heights	139,266	602
County average	$ 44,240	
State low	11,925	
State average	93,735	
State high	16,859,078	

[a]Governor's Office of Economic Resources, market values.

Figure 7.1 displays the annual combined state and local funding per pupil during the 1970s, including the post-*Rodriguez* "equalizing" period.[69]

The reform measures had several consequences. First, educational funding increased significantly in all districts. Second, the relative rankings of the districts over the five-year period remained stable. The affluent districts such as Alamo Heights and North East began and remained at the top; the poor districts remained at the bottom. In 1970–71, there were four "poor" districts in San Antonio—that is, districts spending less than $500 per pupil in state and local funds; in 1978–79, four "poor" districts remained (districts spending less than $1,200 per pupil); not surprisingly, they were the same four ISDs—Edgewood, Somerset, South San Antonio, and Southwest. Third and most apparent, the state reforms did not eliminate the inequality among the districts in pupil expenditures. Although one can detect a slight equalizing effect in 1975–76 following passage of HB 1126 in 1975, Figure 7.1 shows that the range of dollar disparities among the districts increased over the years. Despite this increase in the range of per pupil expenditure levels,

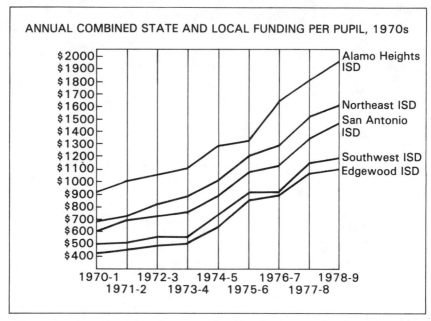

Figure 7.1: Annual combined state and local funding per pupil, selected San Antonio districts, 1970–79.

more sophisticated statistical measurements do show a slight equalizing effect among the districts following the 1975 reform.[70] Post-1975 reform efforts, however, did not equalize further the per pupil expenditures among Bexar County districts, although they did sustain generally the slight equalization achieved in 1975–76.

Further analysis shows that today the state contributions to the foundation school program (FSP) disproportionately assist the poorer school districts. Indeed, this represents significant change from the pre-Rodriguez period, when the state, independent of local enrichments, funded the affluent districts to a greater extent than the poorer ones.[71] For example, in 1978–79, Edgewood received $960 per pupil from the state while Alamo Heights garnered only $667, thus reversing the unequal foundation support of the years prior to the 1975 reforms.

Retention of local enrichment provisions, however, has undermined the mild equalization effects of the distribution of state revenues under the FSP, because disparities in locally generated funding have increased dramatically. Edgewood and many other poor districts were already straining the limits of their local revenue-raising potential prior to 1973. Without a dramatic increase in taxable wealth, their local enrichment revenues will remain rather constant and woefully small. For example, in 1973–74 Edgewood could raise only $38 per pupil in local enrichment funds. By 1977–78 the figure stood at $42. Over the same period Alamo Heights had increased its local enrichment support from $378 to $723 per pupil, and still had not exhausted its revenue-raising potential. Alamo Heights ISD, in other words, generated over seventeen times the local support per pupil that Edgewood did or could in the 1977–78 school year. Today, although the state consistently contributes more to each child's education in Edgewood than in Alamo Heights, this difference is more than compensated for by the extraordinary increase of local enrichment revenues in Alamo Heights and other affluent districts in Bexar County. In school year 1978–79, the per-pupil state and local revenues for Edgewood and Alamo Heights, including local fund assignment revenues, totaled $1,100 and $1,973, respectively. After the Rodriguez litigation, ten years of diverse reform efforts, and the passage of two "equalization" bills, the disparity in state and local funding between the two districts increased from $310 in 1967–68 to $873 per pupil in 1978–79.

Ironically, then, the equalization reforms ended in an increased dollar disparity between Edgewood and Alamo Heights. Yet, in view of nearly two hundred years of educational policy in Texas, that ironic development should hardly be surprising. Statutes consistently publicized as equalizing provide only symbolic, not actual, relief from the traditional unequal opportunity. This is as true today as it was in the nineteenth century. Those with advantage remain the beneficiaries of policy formulae that distribute tangible resources unequally. Owing to incremental reforms, these formulae have become so complicated[72] that the inequality is camouflaged by the complexity of the finance method.[73]

On the positive side, however, the state reforms have increased significantly the level of per pupil expenditures of the poorer districts, greatly facilitating the provision of basic education within those districts. It must be remembered also that marginal, though not remedial, equalization effort did occur following the 1975 reforms. This is attributable to the increased FSP funding and the equalization aid granted the poorer districts. Yet the Texas method of school finance still results in highly different amounts of money being invested in the public educations and futures of children in twelve different districts within Bexar County.

Educational expenditure levels are only one indicator of the quality of education in particular school districts. Nevertheless expenditure levels are the best indicator of the quality of education. A governor's report and extensive testimony in *Rodriguez* clearly demonstrated that the Edgewood

ISD, compared with the North East ISD, had much higher teacher-pupil ratios, dropout rates, and percentages of instructors holding only temporary teaching permits.[74] In addition, Edgewood students had fewer resources, including far fewer counselors, library books, and course offerings. Thus, the disparities among these districts had dramatic consequences. The impact of these disparate resources is demonstrated in a recent Texas Assessment of Basic Skills (TABS) test scores among the Bexar County districts. Edgewood's students achieved significantly lower TABS scores than did students from the affluent districts in all areas tested. For example, in reading and math, fewer than half of Edgewood's ninth grade students passed the TABS exam, while approximately 90 percent of North East's students passed. In fact, in all skills areas, twice as many North East students as Edgewood students passed the exams.

The disparities in funding and resources have racial implications as well. School districts with the highest funding and performance scores are overwhelmingly Anglo, while those with the lowest scores have much higher minority enrollments.

Thus disparities in educational resources have lasting impact in San Antonio, by perpetuating the racial and economic stratification which has characterized the city for generations.

Sidney Plotkin

Chapter Eight

Democratic Change in the Urban Political Economy: San Antonio's Edwards Aquifer Controversy

The land on San Antonio's northern rim is the city's prime real estate market as well as the geological residence of its sole water source—a portion of the Edwards Aquifer. The attempt of environmentalists and Chicanos to redirect market forces off the aquifer—and of builders to protect their access to it—is full of clues to the dynamics of urban political economy.[1] It exposes how some of the givens of the local political economy—the real estate market, the planning and zoning bureaucracies, the form and ideology of urban government—can affect in fundamental ways the life and direction of a community. No less important, it provides an example of how these givens may be challenged and to some extent modified by citizen action. In the end, though, it reveals the limits of urban political change. For while the expanding conflict over the Edwards Aquifer does help propel San Antonio toward a more pluralistic public order, that order is one whose future is stamped by the logic, rules, and legally protected power of capitalism.[2]

The Political Economy of the Edwards Aquifer

The Edwards Aquifer is a great underground reservoir stretching more than 175 miles across South Central Texas from Kinney County in the west, through Uvalde and Medina Counties, and then northward through Bexar, Comal, and Hays Counties. Its porous limestone is estimated to hold between 15 and 30 million acre feet of pure water cradled in a complex network of geologic faults and channels. Although scientists admit they have much to learn about the aquifer, it is generally believed the water is annually replenished, or recharged, by the absorption of rainwater directly into the land and even more importantly, by the seepage of surface streams flowing across the outcrop of the limestone formations. The area in which this process occurs is called the recharge zone.[3]

Environmentalists contend that urban development over the recharge zone pollutes surface streams which feed the underground supply. Builders respond that no scientific evidence exists to support this view, but add that even if it is true, San Antonio's water problem can be solved by building purification plants or importing surface water from nearby lakes. Since this would inevitably raise the city's extremely low water costs, the Edwards' defenders charge the builders with seeking to shift the costs of obtaining pure water from themselves to the city as a whole.[4] Hence, there is no consensus inside San Antonio about the definition of the water issue. Conservationists view it as a matter of water quality, while the city's businessmen want to increase water supplies and thereby avoid having to accept limits on their economic freedom. Since Texas law treats groundwater as part of the private property rights inherent in land ownership, the environmental definition of the issue bears the onus of opposing the established legal bias favoring capitalist development.[5] And it is fundamentally the dynamic of capitalist development, and especially the real estate market which affords it a spatial setting, that generated the issue in the first place by commanding construction in the recharge zone as a matter of pecuniary rationality. To see the significance of the land market, it is only necessary to consider why San Antonio is growing mainly toward the north rather than in other directions, why, in spite of public sensitivity to the recharge zone, builders persist in their demand for access to just this space.[6] The answer begins with an appreciation of the fact that economically speaking, builders are not free to construct and sell houses where they please. Their behavior is constrained by their role as house merchants in a competitive, profit-oriented economic system.[7] The intrinsic logic of the home-building industry, its need to realize profits from the manufacture of new homes, causes it to push constantly outward toward unused space where modern fabrication techniques can be applied to the production of tract housing. This logic is strengthened by the fact that these new use values must be fashioned carefully to satisfy the middle-class tastes of home buyers interested in future exchange values. Thus the houses must be located in a spatial setting designed to enhance their attractiveness as commodities.

Although builders feel these imperatives as an external necessity controlling their investment and sales plans, it is one not totally beyond their control. To confirm the accuracy of the market's direction, construction and real estate interests work hard politically to influence the siting of government capital investments in places signaled by it as likely candidates for development. In San Antonio, such activity led to siting of the University of Texas at San Antonio, the South Texas Medical Center, an interstate highway, and the subsidized extension of public utilities to private subdivisions—all on or near the recharge zone.[8] Once this process begins, private investment in unsubsidized areas is rendered irrational. The political economy of the urban real estate market becomes a continuing lesson in self-fulfilling prophecy. In San Antonio, as well as across the country, it breeds uneven spatial development: expanding production of homes, shopping centers, and factories on the urban fringe while old but still usable capital is left to decay in the city's core. Constant replication of this pattern in city after city suggests the operation of a basic and formidable mechanism of social power: capitalist rationality guiding the use of social space.[9]

Of course, the abstract logic of the real estate market is molded in each community by factors peculiar to that city's geography and social structure. For example, San Antonio's land market drives northward because space for the construction of new middle-class homes is economically restricted in other parts of the city. On the south side, not only is the terrain flat and unattractive as compared with the wooded hill country to the north, but this area contains several large and noisy Air Force bases. Nearby live many of the city's Anglo working class. The southwest and west sides are occupied by the very poor Mexican-American barrios. Growth to the east is hemmed in by a black ghetto. Along with an aversion to low-flying aircraft and young recruits, snobbery and racism keep middle-class Anglo home buyers away from these parts of San Antonio.

Yet, just as the poor and working class limit expansion to the south, the wealthier members of the population restrict development on the near north side. Unlike the typical modern city whose suburban wealth lives on the metropolitan fringe, many of San Antonio's upper- and upper-middle-class people live in exclusive enclave townships near the heart of the city. These are small and fully occupied communities offering little space for new construction. Thus to the degree young or new San Antonians aspire to the conventionally defined "good life" they must move beyond the enclaves to the northern tier where new single family homes can be built. The significance of this upwardly mobile middle-class market to the health of the local building industry prompts the latter's yearning for access to the recharge zone.

In sum, the most direct and pressing social control affecting the fate of the aquifer is the process of capitalist expansion itself, a force channeled not only through the real estate market but through the cultural and political systems as well. That these forces are mutually influencing, imparting a common direction to San Antonio's development, is an expression of the social power of capital to establish the predominant framework, expectations, and rules of behavior in this society. But to understand fully the impact of the aquifer issue on San Antonio, one must appreciate the social implications of its governmental apparatus.

In the postwar era, San Antonio politics has been framed by council-manager government coupled with a nonpartisan, at-large election system. The businessmen and reformers who pushed adoption of this arrangement in 1953 wanted to limit the contentious and often corrupt practice of San Antonio politics by introducing professional administration of the civic machinery.[10] Like their predecessors in other cities, San Antonio's reformers believed that "the interest of the community 'as a whole' should be determined in disinterested ways and then be carried into effect expeditiously and efficiently by technicians."[11] In their pursuit of the city's corporate good, the reformers dismantled the wasteful and tired commission government but retained the at-large election system which was its base. In a community where social inequality was reflected in spacial separation of races and classes, the absence of geographic districts led to the sacrifice of certain legitimate nongeneral interests.[12] Thus, since rich San Antonians retained preferential access to the political system by financing the required citywide campaigns and since the middle class had a regular habit of voting, the losers in the at-large electoral system were those parts of the city where nonvoters were most likely to live—the working-class and poorer areas. Between 1955 and 1971, when the city was dominated by the Good Government League (GGL), only five councilmen were elected who lived on the west or southwest sides; the barrio was politically muted.[13] Of course, the existence of single-member districts would hardly have meant that the interests of nonvoters were protected. But at least the district system might have established the formal responsibility of elected officials to define and defend neighborhood interests. Absence of single-member districts all but assured the burial of Chicanos' spatially defined interests outside the civic arena. Whether the reformers intended it or not, at-large elections in San Antonio meant that, in the words of Banfield and Wilson, the "underdogs" were kept "in their places" and out of city government.[14]

Reform government in San Antonio—that is, the GGL's power—was rooted in more than subordination of neighborhood and class interests, however. Crucial to its success was a consensus within the city's dominant business class that municipal government should be extremely deliberate in its pursuit of outside investment while endorsing the northward flow of capital by accepting petitions for annexations of land promoted by area developers. The anchors of the local economy in tourism, light industry, finance, and the strong military presence were not to be supplemented by heavy industrial capital and its complement of organized labor.[15] Meanwhile, spatial expansion helped dilute the political power of the Mexican-American community and provided economic opportunities for the city's enterprising real estate, construction, and financial interests. Between 1950 and 1970, for example, the developers' voracious appetite for land led, though annexation, to a 70 percent increase in the city's size. In the early 1970s, however, the consensus underlying these policies was strained by disagreement within San Antonio's oligarchy over the pace, scale, and to a lesser extent, direction of the city's growth.

The problem stemmed from a major proposal to accelerate the outward drive of capital and population by construction of a New Town, called San Antonio Ranch, over portions of the recharge zone. Backed by several prominent Texans and by an $18 million loan guarantee from the Department of Housing and Urban Development, the project was aimed, over a thirty-year period, at adding a city of 88,000 people to the San Antonio metropolitan area.[16] Environmentalists warned that this would cause severe pollution of the Edwards' groundwater. This, they emphasized, was not a question of preserving a pretty landscape but of conserving a natural resource indispensable to the community's survival. Several prominent local officials shared that anxiety. A Bexar county judge, for example, proposed "establishment of a national park" over the recharge zone. San Antonio's congressman, Henry B. Gonzalez, joined conservationists and called for government purchase of development rights to the land.[17] Thus, a coalition of the city's environmental groups was allied with several governmental authorities, including the Bexar County Commissioners Court, the Edwards Underground Water District, and even the conservative Texas Water Quality Board, in a suit challenging HUD's support for "Ranchtown."

For the first time, organizations and officials close to, if not actually part of, the GGL oligarchy challenged an assumption basic to its governance of San Antonio. Equally important, as one regional official pointed out, was the fact that the New Town project focused general public attention on the direction of the city's growth.[18] Until Ranchtown, many San Antonians did not perceive the northward development pattern as a fundamental shift in the community's center of socioeconomic gravity. But the massive flow of investment and population it represented illuminated as a potentially dangerous social movement what heretofore passed as a series of harmlessly unrelated private and government decisions. As a result, many San Antonians became less sure of the wisdom of unplanned economic and political expansion.

Revolt at the Top

While Chicanos were all but symbolically excluded from the inner sanctum of San Antonio politics, widespread opposition to Ranchtown made the younger, more enterprising generation of real estate and construction interests feel increasingly unrepresented by, and isolated from, what they perceived as the stodgy leaders of the GGL. The GGL was not enamored of the developers, either. As one councilman put it, the older leadership of the GGL "didn't like the strong influence of the developers" and their overtly aggressive, "positive push to laissez-faire."[19]

It was not so much that the GGL opposed growth over the aquifer, or that local builders were outraged by the city's resistance to outside investment in local land operations. Indeed, some local construction men were themselves hostile to what they perceived as inexperienced outside builders who naively thought it was possible to come in and build a city from scratch. At the same time, former mayor Walter McAllister, Republican patriarch of the GGL, favored the Nixon administration's support for Texas enterprise.[20] The situation was more complex than such a simple dichotomy would suggest. What embittered the north side interests was the apparent ambivalence of the city's leadership about growth and its hesitancy to reward instantly claims for economic expansion to the north. In concrete terms, this meant that developers feared their "positive push to laissez faire" was in danger of losing complete government backing. Free utility hookups, zoning clearances, and other steps which facilitated and subsidized private investment would now be contested, if not rejected. The fact, for example, that the environmentalists' suit against Ranchtown failed at every level of the U.S. judicial system, including the Supreme Court, was less important than the filing of the suit itself. The machinery of law and government was less surely on the side of private development. After all, the federally subsidized Ranchtown, despite its failure as an economic venture, brought with it the strongest land use controls ever applied to development in South Texas. Thus, government aid for north side investment could no longer be assumed. It had to be worked for politically.

In 1973, a split within the city's oligarchy became public and politically focused. After a series of personal and policy disputes, Charles Becker, a city councilman and owner of a local supermarket chain, led San Antonio's land and house merchants in successful revolt against the GGL. Upon taking office as mayor, Becker and several prodevelopment colleagues on the council, including one of the city's major builders, sought control of key municipal agencies. The chairman of the City Water Board, for example, a man who "resisted the builders' influence on the Board's expansion policies,"[21] was replaced by a major San Antonio developer with interests on the north side. In 1975, the north side group attempted to consolidate its power by forming a new political organization, the Independent Team, to replace the GGL as the city's ruling party. As one builder explained, the new entity grew "out of a fear that the vacuum left by the GGL" would lead to control of San Antonio government "by forces alien to business."[22] Bankrolled almost exclusively by developers, the new party carried a majority of six council seats, although it lost the mayorality to the GGL candidate, Lila Cockrell.[23]

The developers' effort to dominate the administrative machinery of growth policy continued. Soon after the election, for example, the deputy director of the City Planning and Zoning Department was fired by the city manager after bitter criticism from several Independent Team councilmen. The planner's sin was his preparation of "An Alternative Growth Study" which included, among other options for the city's future, the idea that San Antonio's growth over the next quarter century could be held *within* the confines of Loop 410, the highway whose northern tier builders viewed as the launching pad of the new urbanization. Indeed, the city manager who did the firing was himself the replacement of a man similarly excused for his opposition to builders. To reduce the likelihood of future resistance, the president of the Greater San Antonio Home Builders Association was appointed chairman of the newly reorganized Planning Commission. He was not asked to leave his private position. Similarly, in October of 1975, the council devised a "zoning overlay" policy to regulate land use in the recharge zone. Several weeks after adoption of the ordinace, the city planning director advised his colleagues within the municipal bureaucracy that the council's new regulation was in full accord with current residential and commercial growth patterns. His memo stated that

Based on the densities permitted under the zoning now in effect on the Recharge Zone, a total of 83,360 people could be accommodated in the residential acreage and the equivalent of sixteen shopping centers the size of North Star Mall [a large suburban style mall on the city's north loop] could be accommodated on the 965 commercial acres. As a point of interest, the combined acreage of the seven largest existing shopping centers . . . is only 430 acres. The possible population of 83,360 represents 27.6% of the expected population increase through the year 2000.

The memorandum next takes the fatal leap from "is" to "ought":

Since zoning is the major implementing mechanism for a master plan and since there is an overabundance of commercially zoned land already over the Aquifer, *allowing the free market forces to determine the eventual use of the balance of the land will have little additional negative impact on the Aquifer.*[24]

To ensure harmony between the environment and "free market forces," the council also established an Aquifer Protection Office. The invitation list to its first meeting of "all agencies involved with the Aquifer" included seven governmental entities and "a representative from the Greater San Antonio Home Builders Association." No other private "agency" was mentioned.[25]

The builders' takeover of local government did not go unchallenged by Anglo middle-class reformers. Fearful of the imminent threat to water purity and anxious over the lack of forthright support from the Texas Water Quality Board and Edwards Underground Water District, environmentalists reorganized themselves to wage their fight for protection of the recharge zone.[26] In August 1974, the League of Women Voters, reluctant to lead an attack on San Antonio's competitive merchants, asked one of its most forceful members, Mrs. Faye Sinkin, wife of a South San Antonio banker, to inquire into the issue of urban growth over the aquifer. Learning quickly about the maze of legal, intergovernmental, and political threats to the underground water supply, Sinkin grasped the need for a group to focus directly and exclusively on the aquifer. Thus, born in the fall of 1974 was the Aquifer Protection Association (APA), the first interest group in the city's history whose *raison d'être* was maintaining the purity of the Edwards Aquifer.[27]

APA's first step was to organize a petition campaign in support of public purchase of land in the recharge zone. It obtained 20,000 signatures and a 5–0 vote endorsing the idea from the Bexar county commissioners. Meanwhile, in Washington, Congressman Gonzalez reintroduced federal power into the equation of local politics. He attached an amendment to the Safe Drinking Water Act forbidding provision of federal assistance to any development or project that might "adversely affect" the underground water supply of a community where such a supply was its sole source. It was designed precisely to fit the needs of the Edwards Aquifer.[28]

Restlessness among the Natives

Thus, in the years 1972–75, when the aquifer issue focused the city's attention on the questions of its future growth and the safety of its sole water source, a fissure was opened within San Antonio's ruling circles. The two developments were intimately related. Environmental resistance to construction over the recharge zone and the GGL's hesitation in supporting capitalist expansion beckoned the construction group to control directly the city government's levers on growth. But the significance of conflict within San Antonio's middle- and upper-class Anglo community transcended the immediate substantive issues of water protection and government support for private enterprise. Most important was the fact that conflict itself was being projected as an acceptable mode of political expression.

While it would be wrong to picture postwar politics in San Antonio as a benign, conflict-free utopia for capitalists—after all, environmentalists bitterly opposed the GGL's North Expressway project in the 1960s—the city's rulers experienced little effective opposition and challenge until the early 1970s. Few questions were raised which refuted the assumption of a harmonious balance of community interests or the universal benefits of expansion. Rarely did public debate specify competing political ideas and values. More often, it involved the comparative personal and moral commitments of candidates to an ill-defined public good.[29] But the effort of the builders to go public with their attack on the GGL, to employ partisan controversy as a mechanism for determining the direction of public policy, emphasized that aggressiveness and competitiveness were no less reasonable in the public realm than in the private marketplace, where such traits are celebrated and rewarded. Dissension within the city's established political community highlighted the usefulness, and more basically, the legitimacy of electoral political conflict in channeling and controlling the machinery of government. In the words of one city councilman, Becker and his allies "unconsciously opened up city politics."[30]

The builders' challenge did more than increase the legitimacy of conflict in political debate. It subverted the myth of San Antonio's common interest. By emphasizing their vested interest in the uneven spatial development of San Antonio, and by pressing their case in the city's most sensitive environment, the construction men illustrated that growth was not an undifferentiated good with benefits flowing to all. To the degree that growth was the logical core of San Antonio's conception of the common good, the aquifer debate exposed its ideological character. This controversy brought home the fact that the city's direction was defined and shaped consciously by and through government, by and through the exercise of political power, by and through conflict. Thus, it could be changed.

The aquifer battle also illustrated the subtle, but nevertheless crucial linkage between interest and place in politics.[31] GGL rhetoric stressed the need for all to join in behalf of the common good. Yet, what was the political unit within which interests were shared? Was it the San Antonio of 1950, 1960, 1970? Why should Mexican Americans accept "San Antonio" as the measure of their interest when public policy periodically extended the city's boundaries to their political and economic disadvantage? San Antonio's leaders undermined the basis of their own ideology by obscuring and manipulating the physical and spatial definition of the community. By 1972, the latter was less a fixed referent in the minds and affections of its population than a visible object of political manipulation. In favoring an aggressive annexation policy to buttress their power, San Antonio's leaders failed to see that to be successful, appeals to common interest require an accepted spatial referent. Thus, they inadvertently sanctioned a growing recognition among Chicanos that defense of the needs of their "place" warranted specific, immediate political representation. Moreover, by adjusting the physical dimensions of San Antonio, and in the process, threatening its water supply, the city's governors accentuated the social and spatial character of uneven development. This led to the most basic consequences of the aquifer debate.

Chicanos were not long in seeing a contradiction in the intensity of conflict over the aquifer. While the city's Anglo middle and upper class hotly debated the fate of empty space and underground water on the north side, the deterioration and waste of resources, human and otherwise, on the south side went undiscussed. As builders debated reformers about the geology of underground water, undrained flood waters wrought havoc in the barrio. The bitterness of controversy over the north side's future underscored the alienation of Chicanos and their needs from the scope of San Antonio's political community. The shifting of governmental services in response to "market forces," the changing spatial definition of the community, and disunity among San Antonio's rulers alerted Mexican Americans to defend the tie between their interest and their turf. Once it became clear that claims for the good of San Antonio no longer obviated clashing interests within the population, and once division within the oligarchy exposed a small vacuum of power, Chicanos developed new modes of organization, participation, and representation. Hence, it was not an accident that when Chicanos reorganized politically, in January 1974, they adopted an essentially federal structure to reflect the new awareness of neighborhood as the basic unit of urban representation.

The new Chicano group was rooted in the west and southwest side parish structure of the Catholic Church and in the experience of poverty politics, but its basic approach was modeled on the Saul Alinsky strategy of direct action against dominant institutions.[32] It took the name COPS—Communities Organized for Public Service—from the deeply felt sense that the San Antonio establishment had not only neglected the barrio, but had exploited its taxes to fuel the city's northward growth. As one participant stated, "You know, they're the robbers and we're the cops."[33] No less important, the reference to organized "Communities" epitomized a denial of the old common interest ideology, a proclamation that San Antonio was a complex of diverse places, each with identifiable interests of its own. Some of these interests—water quality, for example—were shared by neighborhoods throughout the city, but others were more locally rooted reflections of the city's uneven development. Thus the flight of capital to the north side did little to benefit the residents of places left behind. Employing Alinsky's confrontation tactics, COPS moved noisily into the arenas of power in San Antonio—its banks, department stores, the city council, and the streets—to raise challenging questions about historic inequities in the city's distribution of public services and private opportunities. The initial drive aimed at getting adequate drainage to control the periodic floodwaters which inundated the city's southern plain. As success was achieved in this fight and the organization increased in numbers, presence, and power, it turned ever greater attention to the jugular issues of growth and development citywide, especially to the northward migration of investment.

Thus, as the assumptions which underpinned the GGL were challenged by controversy over the direction of San Antonio's growth, that organization was displaced by new political forces: COPS, APA, the Independent Team, and a host of other new neighborhood associations representing middle-class and working-class neighborhoods. These offered, not a singular vision of the common interest, but particular interests consciously proclaimed in terms of the public good. The difference was crucial. Whereas the Good Government League promoted a doctrine which precluded conflict and the expression of discrete, spatially defined interests, the new groups demonstrated that the public interest was basically a dialectical idea: a contradictory, dynamic, shifting notion expressing general and narrow values in the context of public conflict. It was now to be seen as a symbol whose meaning was provided by politics rather than a value to be achieved at the expense of politics. The geographic and political scope of conflict thereafter included streets and neighborhoods across the city. San Antonio's uneven economic development was in glaring contradiction to its increasingly balanced political power.

None of this should be taken to mean that San Antonio had become a South Texas polis. Much suspicion remained about the integrity of government and its officials. COPS was formed, after all, in the year of the first U.S. Presidential resignation. To its members and to most San Antonians, politics and politicians still connoted the seamy underside of community life.[34] Newspaper editorials and radio personalities continued to call for citizens to suspend their differences on behalf of "the good of the whole," to avoid "political" displays. Yet despite the loathing of politics, San Antonio was politicized by the aquifer debate to a greater extent than it had been since the end of World War II and the emergence of the Good Government League. This became especially obvious after October 1975, when the city council voted to permit construction of a large regional shopping mall on 129 acres over the recharge zone.

From Mobilization to Conflict

The council's decision was quite within the boundaries of its zoning "overlay" policy discussed above. Immediately however, APA and other environmental groups charged that the policy was a sham, for it appeared to ratify rather than regulate precisely those growth trends which endangered the city's water. COPS demanded the resignation of the chairman of the City Planning Commission because he refused to give up the presidency of the Builders Association. For two weeks after its decision, council heatedly debated the mall issue. The city was in turmoil over growth policy. Even more vividly than Ranchtown, this decision generated public concern about the safety of its water.

Within weeks, APA joined with COPS in a successful petition campaign to promote a referendum on the council's decision. During December of 1975, APA and COPS lobbied the north and southwest sides of the city, respectively, insisting that storm water runoff from the mall's parking lot represented a basic environmental threat to the recharge zone and the integrity of drainage and sanitary sewers.

The mall's backers replied with an intensive advertising campaign of their own, emphasizing the view of local water experts that no evidence currently available supported the environmentalists' charges.[35] Existing Texas Water Quality Board regulations were adequate, they said, to safeguard the groundwater from pollution. But as the antimall forces well knew, neither the TWQB nor the Edwards Underground Water District were proponents of vigorous environmental protection if that meant restricting the freedom of private enterprise. Nor could the Gonzalez Amendment, passed to protect aquifers where they were a sole source of urban water, guarantee the support of EPA. Indeed, in June of 1975, when that agency's regional administrator first visited the city, he was welcomed at a reception in his honor financed and attended by some of San Antonio's weightiest economic powers. Not an ungracious guest, he told his assembled hosts that the bureau's presence in San Antonio "could make a difference . . . but I don't know that it would."[36]

For APA and other environmentalists, such institutional hesitancy meant that even if the experts were correct in their view that present regulations were adequate, more than a reasonable doubt remained about their enforcement. Faith in the administrative defense of the recharge zone did not exist among conservationists. By going to the streets and neighborhoods for a declaration of broad public interest in strong aquifer protection rules, APA acted to restrict the discretionary power of administrators. COPS joined this fight in part to protect the city's water. But it was equally if not more concerned with stemming the northward migration of capital and jobs. As one of its leaders explained, "When we first became active in the Aquifer issue it was clearly a growth issue," a means for rechanneling the movement of urban investment.[37]

The mall's opponents won resoundingly. By a margin of nearly 4 to 1, San Antonians rejected the shopping center and their city council's policy. An important decision shaped by the dominant political economy was overturned by a democratic decision shaped in the crucible of open debate and controversy.[38]

In the early months of 1976, San Antonians reexamined their growth policy. APA once again promoted the idea of public ownership of the land's development rights. COPS, stressing its main interest in the politics of investment, urged a ban upon further extension of utility lines and subdivision plats in the area and also advised formulation of a master plan including policies to confine growth within the city's highway loop. With the mayor's support an attempt was made to pass a temporary moratorium on growth in the recharge zone, but the council voted it down fearing it would infringe on private property rights.[39] The council did agree, however, to hire an independent engineering firm to make a geological analysis of the land and water. It was hoped that more knowledge might preempt political conflict.[40]

The months that followed failed to bring a lessening of tension over the issue. In March 1976, for example, a north side suburban school district voted to begin construction of a high school directly above the recharge zone.[41] Even more ominous was the announcement several weeks later that the Texas Water Quality Board intended to make its 1975 aquifer protection order effective on a county-by-county basis with a local option to determine whether and how to apply the environmental regulation.[42] This would permit rural Uvalde County, long an opponent of land use controls, to opt out of the program. Since nearly 60 percent of the Edwards Aquifer water enters through streams in the western counties such as Uvalde, the effect of the new order was to undermine even the toughest metropolitan controls.

These developments disappointed and frustrated APA, COPS, and other local groups. Once more they turned to city government to protect their water and to plan the city's growth. But owing to a crucial change imposed on the city from outside, the structure of local government was soon turned radically in their favor.

In the fall of 1975, Texas was brought under the jurisdiction of the 1965 Voting Rights Act. San Antonio's annexations of surrounding territory were subjected to federal scrutiny with respect to their impact on the voting power of the city's Chicano population. Objections made by the Justice Department, as well as a suit brought by the Mexican-American Legal Defense and Education Fund, compelled the city to change its election system. The at-large plan had to yield to an arrangement which included at least some single-member districts. After much political wrangling a "10-1" plan was offered to the city's voters in a January 1977 charter revision election which allowed for ten councilmanic districts, including six from the southern portion of the city, and a mayor chosen at large. In a very close vote—51 percent to 49 percent—the new plan was adopted. But as important as the victory was the manner of its achievement.

With a turnout of only 19 percent of the registered voters, and a large drop-off among the Anglo middle class, COPS' ability to deliver a block of pro 10-1 votes was an important, if not a decisive factor in the election. Perhaps more significant than the votes it supplied were the potentially negative votes it may have influenced to stay home. COPS apparently succeeded in convincing many middle-class whites that the developers' interests were not necessarily identical with their own. Consequently COPS enhanced its reputation as a public-spirited defender of citywide interests. Thus, while it fought mainly for the Hispanic, working-class districts, its ability to link that cause with so enduring a common interest as pure water gave it much-needed credibility in the later struggle for a new electoral system. As one politically active builder lamented, defense of the aquifer earned COPS "a great deal of prestige" in San Antonio.⁴³

April 2, 1977, marked the first election held under the new format. Predictably, it resulted in a very different council. Mexican Americans captured five seats, a black took one, and an Anglo female from the south side won another. All told, "seven persons were elected from areas within the city which had experienced little or no representation during the previous two decades."⁴⁴ The linkage between interest and place was formally reestablished. Neighborhood grievances already voiced against the uneven spatial development of San Antonio's economy were given a legal basis for representation.

Immediately after the election, expectations ran high among the newly represented constituencies that their spokesmen would act quickly to assert authority over the developers. COPS and APA demanded speedy enactment of an eighteen-month moratorium on all new construction over the recharge zone, on utility extensions to subdivisions presently under construction, and on the platting of new subdivisions. Both the city manager and the Planning Commission opposed the idea. Interim controls could be fashioned, they said, which would protect the water without giving the city "a bad image which might hurt economic development."⁴⁵ Similarly the city attorney warned that the moratoria being contemplated against subdivision platting and utility extensions already under contract were probably illegal, since these were controlled by state legislation and county authority. Rumblings of capital flight could be heard from the business community. The *San Antonio Express* warned that "investment capital does not go where there is a lot of controversy."⁴⁶ Yet by June the political chances of an interim regulation were nil. The only question was whether the moratorium chosen would be limited to zoning or extended to all activity on the city's portion of the recharge zone. Thus the face of San Antonio politics was at least temporarily transformed. Suddenly the Left was forcing compromises on the Center. The Right had nowhere to turn but the courts.

On June 10, 1977, the key vote was held. By a margin of 6–4 (a young Chicano moderate abstained) the city council adopted the temporary total ban on development over the recharge zone. It was to last eighteen months, or until completion of the technical studies if that was sooner.

Reaction to the decision was swift and angry among the city's older, more experienced officials. "This is not government, but an anarchy," cried a member of the Planning Commission. Bexar County Judge Blair Reeves, long a proponent of tough aquifer protection rules, called the action "puffing in the wind," adding that the county government would continue to control subdivision platting in the five-mile extraterritorial jurisdiction surrounding the city's fringe.[47]

Business reaction was predictably hostile. The president of the Greater San Antonio Home Builders Association responded that the council should not expect "certain magical things" to happen in other parts of the city just because north side growth had stopped. A day after the decision the president of a north side computer company announced the dropping of plans to enlarge its operations in the city. Banner headlines in the *San Antonio News* screamed of "Job Losses Feared Over Aquifer Ban."[48] Supplementing these threats, local landmen sued the city for $1.5 billion in damages. A federal court injunction was soon imposed enjoining San Antonio from enforcing its new rules.

Most promoratorium councilmen were confused and dismayed by the critical reaction. But though there was some talk of repealing the moratorium, the council after extensive debate chose to keep the ordinance and hire outside legal assistance. They contracted with the prestigious Chicago land use law firm of Rose, Hardies, O'Keefe, Babcock and Parsons to defend the city against the developers' suits and assist the council in formulating the framework of a land use plan capable of controlling growth and protecting the aquifer.

Within weeks the Chicago lawyers confirmed the illegality of the council's limits on utility extensions and subdivision plat approval in the extraterritorial jurisdiction. They insisted, however, that the ordinance governing zoning and building permits within the city was enforceable.[49] With the injunctions on the illegal portions of the ban in place, the city's lawyers went to work on a defensible ordinance to remain in effect until the technical studies and master planning process were finished. The chance of obtaining a new set of rules allowing existing contracts to be fulfilled and new projects to be undertaken inspired the developers to agree to a delay in their suit pending the writing of the new ordinance.

By September the legal experts convinced council to repeal the total moratorium in favor of a limited, interim ordinance based on rigid control of development within the city limits. In San Antonio's portion of the recharge zone no construction would be permitted on less than a five-acre lot, and all applicants for building permits were required to furnish a detailed natural resource disclosure statement showing that their project would not harm the aquifer. The Chicago lawyers also advised the City Water Board to refuse service to developers who did not obey the new standards. Remaining in effect until December 1978, when the technical analysis was expected, the council's new ordinance came close to being a moratorium in effect. For the first time government power in San Antonio was being used to channel the movement of private capital in a fashion not predetermined by "free market forces."

Recent Events

Since the moratorium battle of June 1977, conflict over aquifer protection policy has ebbed. The prevailing trend in this period has favored the business view. In January 1978, for example, the Fourth Court of Civic Appeals of Texas reversed San Antonio's 1976 referendum prohibiting construction of a mall on the recharge zone. Since the state constitution omits referenda as tools of citizen action, the court reasoned that voters may not employ this vehicle to abrogate the city's legitimate exercise of a delegated state power— i.e., land use control or zoning. Appeals to the Texas and U.S. Supreme Courts were fruitless.[50]

In mid-1979 the Massachusetts firm of Metcalf-Eddy completed its technical survey of the Edwards Aquifer and its tolerance for pollution. Science did little to clarify the political muddle. The report confirmed the groundwater's susceptibility to pollution unless effective controls are constituted to regulate development. Existing standards, it emphasized, are inadequate.[51] Needed is a regional authority capable of overseeing land and water use throughout the recharge zone. In the face of the continuing reluctance of the state water agencies and the Edwards Underground Water District to articulate a regional conservation view, Metcalf-Eddy concluded that the area's "municipalities and counties may be helpless in protecting the health, welfare and safety of their citizens" from groundwater pollution.[52]

Such statements of public helplessness have contributed to a considerable rise in optimism about the future marketability of San Antonio's north side real estate. A second "supermall" has been proposed for the northwestern portion of the city to balance the earlier mall project slated to appear in the northeast quadrant.[53] Attorneys for local builders are convinced public policy will not stand in the way. As one snarled recently, "Someone will have to come up with $160 million" in compensation if the city tries again to preempt the "reasonable" use of land within its jurisdiction.[54]

Conservation interests are stymied by the poverty of law and jurisdiction favorable to groundwater protection. They lack an institutional channel through which to focus public policies of resource protection. The more creative of local officials suggest delegation of water protection responsibilities to private homeowner associations. Even this meets the stern resistance of Texas jurisprudence. Thus the city attorney doubts whether any municipal agency possesses the authority to require membership in such associations.[55] Meanwhile city officials periodically trek to Austin to lobby for stronger controls. They have met with little success.

Defense of the aquifer helped propel San Antonio in a democratic direction. It united middle-class whites and working-class Hispanics for some creative experiments in practical pluralism. There are few signs, however, of the permanance of this dissenting alliance. To the contrary, there is currently much talk in the city of a more traditional unity based on the "common interest" in economic growth. A new "grand alliance" of the city's main economic and political interests has been formed—United San Antonio—to attract "new business and jobs."[56] Thus as the nation struggles with what *Business Week* terms the "Run-Away Economy," San Antonians are banking their political-economic optimism on the hope that northern and midwestern capital will run away to a "United San Antonio."[57] After raising its voice against the business community's policy of selling San Antonio as a "cheap labor" town, COPS has recently adopted a more passive voice, disciplined by the city's temporary blacklisting as a hospitable industrial site, and tacitly supports USA.[58]

Whether the quantity and quality of future growth in San Antonio will preempt or postpone the decade-long struggle over its direction is, of course, an open question. For the moment at least, the divisions of the late 1970s have been subordinated somewhat. There is a revival of deference to capitalism's capacity to coopt its poorer critics by delivering the goods in rough proportion with the rise in expectations. COPS, the noisiest of the city's few dissenters, has, it appears, been persuaded that the legitimate price of economic growth is a less truculent, more businesslike stance, a refraining from political belligerence, and participation in "a unity that cuts across all lines in the city's population."[59] But those "lines," economic, racial, and political, are inexpungable. Capitalism, even at its most triumphant, does not, after all, erase social cleavages. It intensifies gradations and divisions of class, status, and power even as these may be rendered more comfortable by a rising standard of living. The question for San Antonio, as for other Sunbelt cities, is whether it can realize promises of municipal prosperity and municipal peace while the national and global economies suffer great turbulence. It is a prospect not to be backed by a sizable wager.

Joseph D. Sekul

Chapter Nine

Communities Organized for Public Service: Citizen Power and Public Policy in San Antonio

"I sir'd him to death." Sitting in her dining room on an overcast February day, Beatrice Gallego, former president of Communities Organized For Public Service (COPS), was recalling one of her first confrontations with a high city official. One evening in August of 1974 she and five hundred other members of COPS gathered in the auditorium of Kennedy High School on San Antonio's west side. They had come for a meeting with the city manager, Sam Granata. Gallego remembers the anger that filled the room. COPS members demanded to know why, for so many years, they had borne the burden of flooded streets and homes in their neighborhoods every time a severe storm hit the city; why hadn't the city built adequate drainage facilities? But Gallego also remembers the fear. COPS was new, not even a year old. And, except for some minor skirmishes with the city over its failure to clean up vacant lots, tear down abandoned houses, and the like, it was untested on the larger battlefield of San Antonio politics. Also, COPS members, like law-abiding citizens everywhere, had been brought up to have a healthy respect for authority figures. So they approached Granata with fear as well as anger. "We were all very nervous," Gallego recalls. And when she addressed Granata, it was, " 'sir, this' and 'sir, that.' I sir'd him to death." After all "he was one of the power people."[1]

Less than two years later COPS itself was being counted among the ranks of the most powerful by the *San Antonio Light*, along with Congressman Henry B. Gonzalez, mayor Lila Cockrell, banker Tom Frost, and builder H. B. Zachary.[2] Other publications, including the *Wall Street Journal*, were writing of COPS' rapid rise from obscurity to prominence and influence.[3] It was unprecedented in urban politics for a neighborhood citizens group to acquire the stature that COPS enjoyed.[4]

COPS' Structure and Goals

The foundation for COPS was laid in 1973 by Ernie Cortes when he trudged door-to-door through the south and west sides of San Antonio. Disillusioned with existing channels for political change in the city, Cortes had left San Antonio several months earlier for training as a community organizer at the late Saul Alinsky's Industrial Areas Foundation in Chicago. Now, upon his return, he began a search for the money, people, and issues needed to build an organization. Cortes first convinced a local Catholic pastor, Father Emundo Rodriguez, of the soundness of his organizing venture. Rodriguez in turn convinced several Protestant churchmen to provide money for Cortes's salary and other expenses to gets COPS off the ground.[5] Soon thereafter a social action arm of the Catholic Church, the Campaign for Human Development, stepped in with money to help COPS meet its expenses. This support lasted until 1977, when COPS became financially self-sustaining.

Cortes and other early leaders like Father Albert Benavides believed that for COPS to last, it had to be anchored by institutions with roots deep in the local communities. They discarded the PTAs as too caught up in school board politics, and settled instead on the Catholic parish networks. The parish networks included members of the parish advisory councils and others who run the festivals and sports programs—the hub of community activity within the parish. These networks became the building blocks of Cortes's new organization, and their leaders became the leaders of COPS.[6] From Holy Family came Andres Sarabia, the first president of COPS (1974–76); from St. James, Beatrice Gallego, the second president (1976–78); from San Martin de Porres, Carmen Badillo, the third president (1978–80); and, from St. Patrick's, Beatrice Cortez, COPS' current leader.

Finally, sticking close to the Alinsky rule of pragmatism, Cortes developed issues from the people. "Causes" like civil rights—issues that lacked immediate importance to the people in these neighborhoods—were avoided. To determine the issues that had pulling power Cortes asked the people in the neighborhoods what *their* problems were. They spoke of drainage, utility rates, traffic problems, and other mundane concerns that blighted their daily lives. Issues, in short, came from the bottom up rather than from the top down.[7]

This "bottom up" principle was later incorporated into the governing structure of COPS. Formally, the basic unit of membership is the "local" (or "area" or "community"—hence the name *Communities* Organized for Public Service). In 1982 only three of these locals were neighborhood groups not based in a church. One was in the northeast part of the city with a predominantly Anglo membership; the other two were black locals on the east side. Otherwise the locals were Catholic parishes. The issues had to come from the locals. If a particular issue did not catch fire in the locals, COPS would not adopt it. Thus COPS ignored problems common to other, more ideological Mexican-American groups. Police brutality, for example, while of concern to people in the locals, has not been pushed by them as a major issue, so COPS has not carried it into the political arena.[8]

Above the locals organizationally is the Delegates Congress. Each local sends delegates to this congress, which meets at least six times a year. Between the annual conventions—at which key officers, including the president, are elected and policies for the coming year are ratified—the Delegates Congress is the formal governing body for the organization. It, not the officers, makes final, binding decisions for COPS. Next is the Steering Committee, and after it the Executive Committee. These committees consist of various officers and committee chairpersons. They are responsible for the day-to-day running of the organization and for developing plans to implement policies. Recommendations on these matters are drawn up by the Executive Committee and submitted to the Steering Committee. The latter reviews these recommendations and submits them for approval to the Delegates Congress.[9]

COPS' agenda of public policy issues flows from its members' commitments to two closely intertwined institutions. The first is the family. COPS members want jobs that provide a decent standard of living for themselves and their children. They want a clean and healthy environment, and place great stock in quality education for their children. When their children grow up, parents want them to settle close by rather than relocating in other neighborhoods or cities in pursuit of higher incomes and more fulfilling careers. Finally, COPS members want their old people to live out their lives in dignity, with decent incomes and access to adequate medical care in their own neighborhoods. The second institution is the neighborhood. This is where the roots are—where the COPS people grew up, attended school, married, and reared their children. For San Antonio's Mexican Americans and for the city's blacks, neighborhood is an integral part of culture. They are proud of these cultures and want to keep them; they don't want to be melted down in the melting pot. Neighborhood defines who they are;

neighborhood reminds them of where they have been; neighborhood is where they want to stay.

COPS' commitment to family and neighborhood also stems from the influence of the Catholic Church. The church is a "member" of COPS, tied to it through affiliated parishes, financial contributions, and the manpower it has supplied for leadership.[10] Doctrinally, the Catholic Church in San Antonio became a part of COPS because it felt an obligation to promote social justice for the poor, a mission advocated by Archbishop Robert Lucey as early as the 1940s. Archdiocesan officials believed that the church needed to enter the secular arena in order to protect family life from the ravages of poverty.[11] More recently, this local tradition has been reinforced within the church by liberation theology, which argues that the Christian virtues of love and charity dictate a quest for social justice. Accordingly, churches have a legitimate role to play in the secular world to try to bring about a more equitable distribution of material wealth.[12]

The second reason the church in San Antonio aligned with COPS was to help preserve itself as a truly neighborhood institution. Residential flight from the older parishes threatened the institution of the neighborhood church. As people moved out of the older, central city areas parishes began to lose their financial base. Zoning changes often made this loss permanent, as residential areas were rezoned for light industry. While the church as a whole continued to receive financial support from people after they moved to their new parishes. it suffered a net financial loss in many cases by having to build completely new parishes. The construction of new churches, new rectories, and new schools greatly increased church debt. The church believed that COPS might help to correct this situation by bringing better streets, drainage, and schools into the old neighborhoods, thus stemming the exodus of people from the old parishes.[13]

COPS and Public Policy in San Antonio

Family and neighborhood may seem to be innocuous issues, but in fact the struggle to preserve and protect them has proven both difficult and controversial in inner-city San Antonio. By working for the well-being of their families in the old neighborhoods COPS members challenged prevailing patterns of private profit and public power.

The private market has usually shaped the contours of American cities. Since profits have recently been greater in the suburban fringes, this is where business and population have gone.[14] By and large San Antonio has mirrored national trends. Its suburban periphery has grown considerably, the result of both a movement of people out of its core and of the Sunbelt migration that has given southern cities so many new residents from northern cities. A major difference between San Antonio's suburban growth and suburban growth in many northern cities is that expansion in the San Antonio suburbs has not meant a decline in the city's population and tax base. San Antonio, like other Texas cities, has enjoyed liberal annexation powers, permitting it to capture suburban growth by expanding its boundaries.[15] Thus the 92 percent population growth that occurred between 1950 and 1980 was accompanied by a 280 percent growth in land area.[16]

This difference aside, economic and demographic growth in San Antonio has followed the usual course of moving away from the older, inner city and into the new suburban areas, mainly on the city's north side. In recent years between 60 and 70 percent of the growth in commercial employment has taken place in the north. While census tracts in other parts of the city have been losing population or registering only small increases, population has been surging ahead in the north. The three northern series of census tracts accounted for virtually all—96 percent—of the net population growth that took place in the country between 1970 and 1976 (see Chapter 2).

Without any government intervention the north side growth probably would have come about sooner or later. But the business-dominated Good Government League (GGL) stepped in to see that it came sooner. It expanded key streets and highways to channel growth northward, and it placed such important growth generators as the South Texas Medical Center and the University of Texas at San Antonio northwest of Loop 410, thereby providing magnets to pull people and investment away from the city's heart (see Chapter 1). Thus the invisible hand of the market got a helping hand from the government.

When COPS stepped forward in 1974 as an advocate of inner city interests, it was thus placing itself in the path of forces that had considerable weight and momentum. This remained so even though the GGL splintered. The GGL's 1975 breakup did weaken the business community's hold on the city council, but business influence in the public sector did not vanish. And the bulk of private sector growth was still earmarked for the north.

COPS did not oppose growth *per se*. To the contrary, its constituency had a vested interest in the social change that growth could bring. But COPS did want to redirect some of that growth into the older areas of the city. To the extent that northward expansion was to continue, COPS was determined to see that residents of its own neighborhoods did not subsidize it through utility rates that rose to cover the costs of extending service to the north side. Finally, if government was to subsidize growth, COPS wanted subsidies for inner-city as well as for suburban development.[17] The issue for COPS was thus not the fact of growth but its direction and terms. More than any other single factor, this tension between inner-city and suburban development has been at the heart of policy debate in San Antonio since 1974.

COPS' Policy Impact

COPS has shaped policies in both the public and private sectors, both positively and negatively in each sphere. On the one hand it has helped enhance the quality of life in its sectors of the city; on the other hand, COPS has blocked policies that it deemed destructive of the well-being of its communities.

In the public sector COPS has targeted its resources and made its weight felt most on the city council, city utility boards, and school boards. Only occasionally has COPS sought to influence county or state level policy, and then with mixed results. On even rarer occasions, such as when it successfully challenged a city council attempt to use urban blight money to buy a golf course, COPS has lobbied the federal government.[18]

COPS' efforts have been concentrated at the municipal level because this is where its power base is most concentrated—and therefore most effective. One extremely significant political victory for COPS was the 1977 adoption of the district-based city council system. (COPS heavily and successfully backed council districting in a close referendum that pitted the group against the Alliance For A Better City, a regrouping of GGL remnants.[19]) Lines for the district system were drawn so as to give Mexican Americans a majority or near majority in five of the ten districts. This fact has, in turn, become a key to increased policy influence by COPS, exercised through the city council. Since 1977, in three elections, these five districts have elected the candidates most in accord with COPS' positions on issues in thirteen of fifteen races. Further, in return for COPS' support of his projects, COPS has been consistently able to win the vote of councilman Joe Webb, representative of the largely black District 2 on the east side.

COPS' influence with the city council is most clearly evident in the distribution of federal funds for neighborhood improvements. It has obtained an impressive amount of money for capital improvements (streets and sidewalks, drainage, and parks) and for housing rehabilitation. The single biggest source of such money has been the Community Development Block Grant (CDBG) program. Instituted in 1974, CDBG consolidated separate federal programs aimed at fighting urban blight in low- and moderate-income areas.[20] Since CDBG began, San Antonio has received annual allotments totaling $138.7 million.[21] Some 62 percent of this money ($86.3 million) has gone to COPS districts (Districts 1, 4, 5, 6, and 7) and been used to fund the type of capital improvement projects COPS has favored. One might argue that such funds would have gone into these districts anyway, regardless of COPS' efforts, because they contain mostly low- and moderate-income persons. Yet, a comparison of lists of projects submitted by COPS to the city with city records on projects granted funding reveals that 91 percent of the $86.3 million, or $78.2 million, went for projects that COPS had specifically requested. Thus, over half, or 56 percent, of the CDBG money allotted to San Antonio has gone to COPS-endorsed projects.[22] A city official knowledgeable about the CDBG program pointed out that no other single citizens' group in the city has come close to garnering this portion of funds for projects that it favors.[23]

COPS's leverage over the CDBG program has stemmed, first, from its several friendly votes on the city council, which must approve the list of projects to be submitted to the federal government. Second, COPS has paved the way for favorable council votes by generating impressive turnouts at CDBG public hearings. Required by the federal government to solicit citizen opinion, the hearings are normally sparsely attended. COPS, however, has regularly been able to mobilize hundreds and, occasionally, a thousand persons for the hearings. Television news coverage is not uncommon. Aiding in the size of these turnouts has been the fact that a certain portion of them are held in schools or parish halls in COPS areas—a concession the organization won from the city early on in the program.[24] All this yields a lesson politicans ignore at their peril: COPS can mobilize voters.

COPS has also been influential in the use of the Urban Development Action Grant program (UDAG). Established in 1977 by the Carter Administration, UDAG was designed to combine public funds with private investment to help revitalize inner-city neighborhoods.[25] In San Antonio, UDAG has provided $20.6 million to underwrite a neighborhood redevelopment program on the near west side, the Vista Verde project. Vista Verde was a victory for COPS not only because the project was approved, but because COPS' version of the project—and not the city manager's—was adopted. COPS preferred Vista Verde to be a combined residential-commercial complex; Tom Huebner, the city manager, wanted it to be commercial only. When at first Huebner refused to discuss the matter with COPS, a delegation of COPS people, led by president Carmen Badillo, paid Huebner a "visit" in his office. They demanded, with TV cameras present, that Huebner meet with them. Eventually a meeting was held, but Huebner stood firm for his business-only plan.[26] Frustrated, COPS changed tactics. To offset Huebner's opposition the organization mobilized an impressive coalition of backers for its version of the project. They included then-councilman Henry Cisneros; labor leaders; state representatives; Robert McDermott, head of the Economic Development Foundation and USAA insurance; and Robert West, president of Tesoro Petroleum. Shortly thereafter, over Huebner's continued objections, Vista Verde was approved by the city council as a residential-commercial venture.

The third major source of federal funds for the city has been general revenue sharing, a relatively flexible program whose funds may be used for any legitimate government expense, including such operating expenses as salaries.[27] Since revenue sharing's inauguration in 1970, it has brought San Antonio an average of about $9 million per year.[28] Because San Antonio, like other cities, forestalled tax increases by using revenue sharing for operating expenses, COPS has not received a major portion of it for capital improvement projects. Thus far only about 13 percent of the revenue sharing money has gone to COPS-endorsed projects.[29]

In the summer of 1978, however, the group did score a striking victory on revenue sharing. Following the defeat of a $98.4 million bond issue that it had strongly favored, COPS set out to obtain revenue sharing money for projects that had fallen in the bond election.[30] It seemed unlikely that COPS would be able to do this because in prior years there had evolved a clear pattern of increasingly using revenue sharing for operating expenses rather than for capital improvements: from spending a high in 1970 of 74 percent of the revenue sharing allotment on capital projects, the city had dropped to alloting only 11 percent for capital projects by 1977.[31] Nevertheless, led by president Beatrice Gallego, COPS mounted an intense lobbying effort on councilmen from its districts. And, despite bitter denunciations from other council members, a council majority voted to allocate 100 percent of the revenue sharing money to capital projects favored by COPS in 1978.[32]

After the CDBG program, the largest source of money for COPS has been city bonds. Apart from the 1978 bond issue defeat, COPS has successfully campaigned for the passage of the two other bond issues since its founding in 1974, the first in 1974 and the second in 1980. As with the CDBG program, COPS' influence is reflected not so much in the portion of money allotted to its districts—bond money of late is being parceled out evenly with about 10 percent going to each district—but in its capacity to select which projects are funded. Combining the 1974 and 1980 bonds, approximately 72 percent of the $60.8 million that has gone into COPS' districts has gone for projects for which it lobbied. In addition a COPS-backed project in District 2 worth $2.1 million was passed in the 1974 bond. Although COPS had only a minimal presence in District 2 in 1974, by 1980 it had established three locals there. In 1980, 49 percent of the $8.2 million in bonds allotted to District 2 went for a COPS-endorsed drainage project. In all, 32 percent of the $145.9 million raised by these bond elections went for COPS-endorsed projects.[33]

Occasionally COPS has moved to the county and state level to procure money. Its biggest county project through early 1982 has been a still unsuccessful attempt to get three neighborhood clinics for the west side.[34] The organization is likely to persist in this venture because members remain bitter that they must travel to the far northwestern corner of the city for affordable medical care. The need for such travel came about in 1968 when the Bexar County Hospital was moved from its central city location. At the state level COPS has successfully lobbied local legislators for increases in state funds for school districts in its areas.[35] These efforts are continuing. As part of a new overall strategy of enlarging its influence at the state level, COPS, during the 1982 gubernatorial campaign, extracted pledges of increased state funding for local school districts from both major party candidates. After the opening of the Texas legislature in January 1983, the new governor, Mark White, renewed his earlier pledge of support for COPS' proposals. Similar promises were obtained from Gib Lewis, the speaker of the Texas House of Representatives, and Lieutenant Governor Bill Hobby, who presides over the state Senate. All three, in fact, agreed to make education their top priority. The final outcome of this campaign awaits the deliberations of the legislature, but COPS could at least claim to have taken some impressive first steps by enlisting key state officials in its cause.

Indeed, improved education for its children has been prominent on COPS' agendas over the years because the organization represents constituencies in some of Bexar County's poorer school districts—San Antonio, Harlandale, Edgewood, and South San Antonio. COPS has sought to lure new business into its west and south side districts and thereby expand the property tax base. It has also tried to shape the budget priorities in the Harlandale, Edgewood, and San Antonio independent school districts.

At first school board members proved unresponsive. COPS' initial demand to several boards in the mid-1970s was merely to see a copy of the districts' budgets. They were refused, being told in one case that extra copies were unavailable. COPS persisted by staging confrontations with school board members at the board meetings: on cue from leaders, COPS members walked out *en masse,* ignored the agendas and speaker sign-up sheets, cheered friendly speakers, and congregated at the front of the room. Security guards were called to restore order on occasion.

Ultimately COPS began to win influence over budget priorities. It obtained copies of the school budgets—once by threatening to send a delegation of parents to the office of the bank where the school board did business.[36] In the case of the San Antonio Independent School District influence grew after a row over the construction of a new $1.6 million administration building. COPS regarded the proposed building as unnecessary because of more pressing needs. When SAISD board president Grace Durr pressed on with plans for the building, she and other board members were defeated in the 1976 election by candidates who agreed with COPS' positions. Plans for the building were dropped by the new board.[37]

In 1980 COPS helped to alter the composition of another school board—the board of trustees of the San Antonio Junior College District. The board had been rocked by scandal involving allegations of contractor kickbacks to school officials, misuse of employee services, and the firing of maintenance workers.[38] Vowing to seek an investigation of these allegations and to reinstate the dismissed workers, dissident board member George Ozuna sought COPS' help in his upcoming electoral battle to unseat board chairman Walter McAllister, Jr. (son of former mayor and GGL head Walter McAllister, Sr.) with a promise to enlarge junior college facilities on the west side. After McAllister blocked COPS' access to a board meeting and took positions hostile to COPS, the organization, under the leadership of Carmen Badillo, sent its workers into the streets on election day with leaflets advertising McAllister's views. McAllister and his running mates racked up large north side majorities but lost the election because of even larger majorities for the Ozuna slate on the south and west sides.[39] Ozuna telephoned his thanks to COPS for its support on election night, and Carmen Badillo was one of the main speakers at the next board meeting chaired by Ozuna.

The Veto Power

The preceding pages have explored some of what COPS has been able to do. But much of COPS' impact in the public arena has been in terms of policy that it has been able to stop. Within its own neighborhoods COPS has, for example, forced the city to end the proliferation of vacant lots that became a dumping ground for refuse,[40] successfully opposed the construction of the proposed Bandera Freeway,[41] and ended the spread of junkyards.[42] COPS leaders cite junkyards as just one example of a larger pattern whereby industries with undesirable side effects, such as air pollution, have been located in inner-city areas, while "clean industries," such as office complexes and medical centers, have gone to the north side. In this connection in 1980 COPS, in an effort spearheaded by local leader Virginia Zamora, fought the south side construction by Barrett Industries of a cement plant. As COPS had expected, Barrett won a permit to build from the Texas Air Control Board. But, demonstrating a capacity to adapt to new forums, COPS' leaders presented its case before an administrative judge and fought the plant through a long series of hearings. The intent was to force costly delays upon Barrett, as well as to fire a shot across the bow of other potentially polluting industries looking at west or south side locations.[43]

In terms of dollars involved, COPS' veto power has been most felt on policies of citywide scope and import, particularly those relating to growth. Intent on the betterment of their own neighborhoods, COPS members are determined to see that the financial resources they believe are due their communities are not siphoned off for the betterment of other neighborhoods. COPS' first major development-related battle was to block construction of a large shopping mall over the Edwards Aquifer, the city's sole source of drinking water (see Chapter 8). COPS feared that pollution of the aquifer's recharge zone would require building water purification facilities which would be funded through higher water rates to consumers. In the end the developers got their way in the courts, but COPS' impressive showing in turning out voters for a referendum against the mall had seized the attention of city decision makers (see Chapter 8). It proved that COPS could affect the outcome of a citywide election—a point worth making at a time when city council candidates ran under the at-large system that forced them to solicit votes from all sectors of the city.

Through a long series of Planning Commission and council hearings from 1977 to 1979, COPS fought the city's proposed master plan. The principal dispute was over how much encouragement the city would give to suburban versus central city development. Neither COPS nor the city's major suburban developers liked the final version of the master plan (albeit for different reasons). After years of wrangling the plan was tabled by the city council in 1979.[44]

COPS has also opposed the City Water Board's (CWB) rate policies and other practices as biased toward north side growth—a view given credibility by the fact that John Schaefer, chairman of the CWB from 1975 to 1982, was a major area home builder. Confrontations with Schaefer have been bitter: Schaefer on occasion has called the police to quell boisterous CWB meetings with large COPS delegations.[45]

By applying pressure to both the CWB and to the city council, which must approve board rates and practices, COPS has thwarted the CWB's will several times: In 1975, led by president Andres Sarabia, COPS forced a rollback on a proposed rate hike from 39 percent to 19 percent. Under pressure from COPS in 1976 the Water Board abandoned its practice of giving developers free materials to build water mains in new suburban subdivisions. At COPS' insistence the CWB was forced to scuttle a contract with a regional river authority for the purchase of surface water. COPS also successfully lobbied against the CWB purchase of a private water company from developer Cliff Morton. After the board's long refusal, it bowed to COPS' long-standing demand to replace old water mains in inner-city areas, allocating $11 million for that purpose.[46] This commitment was reaffirmed just recently when, in the wake of COPS pressure on the city council, the CWB made the replacement of old mains its top priority after earlier omitting reference to it in a master plan designating future needs.[47] As part of the same decision, another long-standing goal of COPS was achieved when the CWB abolished the Community Water Development Fund (CWDF).[48] Over the years COPS has attacked the fund as an unfair subsidy to home builders. In 1976 COPS advocated doing away with the fund but had to settle for a council decision to disburse it only to projects within San Antonio's city limits.[49]

COPS has also clashed with the city-owned power authority, the City Public Service Board (CPSB), over utility rates and charges for extending service to new customers. COPS has consistently lobbied against rate increases, and it forced CPSB to increase charges to developers and new customers for extending service.[50]

COPS' most significant battle with CPSB has been over the South Texas Nuclear Project (STNP). The business community and others have backed the project as the cheapest available source of power for the future, given all the alternate power sources, such as coal. However, as the cost of the project rose severalfold through the 1970s, so did COPS' anxiety about it. In 1980, after astronomical cost overruns had pushed the price of the project from $933 million to $4.8 billion—with promises of yet more increases—COPS called for the city to limit its share to 14 percent of the project, or half its original 28 percent investment.[51]

The late 1981 firing of Brown and Root as both designer and builder of the STNP, combined with cost overruns and concerns over the project's safety, could eventually force San Antonio out of the project. (Austin voters have already approved a referendum to sell that city's share.) Or, as Mayor Cisneros has suggested, the project might be scaled down from two plants to one.[52] While COPS cannot take full credit for either one of these new reservations about the project, the organization did push the issue to center stage months before the project's fall 1981 crisis. By some two years of queries and pressure applied to the city council demanding justification of the STNP, and in the face of intense business community support for it, COPS placed a pullback from the project on the city's agenda.[53]

COPS and the Private Sector

In a free enterprise economy, government has limited potential to effect fundamental economic change because control over the economy rests largely in the hands of business leaders. They make most of the strategic decisions on investment that determine the level and distribution of wealth.[54] In their drive to improve their lives and the lives of their children COPS members inevitably encountered the limits of government-induced change. From its inception, the organization had always seen higher-paying jobs as a prerequisite for real material progress. But up until 1977 it had never seen a way to make headway on that issue. Its power base was tailored to put pressure on politicians and their appointees. But, as former COPS president Carmen Badillo recalled, COPS' inquiries around town revealed that the key decisions on recruiting new and potentially higher paying industries were in the hands of the business community and, in particular, in the hands of the Economic Development Foundation (EDF).[55] This was an organization of San Antonio business leaders formed to attract new industries set up mainly because of dissatisfaction with the industrial recruitment efforts of the Greater San Antonio Chamber of Commerce.

Since COPS wished to influence industrial growth, the question for COPS became how to influence the EDF. One answer came when COPS obtained a report of the Fantus Company, an industrial relocation consulting firm, on San Antonio, commissioned by the EDF. The study analyzed the strengths and weaknesses of San Antonio as a location for new business. To COPS's outrage, the Fantus report cited San Antonio's low wage structure as one of the city's strong points and recommended that industries that might upset that structure not be wooed by the EDF.[56] After reading these recommendations COPS, led by president Beatrice Gallego, attacked the EDF for attempting to perpetuate poverty in San Antonio by limiting its recruiting efforts to low-wage industries.

With the media giving it extensive coverage, a bitter battle ensued. The EDF denied COPS' charges and countered that COPS was scaring away new businesses with its demand that new firms pay a minimum annual salary of $15,000 as a prerequisite for settling in San Antonio. COPS countered that the $15,000 figure was a goal, not a prerequisite.

At first the EDF refused to meet with COPS, citing an earlier stormy meeting as the reason. But the glaring media publicity frightened other sectors of the community interested in growth, and probably the EDF as well. A number of meetings finally did take place, beginning in March of 1978. On May 30, 1978, COPS and the EDF ostensibly patched up their differences, signing an historic agreement to, among other things, work together to recruit high-paying industries. In addition, a committee was set up to promote higher skill levels among San Antonio workers.[57]

This dispute showed that political instability was the Achilles heel of business. If COPS could not use its political resources directly to influence business decisions, it could indirectly pressure business by creating an unsettled climate that frightened new investors. COPS did not realize this at first, but as the conflict wore on, COPS' leaders recognized the source of their leverage—the potential role of spoiler to the city's economic growth. COPS agreed to work with the EDF not because it was interested in the role of the spoiler for its own sake, but rather because it sought to promote more and better jobs. To the extent that the EDF and other members of the business community were frightened by the prospect of future turmoil, COPS had accomplished its objective. It had called attention to the problem of the low wage structure of the city and had given the business community an incentive to change that structure.

COPS had kicked open the door to the private sector, but to what avail? Would the private sector concede to COPS permanent participation in setting business policy? Or would business leaders somehow try to keep COPS quiet? For over a year after the agreement with the EDF was signed little came of it. COPS suspended its confrontation tactics and waited to see if the pact would bring better jobs. It didn't; only a handful of new jobs came into the city. And the ad hoc committee for raising worker skill levels met only once or twice.[58] Then, in the summer of 1979, prospects for cooperation with the business community brightened after the EDF supported COPS on the Vista Verde project. Encouraged, COPS seriously considered a permanent alliance with the city's economic elites. Ultimately,

COPS dropped the permanent alliance idea. Its leaders were uncomfortable with a general shift in tactics from confrontation to negotiation. And they were fearful of the impression that closed-door bargaining sessions might give to the grass-roots leaders in the locals.[59] But before the organization could develop other strategies, Robert McDermott confronted COPS with his version of citizen influence in the private sector—United San Antonio.

Formed in January of 1980, United San Antonio (USA) is a trisector alliance ostensibly designed to involve business, government, and the public in economic development. At the same time, it is intended to demonstrate that the city is united in its resolve to bring economic growth. In an obvious reference to his battle with COPS, McDermott said that he had formed USA because past experience had taught him that industrial recruitment could not be viewed as the exclusive province of business.[60]

COPS declined to join USA because it saw it, at best, as a public relations body, and at worst, as a sinister attempt to coopt dissenting groups. At the end of 1980, however, still convinced of the need for private sector backing in realizing significant social change, COPS put aside its earlier misgivings on negotiating with business. It called for meetings between COPS and key business leaders to enlist their support in solving such problems as drainage and the ever-diminishing tax base of its communities. This call was coupled with a warning that if COPS was rebuffed, it would go back to being the old COPS that disrupted meetings, browbeat business leaders in parish halls, and made those unseemly headlines.

At first the reaction to its invitation was frustrating. While key business leaders such as Glenn Biggs and McDermott met with them, COPS leaders were repeatedly told to work through USA rather than dealing directly with them. COPS refused, reaffirming its position of working only with the real power brokers.[61] In November of 1981, this impasse was broken when thirty-five key business leaders consented to sit down with COPS in what the group styled a community-level summit conference. (At this writing, preparations for the meeting are in progress.)

The proposed conference is part of a recently adopted broader COPS policy to seek direct involvement in key decisions that affect its members. Three recent events indicate that this policy is working thus far. First, the EDF has complied with COPS' request that representatives of industries considering a San Antonio location be sent to COPS so that it can discuss with them the advantages of locating in its communities. Representatives of Sprague Electric met with Beatrice Cortez in August of 1981, and in January of 1982 Sprague broke ground for a plant in the Edgewood area.[62] Second,

COPS accompanied Mayor Henry Cisneros on his recent trip to Mexico to discuss alternate energy sources with President Lopez Portillo and other Mexican officials. Finally, COPS recently met with the president of Houston Power and Light, Don Jordan, to discuss the STNP. Jordan had come to San Antonio to attend a meeting of all the partners in the nuclear power project, and briefed COPS on that meeting.[63]

Conclusion

Only time will tell how far COPS will be able to go in shaping private sector policy or in winning business cooperation. But one thing is clear: COPS has come a long way since that night in Kennedy High School when its members diffidently approached city manager Sam Granata. It has evolved into a force to be reckoned with in city politics. In the years since its founding tens of millions of dollars have flowed into its communities, most of it in accord with COPS' priorities. Numerous government policies that threatened the vitality of its neighborhoods have been checked. Even if USA is a sham intended only to give the illusion of community influence, its creation shows that COPS has made its point: private policies have public consequences. Thus, business leaders now recognize a need to seek approval for growth policies from persons outside cooperate boardrooms.

Such changes may not reverse completely the tide of suburban growth that has threatened COPS' communities, but it has slowed and shaped this growth. It has also convinced at least a few companies to locate in inner-city San Antonio. Finally, COPS has taken giant steps toward raising the quality of life in older neighborhoods, some of which may now become places where people can stay if they choose, rather than leave because they must.

Part IV: Conclusions

John A. Booth

Chapter Ten

Political Change in
San Antonio, 1970–82: Toward
Decay or Democracy?

San Antonians saw their city's politics turned upside down between 1973 and 1982. The transformations of the period were remarkable both for the ethnic and class tensions they engendered in the political arena in the late 1970s and for the speed with which such problems apparently subsided after 1981.

In the late 1970s the city's media noted with alarm the political mobilization of blacks and Chicanos under the leadership of groups like Communities Organized for Public Service (COPS). Signs of increased ethnic conflict and newly expressed demands by formerly silent lower-class groups aroused considerable unease among upper- and middle-class Anglos. Some feared that the election of a Chicano mayor—by then something that appeared inevitable—would probably institute a powerful and biased new political machine in San Antonio.

Another frequently voiced concern during the late 1970s was that the quality of policy making by city government had declined as the result of the changes undergone by the system. The 1976 demise of the Good Government League (GGL) brought anguish to those nostalgic for the departed era in which that organization had ruled the city with great firmness and unity. To many observers, the disappearance of the GGL, the angry crowds at City Hall, and the testiness of "upstart" or "radical" minority politicians signified severe political decay—a breakdown of the city's political institutions due to an excess of citizen participation.

Yet despite such portents and fears, San Antonians in 1981 elected as their mayor Henry Cisneros, the first Mexican American to hold that post in over 140 years. Cisneros ran well not only among Chicanos but among Anglos, too; and ethnic and class issues played little part in the campaign. The 1981 election thus appeared to have ushered in an era as much marked by its ethnic and class political harmony as the previous six years had been marked by conflict. San Antonio had apparently passed from an Anglo elite–dominated machine system to a coalition system in which no single class or ethnic group held complete power over political decisions.

From Machine to Coalition Politics

The Decline of the GGL

From 1955 to 1975 the Good Government League controlled city politics in San Antonio with a silk-gloved fist of steel. The GGL, dominated by business leaders from the San Antonio area (but not necessarily city residents), had sprung from the movement that utilized a council-manager reform of the city charter to oust a thirty-year-old, lower-middle-class political machine from City Hall (see Chapters 1 and 5). Though differing vastly in style and means from the organization it vanquished, the GGL soon became a machine in its own right.[1] The GGL era was one of unprecedented city council harmony because the league's secret nominating committee chose candidates only after careful screening for agreement with central GGL growth policies.[2] The city council chose city managers and city board and commission members from within GGL leadership ranks. The GGL also created and then quietly controlled several elective policy-making boards, including those of the San Antonio River Authority, the Edwards Underground Water District, and San Antonio College. Public policy in this era provided public subsidies for suburban developers, promoted such nonpolluting, nonunionized, and low-wage industries as tourism, bureaucracies, and military installations, and permitted the deterioration of public services in older portions of the city.[3]

But in the early 1970s the league began to lose its hold as an insurgent faction arose in a feud over downtown versus suburban growth priorities, formed its own candidate-slating organization with the ironic tag of the Independent Team, and spent heavily on its electoral challenge to the GGL.[4] The short-lived Independents succeeded: They first pared the GGL's share of the 1973 council to only five of nine members and then to a mere three of nine in 1975, only to disappear by the 1979 election.

The final nail in the GGL's coffin came in early 1977, when voters transformed the at-large city council into the present district-based representation format. The at-large system had made the formidably endorsed and heavily financed league slates extraordinarily tough to challenge, except by slates with equal resources—such as the Independent Team's. Things began to change, however, when the U.S. Congress passed the Voting Rights Act of 1975, which provided the minority populations of several states, including Texas, special political protections. Under the provisions of this new law, the Mexican-American Legal Defense and Education Fund challenged San Antonio's 1972 annexation of a large Anglo area on the northwest side. The U.S. Justice Department agreed that this annexation diluted the Chicano population below its former slight majority status in the city, thus harming Chicano political strength. Justice thus presented the city with the Hobson's choice of voiding the annexation and suspending elections indefinitely, or of adopting a district-based council representation system. The required charter change referendum passed in January 1977. Support for the measure came especially from blacks and Mexican Americans, who clearly saw the prospects of increasing their representation in city offices. With each council seat tied to a specific district, the citywide slating strategy of the GGL and the Independent Team had lost its power. No longer could such business- and north side–dominated groups always depend upon Anglo voter turnout to control the city council.[5]

The Rise of Mexican-American Participation and Representation

If the GGL and other socioeconomic elite interests forfeited some of their power over the city's government, who, if anyone, rose to replace them? One answer is that Mexican Americans have come to wield growing political clout in San Antonio.

The citizen advocate group COPS supplies an excellent example of this new power. COPS is not a Chicano organization per se, though it is predominantly so by membership. This admired and feared (but widely misunderstood) group grew out of dissatisfaction among many lower-middle-class homeowners and other residents of the largely poor west side with their substandard public services. With seed money from Catholic Church community development funds and with the guidance of a Saul Alinsky-trained organizer, groups began to form around the natural community nucleus of the parish and joined together under the COPS umbrella.[6]

Not a civil rights group, but a coalition of pressure groups dedicated to the pursuit of concrete improvements in the everyday standard of living, COPS mobilized Chicanos and other service-poor communities with amazing speed. Astounded city politicians found their economic dogma of two decades challenged by this long-ignored, once-passive element. When first rebuffed by policy makers, COPS raised its voice by using confrontational tactics to gain a hearing. COPS came of age as a political force when it allied with the Aquifer Protection Association to support a referendum to restrict further north side growth. COPS' skillful voter mobilization overwhelmed their opponents and stunned San Antonio politicos.[7]

Some of COPS' detractors have portrayed the group as an unstoppable juggernaut, but its success has varied according to arena and issue: The group has lost on school district and city capital improvement bond issues. In contrast, COPS has proven very effective in persuading the city to allocate federal funds to projects in the organization's neighborhoods. COPS began the decade of the 1980s by challenging the city's economic policy makers over industrial development policy. This struggle promises to continue for many years. Although COPS won a voice in the process early on, its true influence upon decisions remained difficult to judge as of 1982.

After the referendum victory, San Antonio city council members began to listen to COPS' demands with greatly enhanced respect. Indeed, by 1980 COPS could usually get the ear of policy makers in city and county governments and on utility boards, so that the group's tacticians resorted to the early feistiness and confrontation only when ignored. In addition to getting its issues on the public agenda, COPS had undoubtedly increased the participation of much of the city's traditionally apathetic lower middle classes in politics, and especially the Mexican Americans, by giving them a model of political success that shattered all tradition. It also called into question the basic economic goals of San Antonio's socioeconomic elite, thus introducing class conflict into city politics to a previously unknown degree.

During the 1970s Mexican Americans also assumed a much higher political profile in San Antonio in ways entirely unrelated to COPS. San Antonio had long been a center of Mexican-American organization, including *mutualista* (self-help) societies originating in the nineteenth century, the League of United Latin American Citizens (LULAC, founded in 1928), and the American G.I. Forum (formed by Chicano veterans after World War II). Civil rights initiatives that began in the 1950s had overturned anti-Chicano restrictive covenants on property deeds, outlawed the poll tax, and won Chicano participation on juries. In 1962 congressional redistricting created a new U.S. House of Representatives district that included most of Bexar County's Mexican-American barrios. Henry B. Gonzalez's election to Congress from that seat represented a landmark event for San Antonio Mexican Americans. In the 1960s, other Chicanos won a handful of public offices in Bexar County, some of them by campaigning on issues of primary concern to their own ethnic group.

The formation of the Mexican-American Youth Organization (MAYO, 1967), the Mexican-American Legal Defense and Education Fund (MAL-DEF, 1967), and the Raza Unida Party (1969) bespoke an awakening political militancy among some segments of San Antonio's Chicano community. In 1972 MALDEF and other groups successfully challenged the multimember state representative district for Bexar County, permitting the election of several new Mexican-American representatives to the state legislature from single-member districts. This key success spurred still greater efforts to increase representation: The Mexican-American Democrats (MAD) arose with the Democratic Party, and the Southwest Voter Registration and Education Project formed in San Antonio in 1974 to work to expand the Chicano electorate. When the 1975 Voting Rights Act extended language minority protections to Texas, MALDEF challenged the at-large council districting of the city of San Antonio and won. The resulting 10–1 council districting arrangement brought a handful of new, young Mexicano politicos to the fore on the council. Some, such as Bernardo Eureste, often raised class and ethnic issues in the council, while others, such as Henry Cisneros, adopted a conciliatory posture toward Anglos and toward the socioeconomic elite.[8]

The Voting Rights Act of 1975 and the changes it wrought in San Antonio and Bexar County represented a major gain in the long drive for Chicano political rights. Nevertheless, the act's effects upon Mexican-American voter participation appear to have been only modest. Even with the voter registration drives by Southwest Voter Registration and by COPS, Spanish-surnamed registration in San Antonio was only about 40 percent of those eligible in 1980, compared to 56 percent among Anglos. Overall, the Spanish-surnamed share of all of San Antonio's registered voters rose only five percentage points, from 37 percent in 1971 to about 42 percent in 1981. Moreover, these modest Mexican-American registration increases did not ensure greater Mexican-American turnout at the polls: turnout levels changed little over the decade. The fact of generally low turnout has helped keep Chicanos underrepresented in public office.

Though still voting at low rates that limited its potential political impact, the Mexican-American populace did benefit from the structural impact of the Voting Rights Act through increased representation among elected public officials. Table 10.1 presents data on the representation of the Spanish-surnamed among elected public officials of the city of San Antonio and Bexar County. The data clearly reveal a substantial rise in representation of

Table 10.1: Representation of the Spanish-Surnamed
among Selected San Antonio and Bexar County Public Officials,
before and after Voting Rights Act Extension of 1975

	1970		1981	
Office	% Mex.-Am. Officials	Index of Under-representation[a]	% Mex.-Am. Officials	Index of Under-representation[a]
Mayor and city council	26%	.50	45%	.75
Commissioner's Court	13	.29	50	1.08
Other high county officials[b]	17	.37	30	.65
Higher judicial officials[c]	17	.37	10	.22
Minor judicial and law enforcement officials	38	.84	53	1.14
State legislators and senators	23	.51	40	.86
All officials	23	.51	37	.80

SOURCES: *Bilingual Elections at Work in the Southwest* (San Antonio: Mexican American Legal Defense and Education Fund, March 5, 1982), p. 85; City of San Antonio Clerk's Office files; Bexar County Election Office records. Figures given do not include interim appointees, but only officials who have stood for election.

[a]The index of underrepresentation is the percentage of Spanish-surnamed officials expressed as a ratio to the percentage of Spanish-surnamed population of the city or county (as appropriate). It indicates the degree to which actual representation approaches parity (equality) with the group's share of the population. A value approaching zero indicates extreme underrepresentation, while a value of 1.0 indicates perfect parity of representation.

[b]Includes sheriff, county clerk, tax assessor-collector, treasurer, surveyor, district clerk, and district attorney.

[c]Includes district judges and county court-at-law judges.

Mexican Americans among public officials as well as general gains toward parity of representation.[9]

Perhaps the most dramatic and visible sign of the new Mexican-American access to public office has been the election of Henry Cisneros as mayor of San Antonio in 1981. Running against an Anglo establishment figure, John Steen, Cisneros won not only most of the Chicano vote but also about a third of the vote in predominantly Anglo districts. Dr. Cisneros, an urban management professor at the University of Texas at San Antonio and a veteran of three terms on the city council, forged this winning coalition with the assistance of heavy financial backing by several big-spending developers. Cisneros' achievement, so widely noted in the national media, must be placed in perspective by noting similar pioneering victories won by similar strategies for Bexar County Judge Albert Bustamante (first elected in 1978) and Sheriff Joe Neaves (elected in 1980). In sum, despite modestly increased participation by Chicanos, their substantially increased representation in public office has brought major growth in Chicano political influence in San Antonio.

To sum up, between 1973 and 1982, San Antonio city politics had been transformed from a system of business elite–dominated, political machine rule to a coalition system. The impact of federal voting laws, growing Mexican-American representation, and the divergence of economic elite interests had created a new district-based city council structure that could no longer be dominated by a citywide slating organization appealing to Anglo votes. These changes created the conditions under which pressure groups seeking to influence public policy had to form coalitions with other political forces. The time was ripe for Mexican-American candidates with electoral appeal outside their own ethnic group and with economic development proposals that could bridge the gap between the demands of COPS, Anglo environmental activists, and at least some factions of the politically active economic elite.

Prospects for the Future and Criticism of Recent Changes

One fear often mentioned by defenders of the GGL status quo ante was that between COPS and growing Chicano representation a new, ethnically biased political machine would arise to raid the city's resources for the exclusive benefit of Mexican Americans and the west and south sides. But such fears are groundless: machine politics is virtually impossible in San Antonio. In the first place, a city manager, not the mayor and council, controls the city bureaucracy. This eliminates the most basic element of the classical political machine—the ability of elected politicians to reward supporters with patronage jobs. The only means for any kind of machine to succeed under San Antonio's council-manager system is the way the Good Government League worked it—with an at-large election system that permitted complete control of the city council by a citywide power group. Such an arrangement appears very unlikely to recur under the present council districting system.

Second, because Mexican Americans comprised only 42 percent of the registered voters in 1981 and turned out to vote at rates consistently lower than Anglos,[10] the charter changes necessary to build the required patronage apparatus would seem, for some years to come, to have scant chance for winning the requisite public approval. In fact, as of 1982, the balance of ethnic representation on city council remained unstable. In 1979, for example, Anglo Bob Thompson unseated incumbent Rudy Oritz in ethnically mixed District 6, a victory repeated in 1981. By contrast, in the same election Henry Cisneros won the mayoralty race with substantial Anglo backing. The effects of the post–1980-census redistricting upon the still shifting ethnic representation balance remains to be seen in the 1983 elections.

Third, the creation of an ethnic machine would require considerable unity of purpose among the city's Chicano council members and other political leaders. Those Mexican Americans who have served since 1977 on the San Antonio city council and in other public offices have been, however, nothing if not diverse in their ideologies, styles, programs, goals, and personalities. In fact, the diversity among Mexican-American council members is probably greater than that among their Anglo colleagues, and therefore more likely to preclude rather than to facilitate their attempting to construct a machine.

Fourth, COPS has so far basically stayed away from the traditional giveand-take of city and county electoral politics. COPS does seek candidate commitments to its programs, and does occasionally endorse and electioneer for certain preferred individuals. COPS has not, however, identified itself with traditional parties nor actually sought to elect its own members to public office. The organization's leaders have avoided such arrangements because they feared that entanglements in the factionalism of west side politics might compromise their pursuit of better services. Therefore, as of this writing, there appear to be neither the votes, the unity among the critical actors, the institutions, nor the organizational will that would be necessary for a successful movement toward ethnic machine rule in the city of San Antonio.

Some critics of council districting have feared that it would intensify ethnic cleavages in San Antonio politics. The blunt affirmation of former GGL mayor W. W. McAllister, Jr., that council districting was "creating racism that didn't exist"[11] best encapsulates this argument. Purveyors of this idea have in effect suggested that increased Chicano participation would spawn ethnic conflict or racism in the political arena. Presumably, Mexican Americans would be the source of this new bias, since they made up the major new element in the political arena.

This argument, however, is logically flawed, patronizing, and perhaps dangerous. Increased participation and ethnic awareness do not necessarily mean ethnically biased and hostile policy making. Community identification and political organization—Anglo Saxon, German, black, and Mexican-American—have a century-old history in multiethnic San Antonio, but open ethnic political strife has been infrequent. It is true that the city's white-dominated political machines have historically exploited blacks and Mexican Americans for electoral purposes[12] while systematically discriminating against these communities in public policy.[13] Despite such a deplorable model of ethnic policy bias by Anglo politicos, however, there is no necessary reason that increased Chicano participation should breed conflict unless barriers were to be erected to block Chicanos, or unless the political arena were to be inflamed with hostile actions and attitudes by the Anglos already in the ring. Further, to argue that the increased Mexicano clout must bring racism smacks of racism itself. This idea's proponents assume the awkward position of arguing against increasingly fair and more democratic participation for long-excluded groups because that would be "racist."

Indeed, one may reasonably argue that increased Mexican-American representation because of the 1970s rights movement and the structural changes occasioned by the 1975 Voting Rights Act has actually diminished tension. These changes may have reduced a growing frustration felt among San Antonio Chicanos, and thus avoided increased unrest and conflict. City councilman Bernardo Eureste, for example, has said that the 1977 districting of the city council headed off "serious disturbances in the city of San Antonio because Mexicans would feel that they were not represented. . . . I truly believe that we were headed in that direction."[14]

Critics of the new Mexican-American role in the system often claimed that ethnic splits in city council voting during the 1977–79 term proved that racially biased decision making had already become institutionalized. For example, the press frequently noted with some alarm that the 1977–79 council's five Mexicanos—inflammatorily dubbed the "Crystal City Coalition" by their detractors—aligned with black councilman Joe Webb against the five Anglos. Ironically, these observers failed to notice that the Anglos, too, were voting *en bloc.*

Three rebuttals to this criticism can be made. First, ethnic bloc voting was rare. An analysis of the many hundreds of votes taken by the city council in 1977 and 1978 demonstrated that less than 1 percent involved such an ethnic division.[15] Second, closer scrutiny suggests that the real issues involved in most such splits were economic rather than ethnic. Many simply pitted the representatives of poor and service-poor districts against those of the more prosperous, better-served areas in a contest over service distribution. Council voting alignments have shifted constantly, taking different forms on different issues according to the views of members and the problems of their constituents.

Third, when Anglos regained an absolute majority on the city council in 1977 because of the election of an Anglo from District 6, charges of ethnic bias and conflicts diminished markedly. This reduced ethnic strife occurred largely because Anglo elite political representatives no longer needed such charges to polarize voters in order to block economic policy changes that they opposed. During the 1979–81 council term a new elite strategy developed: the business community initiated a conflict-containment program for city politics through the United San Antonio (USA) organization. So defused had ethnicity per se become by 1981 that the candidacy of Henry Cisneros was heavily endorsed and financed by important leaders within the Anglo economic establishment.

Despite the decline of ethnic tension in 1981–82, the danger of polarization still lurks among the city's possible political futures. But this danger resides far less in the new Chicano activism than in potential recourse by Anglo political figures to ethnic fear-mongering in order to cloud discussions of ordinary substantive policy matters. The more public figures cry "Wolf!" the harder it could become to defuse true ethnic tensions should they arise. There is also the self-fulfilling prophecy danger of provoking such racial hostility under the guise of constantly warning against it.

The 1977 campaign against the 10–1 council districting plan, waged by many former GGL and Independent Team heavyweights, took a nasty turn with the distribution to homes on the Anglo north side of propaganda appealing to racist fears of a possible Chicano takeover. Moreover, the victory of the 10–1 plan failed to halt such tactics. From the outset of the council districting system in 1977, opponents argued for changing the city charter to provide for some sort of mixed system of at-large and district council members. All such plans would increase Anglo representation on the council and perhaps enhance the likelihood for the emergence of a reconstituted GGL. Early advocates of such a system included ex-mayor W. W. McAllister and former councilman Phil Pyndus. Most trial balloons for such a charter change have been justified by proponents by references to the "divisiveness" and "irresponsibility" of "ethnic minority members" of the 1977–79 council, a clear indication of the racist potential of such a campaign. Racism also blighted campaigns for the 1978 city bond election and the May 1978 Democratic primary election for county judge. Of course, such campaigns were part of an old pattern; ethnic fear tactics had previously been used several times by the GGL.[16] Though dormant in the early 1980s, such strategies remained part of the repertoire of political discourse of the city's political forces and could be brought back into service with ease.

Commentators and activists on the political Left have voiced a third fear. They believe that the emergence of the economic elite–backed USA and its call for harmony, the incorporation of COPS into the development-promotion process through the Economic Development Foundation, and the real estate developers' backing for Albert Bustamante's and Henry Cisneros' successful bids for major public offices constituted aspects of an elite strategy of co-optation of Chicanos. One goal of this process of co-optation is said to be the denial of true ruling power to the Mexican-American community by keeping the Anglo elite ruling through "safe" or "acceptable" conservative Hispanic politicians. Another goal of the economic elite is, supposedly, to defuse the potential for the growth of a lower-class political movement. In sum, the emergent system is viewed as simply another, more complex, yet efficient vehicle for excluding Mexican Americans and the poor from real influence over public policy.

This argument has the virtues of accurately portraying many of the political forces at play in San Antonio and of accounting for much of their behavior. But this approach also makes some erroneous assumptions. First, these arguments assume a considerable harmony of interest among San Antonio Chicanos (leaders and followers), along both ethnic and class lines. Even were there no USA or elite co-optation strategy in San Antonio, one would be hard pressed to imagine the emergence of a coherent and persistent class-conscious or ethnically self-conscious political movement from within the San Antonio Mexican-American community. A case in point is the dissensus and disarray of the Raza Unida Party's forces in Crystal City after only a few years in power. San Antonio's Chicano community is much more complex and diverse than that of Crystal City and lacks the strong common experience of frustration and complete exclusion from power that sparked the Crystal City movement. The potential for unified political struggle in San Antonio therefore appears far less than in Crystal City, and the potential for disunity seems far greater.

The argument from the Left, moreover, assumes that no true community of interest, nor even coincidence of interest, across ethnic or class lines is possible in San Antonio. This assumption lacks credibility when examined in the light of day. Indeed, the coalition forged by Henry Cisneros in 1981 represented the emergence of a coincidence of interests among Anglos and Chicanos: Cisneros was the articulate, competent, and reasonable mayoral candidate wanted by Anglos, as well as the credible representative desired by Mexican Americans. This coalition also benefitted from a key community of interests between the developers who funded the Cisneros campaign and the constituents of COPS who voted for him—the pursuit of an aggressive policy of industrial development.

A Question of Democracy

One may argue that the political transformation of San Antonio treated in detail in this volume has made the city's government more democratic. Three key elements of democracy are citizen participation, majority control of representatives, and discussion. The more of each of these present in a political society, the more democratic it is. The Greek roots of the word *democracy* itself mean rule by the people, revealing directly the participatory heart of the idea. Democracy literally consists of members of a community participating in making decisions for that community.[17] Thomas Jefferson, author of the Declaration of Independence and an important democratic theorist, described democracy as "government by . . . citizens in mass, acting directly and personally, according to rules established by the majority."[18]

Democracy therefore involves citizen participation, but in a large community such as San Antonio not everyone can take a direct part; thus some sort of representation is required. This poses the key problem which political philosopher. A. J. Lindsay has dubbed the "necessary evil of the representative": how to approach rule by majority preferences with decisions made by a small minority of delegates.[19] Thus, a second principle of representative democracy requires that the delegates must be as close as possible to the people in order to do their bidding. Among the solutions for this problem recommended by Jefferson and adopted by the framers of the U.S. Constitution were division of government powers, free election of delegates, and a system of regional representation to protect the rights of diverse interests. If every citizen cannot feasibly take direct part in decision-making, the next most democratic alternative is to give the people access to and control over their representatives.

Third, democrats give a critically important role to discussion. Jefferson states that "where man is free to think and to speak, differences of opinion will arise," to be resolved by "free discussion."[20] Lindsay argues that government without the "free give and take of discussion" is not democratic at all, but "a makeshift, or a compromise, or means of keeping people quiet by the production of a sham unaminity."[21] Just as citizen participation and majority control of leaders are keys to democracy, so too is discussion, the open consideration of policy alternatives by both the public and their representatives. Let us now look at each of these principles separately to see how San Antonio's political scene has become more democratic in the last few years.

Several factors permitted more citizens to take an active role in community politics in 1975–82 than during the GGL era. First, the disappearance of the Good Government League made it easier for individuals and previously excluded groups to affect who got elected to council. This occurred because there was no longer a monolithic political machine, dominated by like-thinking candidates almost certain to win. The GGL had for two decades stood as a barrier between much of the San Antonio community and elected officials and policy. Without this juggernaut that steamrolled over 90 percent of its slate into office through heavy financing and sophisticated electioneering, the makeup of the council changed. Chicanos came to hold a number of council seats that much more nearly approximated their proportion of the population, while during the GGL era they were usually substantially underrepresented on the GGL slates and the council.[22] The preponderance of businessmen and other highly paid professionals on the councils diminished, and middle-class representation increased. Still, no poor nor even nearly poor people became council members. But at least the inner circle of the GGL no longer maintained its iron grip on political power in the city, and that power became dispersed among a wider constituency.

The second reason for more participation was the new council districting plan. While it was the Independent Team that first broke the GGL's council monopoly, it was the parcelling out of representatives to the variegated neighborhoods of San Antonio that prevented the reconcentration of power in another GGL-like group. In fact the Independents lasted only briefly as an organization. Nor did the Alliance for a Better City, created to fight the 10–1 districting plan in hopes of reconstituting business's political power base, survive beyond its first major battle. No longer could a single group consistently dominate the city council by appeal to the north side

Anglo vote in council elections. The city's once monolithic economic elite had divided and declined in stature from a ruling group to simply a handful of pressure groups.

A united business elite could still exercise great sway in city politics, however. For example, in 1978 many elements of the previously divided Anglo political establishment reunited to oppose approval of a $100 million bond package. As a result of their campaign, the Anglo majority of voters soundly defeated the bond issue, which was strongly favored by Mexican Americans on the city council. Moreover, during the 1977–82 dispute between COPS and the economic elite's Economic Development Foundation over development policy, the elite strengthened its hand by enlisting outside aid to outmaneuver the west side challengers. In essence, they backed COPS down by contriving a possible industrial relocation boycott of the city should challenges to the foundation's policy continue and by including COPS on an advisory board.

Out of the development policy conflict grew the new organization United San Antonio. Its goal was to minimize conflict and to promote economic growth according to the policy preferences of the newly reunited business elite.[23] USA's goal, as described privately by one Chamber of Commerce spokesperson, was to "co-opt the hell out of everybody" in order to promote economic growth and urbanization with maximal public sector subvention and minimal regulatory restraint and public criticism. Nevertheless, the new district-based representation system for city council had already given a much broader segment of the community an opportunity to select representatives who lived near them and shared their problems, which in turn encouraged more citizen communication with those officials once elected.

A third factor increasing participation has been the emergence of groups like Communities Organized for Public Service and the east side's Residents Organized for Better and More Beautiful Environmental Development (ROBBED). These groups have mobilized ever greater numbers of Mexicanos and blacks into city politics. Following the successful example of COPS and of other neighborhood improvement and preservation organizations, such as the King William Association and the Monte Vista Association, many new neighborhood groups have recently formed. Many people who never before took part in any public arena were contacting their elected and appointed officials to voice their opinions. More people from throughout the city and from all ethnic groups are voting in city elections.

As for the democratic principle of majority control of representatives, the citizenry at large made definite gains. During the GGL era, a business-elite committee secretly chose most of the city council members from among north side business and professional leaders. But after 1977, with district-based council seats, more people than before felt encouraged to run for city council, and still more worked to elect their favorite candidate since the intimidating big slates no longer existed. North side Anglos could still elect representatives that suited them, but their choices were no longer imposed upon them and upon everyone else in the GGL's secret-lodge style. What is more, council members now had more in common with their constituents and appeared to understand neighborhood problems better. Middle-level groups, especially those long connected with school system politics and with the city's west side state legislative districts, have become important new power bases in community politics. Both of these changes have made city council members more sensitive to the interests of their constituents than they were under the at-large system.

Finally San Antonio politics has become more democratic because district-based representation provides a voice to much more diverse economic, cultural, and service concerns. The diversity among city council members and the greater variety of groups taking part in city politics caused a virtual explosion of discussion of public policy issues. To some, these different voices sounded like a tower of Babel, since in the GGL era councilmen argued little about public policy, having previously been selected for their agreement with certain major goals. GGL councils, basically without challenge, had pursued development by working to attract bureaucratic, non-polluting service industry (military, government, health, and educational institutions) and to stimulate the low-wage tourist industry. Such politics had protected downtown real estate and financial interests. These councils had also promoted steady north side suburban growth, which San Antonio taxpayers subsidized for developers with water, sewer, gas, and electric extensions courtesy of the City Water Board and City Public Service Board. The city's poor, especially Chicanos and blacks, bore the major costs of such economic development policies. Among those costs have been discrimination, deterioration of public services in older areas, high unemployment, and high employment concentration in the low-skilled service sector (see Chapters 2, 3, and 7).

After years of harmony, however, differences of opinion among business leaders about some details of these plans emerged, then sharpened, and eventually undermined the GGL. Then policy discussion broadened even more because COPS boosted previously excluded people into the area, and because the new districting system ensured a voice on the city council to a wider ethnic and economic spectrum. As mentioned above, one vigorous dispute recently boiled up over the efforts of city economic leaders on the Economic Development Foundation to attract industry and the accompanying wage policy. In another, residents of older neighborhoods with inferior and deteriorating services loudly challenged public service board subsidies to unincorporated suburbs. For decades such subsidies have made services more expensive to (often poor) inner-city residents, while making suburban development more profitable.

Other groups have attacked the continued north side development which may threaten the city's underground water supply and the downtown's commercial viability (see Chapter 8). The allocation of capital improvement funding now sparks sharp debate, especially among the victims of poor drainage control. Debate has arisen and intensified as to the wisdom of continued participation by City Public Service in the South Texas Nuclear Project (designed to increase the city's future electrical supply). In short, fundamental and competing economic interests of different economic classes entered the decision-making arena, where the economic elite alone had once held nearly consensual sway.

The sparks that have flown over these and other issues in city council and on other boards simply revealed, to the dismay of some and the glee of others, that alternative policies were being discussed in the light of day. No longer did a narrow business clique impose its self-serving vision upon public policy with no challenge. This does not mean, however, that such challenges always prevailed or that the insurgents gained control. Powerful economic interests continued to dominate key policy-making bodies other than the city council. Indeed, the 1979–81 growth of United San Antonio's program to harmonize development policies represented an attempt to contain challenges to traditionally probusiness public policy in the wider arena of the many governments and pressure groups in the San Antonio area. Nevertheless, between 1975 and 1982, policy alternatives were receiving much more vigorous media and popular scrutiny than in the previous half century. In this light, City Hall wrangling and interest group posturing on issues may be seen as a sign of democracy. Decisions were not being made by mobs in the streets, as some tended to argue in San Antonio's popular press during the late seventies. But it had become less common for public policy to be made uninformed by popular opinion. The chorus in this pluralist heaven had indeed begun to "sing with an upper-class accent," as Schattschneider has said, but at least there is now a chorus.

To summarize, democracy involves citizen participation in decision making, majority control over elected representatives, and free discussion of policy options. San Antonio politics has become somewhat more democratic because it displayed more of these in 1980–82 than during the two decades prior to 1975. But a word of caution is in order. Policy making has become more democratic, but such changes must still be classified as limited. The 1977–81 city councils failed to follow majority preferences many times. For instance, despite 1977 poll data revealing a voter preference for greater city council control over utilities,[24] the council in 1978 scuttled a proposed citizens utility review commission. Nevertheless, with the passing of the GGL and district-based representation, the San Antonio city government has become somewhat more responsive to its constituents. For all their strife, the 1977–81 councils appeared no less competent than other legislative bodies, and may well have been more responsive to their constituents' policy interests than many similar institutions.

Conclusions

Overall, then, there was in 1982 more democracy in San Antonio than during the half century preceding 1975. From about 1925 until 1952, the city had been controlled by a machine of middle-class professional politicians who entrenched themselves in the mayor's and city commissioners' chairs through patronage, vote manipulation, and election fraud. The 1952 council-manager reform corrected such abuses, but opened the way for takeover of the redesigned city government by a narrowly based business elite which then controlled policy to its benefit through the Good Government League. Events of the late seventies introduced new contenders for power into the game and swept away much of the predictability and order that marked the GGL era. But the stability, order, and good manners of elite machine rule should not be confused with civic virtue or universally beneficial public policy. The more democratic nature of policy making under the new system inevitably sparked greater contention over public issues, because new community and class interests had come to impinge upon the decision making.

As of 1977 no single group had the resources—financial, electoral, or organizational—to monopolize public policy. More citizens than ever took part in politics. Previously excluded groups began to get a somewhat fairer shake in terms of public policy outputs. Citizens gained new access to and control over their elected officials. City council members began to make policy in an atmosphere of debate and discussion that reflected their heightened sensitivity to popular preferences. Despite the business community's renewed and reunited efforts to control policy and access to the public agenda through USA, the political game in San Antonio, more than ever before, was being played by a greater fraction of the citizenry.

Need a more democratic future under such a system bring about ever more intense class or ethnic cleavage in San Antonio? Not necessarily. If the economic elite remains committed to the newly pluralistic context for policy making and responsive to certain needs of non-elites, conflicts damaging to the interests of all groups might be avoided. This would require a growth policy that would reduce economic inequality and a willingness to permit political participation and policy influence of groups regardless of ethnic and class lines.

It remains to be seen, however, to what degree such policies can success-fully be implemented because they require more than just symbolic sharing in order to work. The capture of both the White House and the U.S. Senate (1980) and of the Texas Governor's Mansion (1978) by fiscal conser-vatives could undermine the present period of harmony. By 1982 funds from intergovernmental aid programs, which had sustained much of San An-tonio's social and infrastructure spending for years, had begun to disappear. This confronted city policy makers with tough decisions about how to divide a shrinking pie, and set off a flurry of intense lobbying with the Reagan administration by San Antonio officials in order to protect federal income sources.

Declines in the resources needed for continuing the city's growth and in the progressive inclusion of the lower classes, Chicano, and black commu-nities among those who share its benefits seemed much more likely in 1982 than at any time in the previous decade. Not even the Sunbelt growth boom could insulate the San Antonio economy from the 1982 national recession, high interest rates, and the slowdown in several key local indus-tries. This circumstance raised the possibility that the future economic development of the city might fail to ameliorate—or perhaps might even exacerbate—economic inequality, thereby bringing interethnic and class conflict back to the foreground of San Antonio politics. Plotkin has argued that such an outcome seems almost inevitable, and that the USA's "unity strategy" and the apparent decline of conflict after 1979 represent merely a temporary remission in the growth of class-based political conflict in San Antonio.

The prospect for greater future conflict in the city does indeed appear great, given the conservative, purse-tightening changes in the larger politi-cal environment since 1980. The fiscal conservatism of the Reagan admin-istration could well throttle important traditional sources of funding for human and physical services that might be used to buy off disaffected recent and future entrants to the San Antonio political arena. The fact of greater political democracy thus makes the prospect of greater conflict throughout the 1980s likely indeed, then, since these groups have greater access than before and may well become angrier as the eighties wear on. This prospect may well render the 1982–92 decade in San Antonio at least as interesting as, and possibly even more clamorous than, the ten years just passed.

Notes

Preface

1. *Power* has been defined in a myriad of ways, but typically definitions treat it as an asymmetrically distributed resource in social interactions, based upon sanctions for noncompliance with the wishes of the party at advantage. Lewis A. Coser presents a useful summary and review of approaches to this concept in his "The Notion of Power: Theoretical Developments," in L. A. Coser and B. Rosenburg, *Sociological Theory* (New York: Macmillian, 1976), pp. 150–61. With Coser, we wish to distinguish power from authority, which involves a capacity to decide based upon status within formal institutions. Power, the ability to compel, may transcend institutional authority. Likewise, power is much more than influence, which is largely persuasive rather than compelling.

2. In addition to Chapters 1, 5, 6, 8, and 10 of this volume, see: Luther Lee Sanders, *How to Win Elections in San Antonio the Good Government Way, 1955–1971* (San Antonio: Department of Urban Studies, St. Mary's University, 1975); Charles L. Cotrell, *Municipal Services Equalization in San Antonio, Texas: Exploration in China Town* (San Antonio: Department of Urban Studies, St. Mary's University, 1976); Sidney Plotkin, "Democratic Change in the Urban Political Economy: San Antonio's Edwards Aquifer Controversy," *Texas Journal of Political Studies* 1 (Fall 1978): 4–31; Arnold Fleischmann, "Sunbelt Boosterism: The Politics of Postwar Growth and Annexation in San Antonio," in David C. Perry and Alfred J. Watkins, eds., *The Rise of the Sunbelt Cities* (Beverly Hills: Sage, 1977), pp. 151–68.

3. Paul Burka, "The Second Battle of the Alamo," *Texas Monthly*, December 1977, pp. 138–43, 218–38; see also Cotrell, *Municipal Services Equalization*, and Plotkin, "Democratic Change in the Urban Political Economy."

4. We usually employ the term *class* not in its economic sense, referring to social strata defined by the standing of their members with relation to the system of production, but rather in the Weberian tradition of status groups. Nevertheless, in

San Antonio, there has traditionally been a considerable overlap between certain class strata based on status and upon production relations. For example, there exists a high correlation between the social status elites (based on family position affiliations and wealth) and economic elites (based on ownership of capital). Likewise, among the lowest-ranked and poorest social status groups in San Antonio—the Anglo, Mexican-American, and black poor—one finds a high concentration of proletarians and subproletarians. For more on class theory, see Reinhard Bendix, "Inequality and Social Structure: A Comparison of Marx and Weber," *American Sociological Review* 39 (April 1974): 149–61.

    5. See Ozzie G. Simmons, *Anglo Americans and Mexican Americans in South Texas* (New York: Arno, 1974); and Burka, "The Second Battle of the Alamo"; Sanders, *How to Win Elections;* Cotrell, *Municipal Services Equalization;* and John A. Booth, "San Antonio: From Machine to Coalition Politics, 1925–1979," in Ernest Crain, Charles Deaton, and William Earl Maxwell, *The Challenge of Texas Politics (St. Paul: West, 1980), pp. 359–63.*

Chapter One

    1. Richard C. Wade, *The Urban Frontier: The Rise of Western Cities, 1790–1830* (Cambridge: Harvard University Press, 1959), pp. 332–36; Howard P. Chudacoff, *The Evolution of American Urban Society* (Englewood Cliffs, N.J.: Prentice-Hall, 1975), p. 33.

    2. David C. Perry and Alfred J. Watkins, "Three Theories of American Urban Development: Introduction," in David C. Perry and Alfred J. Watkins, eds., *The Rise of the Sunbelt Cities,* Urban Affairs Annual Reviews, vol. 14 (Beverly Hills: Sage, 1977), p. 15.

    3. Alfred J. Watkins and David C. Perry, "Regional Change and the Impact of Uneven Urban Development," in Perry and Watkins, *Rise of the Sunbelt Cities,* pp. 19–54; David U. Gordon, "Class Struggle and the Stages of American Urban Development," ibid., pp. 55–82; Walt W. Rostow, "Regional Change in the Fifth Kondratieff Upswing," ibid. pp. 83–103.

    4. Watkins and Perry, "Regional Change," pp. 27–48.

    5. Wyatt W. Belcher, *The Economic Rivalry between St. Louis and Chicago* (New York: Columbia University Press, 1947); Julius Rubin, *Canal or Railroad: Imitation and Innovation in the Response to the Erie Canal in Philadelphia, Baltimore, and Boston* (Philadelphia: American Philosophical Society, 1961).

    6. The literature on urban politics from an historical perspective has traditionally viewed local conflicts as battles between reformers and bosses over such issues as honesty, efficiency, and civil service reform in government. But that viewpoint overlooks the broader context of those issues. As we hope to demonstrate in this paper, conflicting ideas about the form and substance of urban growth often shaped

political controversies and influenced their outcomes more fundamentally than ephemeral disputes over the traditional issues associated with bossism.

7. Thomas A. Baylis, Chapter 5, this volume. Our definition of elites, like that of Baylis, combines elements of the "decisional" and "nondecisional" approaches to community power, eschewing the "reputational" approach. See, for example, Charles M. Bonjean and Michael D. Grimes, "Community Power: Issues and Findings," in J. Lopreato and L. S. Lewis, eds., *Social Stratification* (New York: Harper and Row, 1974), pp. 377–90; Robert Presthus, *Men at the Top* (New York: Oxford University Press, 1964); Robert A. Dahl, *Who Governs?* (New Haven: Yale University Press, 1961); and Peter Bachrach and Morton Baratz, "Two Faces of Power," *American Political Science Review* 56 (December 1962): 947–52. For a more detailed discussion and further citations, see Baylis's essay.

8. Watkins and Perry, "Regional Change," p. 29

9. Kenneth W. Wheeler, *To Wear a City's Crown: The Beginnings of Urban Growth in Texas, 1836–1865* (Cambridge: Harvard University Press, 1968), pp. 35–45, 151, 155–58, 164; Ray F. Broussard, *San Antonio during the Texas Republic*, Southwestern Studies Monograph no. 18 (El Paso: Texas Western Press, 1967).

10. This description of the elite's early development has been compiled from an analysis of data in Frederick C. Chabot, *With the Makers of San Antonio* (San Antonio: Privately printed, 1937); and in "Mayors and Aldermen, 1836–1915," vertical file, San Antonio Public Library.

11. Caroline M. Remy, "A Study of the Transition of San Antonio from a Frontier to an Urban Community, 1875–1900" (master's thesis, Trinity University, 1960); T. R. Fehrenbach, *The San Antonio Story* (Tulsa: Continental Heritage, 1978), pp. 103–64.

12. "Mayors and Aldermen, 1836–1915."

13. Remy, "Transition of San Antonio," chap. 1.

14. Watkins and Perry, "Regional Change," pp. 32–38.

15. Randall L. Waller, "The Callaghan Machine and San Antonio Politics, 1885–1912" (Master's thesis, Texas Tech University, 1973), pp. 30–43.

16. See Remy, "Transition of San Antonio," chap. 3; and Waller, "The Callaghan Machine," passim.

17. This structure, now restored, once housed the Spanish colonial system's provincial governor.

18. *San Antonio Express*, February 1, 1889; Mary B. Edelman, "Bryan Callaghan II: His Early Political Career, 1885–1899" (Master's thesis, Trinity University, 1971), passim.

19. George H. Paschal, Jr., "The Public Service Aspect of the Medical Career of Dr. Frank Paschal in San Antonio, 1893–1925" (Master's thesis, Trinity University, 1956).

20. Waller, "The Callaghan Machine," pp. 87–108.

21. Ibid., pp. 97–104.

22. Ibid., p. 103.

23. Ibid., pp. 109–10.

24. Ibid., p. 115, table 7, indicates that Callaghan's organization reestablished support in critical wards which had been lost in 1899. The change in the organization's composition is still largely conjecture, based upon an analysis of the backgrounds of aldermen elected with Callaghan in 1905 using the list from "Mayors and Aldermen, 1836–1915" and San Antonio's city directory for 1905. On Callaghan's changed attitude toward expenditures, see the *San Antonio Express*, January 1, 1911, p. 9. See also Stacy R. Lester, "Bryan Callaghan versus the Reformers, 1905–1912" (Master's thesis, Trinity University, 1976).

25. *San Antonio Express*, September 7, 1911, pt. 4, p. 3.

26. Ibid., January 1, 1911, p. 9.

27. Ibid., May 7, 1911, p. 3; July 9, 1911, p. 3; September 7, 1911, pp. 11–12; Waller, "The Callaghan Machine," p. 127; *San Antonio Express*, May 3, 1911; Lester, "Callaghan versus the Reformers," pp. 66–71.

28. *San Antonio Express*, February 5, 1911.

29. Waller, "The Callaghan Machine," p. 127; *San Antonio Express*, May 3, 1911, p. 18; and Lester, "Callaghan versus the Reformers," pp. 57–58.

30. *San Antonio Express*, April 30, 1913, p. 3; May 4, 1913, p. 6; May 8, 1913, p. 5; May 14, 1913.

31. Brown numbered among his supporters Albert Steves, scion of one of San Antonio's oldest families and businessman who sat on the board of directors of the Alamo National Bank; Clinton Kearney, a civil engineer and a director of the Gross National Bank; and Louis Heuermann, a leading merchant and director of the Casino Association, one of the city's most prestigious private clubs. Steves would serve as the first police and fire commissioner; Kearney and Heuermann served consecutively as street commissioner after the charter change. For additional details see Frank Bushick, *Glamorous Days* (San Antonio: Naylor, 1934), and Lester, "Callaghan versus the Reformers," pp. 57–58.

32. The *San Antonio Express*, February 14, 1914, p. 18, contains a summary of the battles within the elite, which lasted from the fall of 1913 until the charter election. See also ibid., January 16, 1914, pp. 1–2. For a general study of the commission idea, see Bradley R. Rice, *Progressive Cities: The Commission Government Movement in America, 1901–1920* (Austin: University of Texas Press, 1977).

33. All these data came from Frank Bushick, *Glamorous Days*, and city directories of the perod.

34. Clinton Uhr, Bexar County Treasurer, interview, March 10, 1978.

35. Richard B. Henderson, *Maury Maverick: A Political Biography* (Austin: University of Texas Press, 1970, pp. 47–48); Nowlin Randolph, *The Citizens League Will Win Again* (San Antonio: Marjorie McGehee Randolph, 1973); Ozzie G. Simmons, *Anglo Americans and Mexican Americans in South Texas,* (New York: Arno, 1974); Uhr interview; Walter W. McAllister, interviewed by William McLellan, April 7, 1977; Melvin Sance, Institute of Texas Cultures, interview, March 20, 1978;

Robert Green, Bexar County Clerk, interview, March 1, 1978; Larry Dickens, "The Political Role of Mexican Americans in San Antonio, Texas" (Ph.D. diss., Texas Tech University, 1969), pp. 47–48.

36. A model for this effort was a similar donation of land to the U.S. Army for the expansion of Fort Sam Houston (1865–72). E. A. Kindervater, "Fort Sam Houston: A Historical Sketch," MS, Ft. Sam Houston Papers, San Antonio Public Library; John E. Conner, *The Centennial Record of the San Antonio Army Service Forces Depot, 1845–1945* (San Antonio: n.p., 1945), p. 6.

37. William D. Angel, Jr., "To Make a City: Entrepreneurship on the Sunbelt Frontier," in Perry and Watkins, *Rise of the Sunbelt Cities*, pp. 109–28.

38. Randolph, *Citizens League*, pp. 6, 11, 25.

39. Henderson, *Maury Maverick*, pp. 52–57.

40. See articles in the *San Antonio Express* dated June 30, 1939, p. 12A; July 29, 1939, p. 8; July 17, 1939, p. 1; July 20, 1939, pp. 7–8; October 6, 1931, p. 10A; October 7, 1939, p. 8A; February 15, 1935, p. 16; February 21, 1935, p. 9; March 23, 1935, p. 7; January 22, 1936, p. 18; May 8, 1936, p. 14; March 13, 1937, p. 18; November 26, 1940, pp. 1–16D.

41. Earle Mayfield, in the *Bexar Facts*, cited in Henderson, *Maury Maverick*, p. 57.

42. Henderson, *Maury Maverick*, pp. 48–49; Randolph, *Citizens League*, pp. 18–19.

43. Such organizations had by this time enjoyed a long history in San Antonio, with elite factions coalescing into transitory "leagues" or political tickets around many issues and campaigns. The Citizen's League and Wednesday Club represent an important departure: their relative permanence produced greater success and a model for the GGL.

44. Henderson, *Maury Maverick*, p. 50; Randolph, *Citizens League*, chap. 2.

45. Randolph, *Citizens League*, p. 19.

46. *In Search of Good Government* (San Antonio: Good Government League, 1972), p. 5; McAllister interview by McLellan; Henderson, *Maury Maverick*, pp. 50–52; and Randolph, *Citizens League*.

47. Randolph, *Citizens League*, pp. 27, 50.

48. Ibid., pp. 80–87.

49. *In Search of Good Government*, p. 5; see also McAllister interview (McLellan); and Walter W. McAllister, Jr., interview on WOAI Radio, "Insight," April 1, 1978.

50. McAllister interviews (McLellan, WOAI).

51. Henderson, *Maury Maverick*, pp. 61–62, 192.

52. Ibid., pp. 188–231; see esp. pp. 229–30.

53. *In Search of Good Government*; McAllister interviews (McLellan, WOIA): Henderson, *Maury Maverick*, pp. 230–31. One incident turned to civil libertarian Maverick's disadvantage was the turmoil resulting from his approval of the use of the Municipal Auditorium for a Communist party meeting.

54. Watkins and Perry, "Regional Change," p. 45; and see also pp. 39–51, and Rostow, "Regional Change."

55. Henderson, *Maury Maverick,* pp. 188–231; Works Progress Administration, *Along the San Antonio River* (San Antonio: City of San Antonio, 1941); Adina de Zavala, *The Alamo: Where the Last Man Died* (San Antonio: Naylor, 1956), pp. 47–54.

56. Paul Burka, "The Second Battle of the Alamo," *Texas Monthly,* December 1977, pp. 138–43, 218–38; and Clinton Uhr interview.

57. The military affairs committee dates from 1894, as a part of the Chamber of Commerce's predecessor organization. In 1937 the committee began to promote the city as a retirement center for military officers. See Charles Smith, "San Antonio Chamber of Commerce: A History of Its Organization for Community Development and Service, 1910–1960" (Master's thesis, Trinity University, 1965), pp. 59–64, 90–91. See also Kindervater, "Fort Sam Houston," and Conner, *Centennial Record.*

58. Arnold Fleischmann, "Sunbelt Boosterism: The Politics of Postwar Growth and Annexation in San Antonio," in Perry and Watkins, *Rise of the Sunbelt Cities,* p. 153.

59. Ibid., pp. 152–54.

60. Ibid., pp. 152–55; and see note 40 above.

61. *San Antonio Express,* April 25, 1949, p. 1A; April 26, 1949, p. 1A; April 26, 1949, p. 1B; April 29, 1949, p. 1A; L. Tucker Gibson and Robert R. Ashcroft, "Political Organization in a Nonpartisan Election System" (Paper delivered at the annual meeting of the Southwestern Political Science Association, Dallas, March 30–April 2, 1977).

62. *San Antonio Express,* April 29, 1949, p. 1A; Luther Lee Sanders, *How to Win Elections in San Antonio the Good Government Way, 1955–1971* (San Antonio: Department of Urban Studies, St. Mary's University, 1975), p. 5.

63. *San Antonio Express,* May 13, 1951, p. 1.

64. *In Search of Good Government,* p. 10.

65. *San Antonio Express,* December 11, 1951, p. 6.

66. Gibson and Ashcroft, "Political Organization," p. 28; Fleischmann, "Sunbelt Boosterism," pp. 154–57.

67. *In Search of Good Government;* Fleischmann, "Sunbelt Boosterism," pp. 157–58.

68. *In Search of Good Government,* p. 17. Names of those on which data in this paragraph are based were drawn from pp. 8–19 of ibid. and from city directories to obtain residence and occupation in 1952–53. Those included were involved in the Council-Manager Association and the founding of the GGL.

69. Sanders, *How to Win Elections,* p. 10, n. 4.

70. Ibid., pp. 9–13.

71. Gibson and Ashcroft, "Political Organization," pp. 6–7.

72. Ibid., pp. 9–17.

73. Sanders, *How to Win Elections,* p. 14.

74. Ibid., pp. 14–17.

75. Ibid., pp. 27–61.

76. John A. Booth, "San Antonio: From Machine to Coalition Politics, 1925–1979," in Ernest Crain et al., eds., *The Challenge of Texas Politics* (St. Paul: West, 1980), pp. 359–63.

77. Sanders, *How to Win Elections;* Green interview; *San Antonio Express,* April 13, 1966, p. 80; April 24, 1966, p. 2B; April 17, 1966, p. 2B; March 31, 1966, p. 12B: March 27, 1966, p. 85; March 10, 1966, p. 19G; October 30, 1966, p. 12A; November 6, 1966, p. 3D.

78. Similar shifts are described by Randolph, in *Citizens League,* for the Citizens League's Frank C. Davis, Robert Uhr, and Albert Hauser.

79. Ibid.; see Randolph's discussion of vacillation with the Citizen's League over whether or not the league law enforcement officials should prosecute gamblers. See also Chapter 10 of this volume.

80. David C. Perry and Alfred J. Watkins, "People, Profit, and the Rise of the Sunbelt Cities," and Peter A. Lupsha and William J. Siembieda, "The Poverty of Public Services in the Land of Plenty: An Analysis and Interpretation," both in Perry and Watkins, *Rise of the Sunbelt Cities,* pp. 277–305, and 169–90, respectively.

81. See Remy, "Transition of San Antonio," and Waller, "Callaghan Machine."

82. Burka, "Second Battle."

83. Lupsha and Siembieda, "Poverty of Public Services," pp. 180–81.

84. Charles L. Cottrell, *Municipal Services Equalization in San Antonio, Texas: Exploration in China Town* (San Antonio: Department of Urban Studies, St. Mary's University, 1976).

85. Harold Arthur Shapiro. "Workers of San Antonio, Texas, 1900–1940" (Ph.D. diss., University of Texas at Austin, 1952); and Kenneth Walker, "The Pecan Shellers of San Antonio and Mechanization," *Southwestern Historical Quarterly* 64 (July 1965): 44–58.

Chapter Two

1. U.S. Bureau of the Census, *1970 Census of Population and Housing: Characteristics of the Population,* Part 1, "General Demographic Trends for Metropolitan Areas, 1960 to 1970."

2. Ibid.

3. The Fantus Company, *Business Climate of the States* (New York: Fantus, for the Illinois Manufacturers' Association, 1976).

4. The twenty-year time span chosen for this analysis, 1956 to 1976, is long enough to encompass a whole series of relevant events—postwar boom, the Vietnam conflict, the energy crisis, the Sunbelt phenomenon, and the period of the Good Government League in San Antonio. Bexar County is taken as the unit of analysis for San Antonio because of the availability of data at the county level.

5. Unfortunately, military and other government employment are not included in these subsectors in U.S. Department of Labor, *County Business Patterns: Texas* (1956, 1976); however, such data were obtained elsewhere (see below).

6. The Spearman rank-order correlation (r_s) between the two sets of rankings is 0.832, a moderately strong correlation.

7. San Antonio Economic Development Foundation, *Greater San Antonio Manufacturers Directory, 1976* (San Antonio: EDF, 1976).

8. Greater San Antonio Chamber of Commerce, Economic Research Department, "San Antonio Military Statistics for Fiscal Year Ending September 30, 1977."

9. Thomas J. Murray, "Booming San Antonio," *Dun's Review* 114 (July 1979): 57–61.

10. John W. Alexander, "The Basic–Non-Basic Concept of Urban Economic Functions," *Economic Geography* 30 (1954): 246–61; Hans Blumenfeld, "The Economic Base of the Metropolis: Critical Remarks on the 'Non-Basic' Concept," in Paul D. Spreiregen, ed., *The Modern Metropolis: Selected Essays by Hans Blumenfeld* (Cambridge: MIT Press, 1967); and Charles M. Tiebout, *The Community Economic Base Study,* Committee for Economic Development, Supplementary Paper no. 16 (New York, 1962).

11. Homer Hoyt, *The Structure and Growth of Residential Neighborhoods in American Cities* (Washington, D.C.: U.S. Federal Housing Administration, 1939).

12. Richard B. Andrews, "Mechanics of the Urban Economic Base: A Classification of Base Types," *Land Economics* 29 (1953): 343–49.

13. San Antonio Convention and Visitors Bureau, Visitor Information Center, *Monthly Reports,* 1976–78.

14. Texas State Department of Highways and Public Transportation, Travel and Information Division, "1978 Report on the Texas Visitor Industry," May 1979, pp. 22–28.

15. Stanley A. Arbingast et al., in *Atlas of Texas* (Austin: Bureau of Business Research, University of Texas, 1976), p. 108.

16. Edward J. Taaffe, "Air Transportation and United States Urban Distribution," *Geographical Review* 46 (April 1956): 219–39; Charles P. Zlatkovich, "Air Travel Patterns and Regional Orientations" *Texas Business Review* 51 (October 1977): 225–31.

17. Edward J. Taaffe and Howard L. Gauthier, Jr., *Geography of Transportation* (Englewood Cliffs, N.J.: Prentice-Hall, 1973), pp. 75–83.

18. Howard L. Green, "Hinterland Boundaries of New York and Boston in Southern New England," *Economic Geography* 31 (1955): 283–300; Phillip D. Phillips, "Newspaper Circulation as a Measure of Metropolitan Influence and Dominance," *Southeastern Geographer* 14 (May 1974): 17–25.

19. Wade Harrington, Research Department of the *San Antonio Light,* interview, October 1978.

20. ABC Audit Report, *Newspaper: "The Light"; "The Express and News"* (Chicago: Audit Bureau of Circulations, 1957 and 1977); and estimates made from decennial data in the U.S. Bureau of the Census, *Census of Population,* 1950, 1960, and 1970.

21. Ibid.

22. "Bank Holding Company Study Completed," *Voice* (monthly publication of the Federal Reserve Bank of Dallas), July 1978, pp. 9–13.

23. Don Heath, "San Antonio Has Mexican Investors," *San Antonio Light*, December 17, 1978; and Geoffrey Leavenworth, "Behind the Foreign Frenzy to Buy Texas Land," *Texas Business* 4 (November 1979): 44–49.

24. Marina Pisano, "The New Carpetbaggers," *SA Magazine*, January 1978, pp. 34–41.

25. Greater San Antonio Chamber of Commerce, *Directory of Largest Employers*, various editions, 1973–78.

26. Ibid.

27. San Antonio Economic Development Foundation, *Greater San Antonio Manufacturers Directory, 1976*.

28. Texas Highway Department et al., *San Antonio Metropolitan Area Traffic Survey, 1956* (Austin: Highway Planning Survey, 1956); and City of San Antonio et al., *San Antonio–Bexar County Urban Transportation Study* (Austin: Texas Highway Department, 1969).

29. John Campbell, "San Antonio: A Century of Progress, 1870–1970" (Position paper for "San Antonio: A Brief Historical, Physical, and Socioeconomic Profile," edited portfolio of papers for Geography 4953, "The Geography of Texas," Spring 1978, University of Texas at San Antonio).

30. U.S. Bureau of the Census, *Census of Population and Housing, 1970*.

31. Dudley L. Poston and Jeffrey Passel, "Texas Population in 1970: Racial Residential Segregation in Cities," in *Texas Resources and Industries* (Austin: Bureau of Business Research, University of Texas at Austin, 1975), pp. 49–54.

Chapter Three

1. The Census Bureau's designation of Spanish-language or Spanish-surname population does not permit precise statements about Mexican Americans owing to the inclusion of other Hispanic people. Nevertheless, the vast majority of Hispanics in San Antonio are of Mexican origin. The terms "Mexican American," "Hispanic," and "Spanish surname," therefore, will be used interchangeably.

2. See Edward Murguia, *Assimilation, Colonialism, and the Mexican-American People* (Austin: University of Texas Press, 1975), chap. 6, for a comparison of metropolitan areas with large numbers of people of Mexican origin.

3. The discrepancy in the patterns for education and income between blacks and Mexican Americans is largely accounted for by the larger percentage of female-headed families among blacks (43% versus 17% in the United States, 1978). U.S. Bureau of the Census, *Current Population Reports*, P-60, no. 120 (November 1979), pp. 6–8.

4. These differences in occupational distribution may be summarized more concisely, but also more technically, with the index of occupational dissimilarity. This

index ranges from o, indicating equality of distribution, to 100, indicating total occupational segregation. Based on the percentages in Table 3.1, the index of occupational dissimilarity comparing blacks to Anglos is 38.6. The index comparing Mexican Americans to Anglos is 31.1. The occupations of blacks, therefore, are somewhat more unequally distributed in comparison to Anglos than are those of the Mexican Americans. See Henry S. Shyrock, Jacob S. Siegel, et al., *The Methods and Materials of Demography* (Washington, D.C.: U.S. Printing Office, 1973), pp. 179, 232–33, 262.

5. See, for example, Tatcho Mindiola, Jr., "Age and Income Discrimination against Mexican Americans and Blacks in Texas, 1960 and 1970," *Social Problems* 27 (December 1979): 196–208; Dudley L. Posten and David Alvirez, "On the Cost of Being a Mexican-American Worker," *Social Science Quarterly* 53 (March 1973): 697–709; Dudley L. Posten, David Alvirez, and Marta Tienda, "Earning Differences between Anglo and Mexican-American Male Workers in 1960 and 1970: Changes in the 'Cost' of Being Mexican American," *Social Science Quarterly* 57 (December 1976): 618–636; Otis Dudley Duncan, "Inheritance of Poverty or Inheritance of Race," in Daniel P. Moynihan, ed., *On Understanding Poverty* (New York: Basic Books, 1968, pp. 85–109); Paul M. Siegel, "The Cost of Being Negro," *Sociological Inquiry* 35 (Winter 1965): 41–57.

6. See especially Steven Thernstrom, *Poverty and Progress: Social Mobility in a Nineteenth-Century City* (Cambridge: Harvard University Press, 1964) and *The Other Bostonians: Poverty and Progress in the American Metropolis, 1880–1970* (Cambridge: Harvard University Press, 1976). Also, Joseph J. Barton, *Peasants and Strangers: Italians, Romanians, and Slovacks in an American City, 1890–1950* (Cambridge: Harvard University Press, 1963). More general sociological discussion is provided in Milton Gordon, *Assimilation in American Life: The Role of Religion and National Origins* (New York: Oxford University Press, 1964). For material focused on Mexicans, see Carey McWilliams, *North from Mexico: The Spanish-Speaking People of the United States* (New York: Greenwood, 1968); Juan Gomez-Quinones and Luis Leobardo Arroyo, "On the State of Chicano History: Observations on Its Development, Interpretations, and Theory, 1970–1974," *Western Historical Quarterly* 7 (April 1976): 155–85; and Edward Murguia, *Assimilation, Colonialism*.

7. Gomez-Quinones and Arroyo, "On the State of Chicano History"; Arthur F. Corwin, "Mexican Emigration History, 1900–1970: Literature and Research," *Latin American Research Review* 8 (Summer 1973): 3–24; Juan Gomez-Quinones, "Toward a Perspective on Chicano History," *Aztlan* 2 (Fall 1971): 1–48; Rodolfo Acuna, *Occupied America: The Chicano's Struggle toward Liberation* (San Francisco: Canfield, 1972). For a concise discussion of the colonialism perspective, see Murguia, *Assimilation, Colonialism*, pp. 6–9.

8. Murguia, *Assimilation, Colonialism*, p. 74.

9. See especially Peter Blau and Otis Dudley Duncan, *The American Occupational Structure* (New York: John Wiley and Sons, 1967); Otis Dudley Duncan, David L. Featherman, and Beverly Duncan, *Socioeconomic Background and Achievement* (New

York: Seminar, 1972); William H. Sewell and Robert M. Hauser, *Education, Occupation, and Earnings: Achievement in the Early Career* (New York: Academic 1975); Richard J. Harris, "The Rewards of Migration for Income Change and Income Attainment," *Social Science Quarterly* 62 (June 1981): 275–93.

10. Gordon, *Assimilation in American Life*, pp. 60–83; Murguia, *Assimilation, Colonialism*, pp. 2–6. For an alternative interpretation of these types of trends based on a convergence model, see Richard J. Harris, "An Examination of the Effects of Ethnicity, Socioeconomic Status, and Generation on Familism and Sex Role Orientations," *Journal of Comparative Family Studies* 11 (Spring 1980): 173–93.

11. For detailed discussions of these developments see Chapters 4, 5, 9, and 10.

12. Gordon, *Assimilation in American Life*, pp. 46–47; Murguia, *Assimilation, Colonialism*, p. 23; Harris, "An Examination of the Effects of Ethnicity."

13. Alwyn Barr, "Occupational and Geographic Mobility in San Antonio, 1870–1900," *Social Science Quarterly* 51 (December 1970): 396–403.

14. Ibid., pp. 398–400. About 61 percent of native whites and 69 percent of European immigrants were manual laborers.

15. Richard Romo, "Work and Restlessness: Occupational and Spatial Mobility among Mexicanos in Los Angeles, 1918–28," *Pacific Historical Review* 46 (May 1977): 157–80.

16. Fernando Penalosa and Edward C. McDonagh, "Social Mobility in a Mexican American Community," *Social Forces* 44 (June 1966): 498–505.

17. For detailed description of the sample, see Crandall A. Shifflett with Richard J. Harris, *Occupational Mobility and the Process of Assimilation of Mexican Immigrants to San Antonio, Texas*, DOL 21-48-78-06 (Springfield, Va.: National Technical Information Service, 1979), PB-299 862.

18. See James A. Davis, *General Social Surveys, 1972–1978* (Chicago: National Opinion Research Center; New Haven: Roper Public Opinion Research Center, 1979). The original samples are full probability surveys of the noninstitutionalized English-speaking population of the continental United States.

19. Some words of caution are in order about the comparisons between the sample of Mexican Americans in San Antonio and the Anglo sample in southern SMSAs. Occupational attainment and mobility are largely a function of the range of occupational opportunities available in different communities. These may vary according to size of community and even between communities of the same size. Traditionally, it is assumed that rural or smaller communities have fewer opportunities than larger metropolitan areas. See, for example, Blau and Duncan, *The American Occupational Structure*. Furthermore, cities with an extensive industrial base are thought to provide greater opportunities for occupational advancement than less industrial cities. San Antonio is a large, service-oriented city, possibly providing greater opportunities than smaller communities, but fewer opportunities than larger, more industrialized cities. (See Chapter 2 for a more detailed assessment of some of these issues.) In the sample of Anglos in southern SMSAs some of the communities of residence are smaller than San Antonio and some are larger. Some

224 Notes to Pages 59–60

have a more extensive industrial base. It is impossible to sort out all of the differences. For this analysis it is assumed that these factors balance each other and that the samples provide useful comparison groups.

20. For a more detailed description of this sample, see Richard J. Harris, "A Comparative Analysis of Hispanic and Non-Hispanic Occupational Mobility in San Antonio: 1948–1978" (Unpublished manuscript, University of Texas at San Antonio).

21. Unfortunately, the city directory does not contain information on such crucial determinants of occupational status as age and education. The analysis of the determinants of occupational position, therefore, is restricted to the smaller samples.

22. See Shifflett with Harris, *Occupational Mobility and the Process of Assimilation,* and Harris, "A Comparative Analysis."

23. The weights were established in direct proportion to the actual sample size of 132. Therefore, they do not bias inferential tests of statistical significance. Comparing weighted and unweighted analyses, the weights have a substantial impact on the estimates of occupational mobility per se, but a negligible impact on the correlation and regression analyses that follow. The actual weights used are as follows: professionals and managers—0.61, clerical and sales—0.84, skilled labor—1.84, and unskilled labor—0.78. These weights produce a percentage distribution by occupation almost identical to that of the Spanish-surnamed males in the 1970 census of San Antonio.

24. Occupational position is an ordinal variable coded as follows: 1—unskilled labor, 2—skilled labor, 3—clerical or sales, 4—professional or managerial. Although correlation and regression analysis generally assume interval or ratio variables, there is a growing literature suggesting that these techniques are acceptable with ordinal data. See, for example: George W. Bohrnstedt and T. Michael Carter, "Robustness in Regression Analysis," in H. Costner, ed., *Sociological Methodology, 1971* (San Francisco: Jossey-Bass, 1971), pp. 118–46; Edgar F. Borgatta and George W. Bohrnstedt, "Level of Measurement—Once Over Again," in George W. Bohrnstedt and Edgar F. Borgetta, eds., *Social Measurement: Current Issues* (Beverly Hills: Sage, 1981), pp. 23–37; Kenneth A. Bollen and Kenney H. Barb, "Pearson's *R* and Coarsely Categorized Measures," *American Sociological Review* 46 (April 1981): 232–39. To test the appropriateness of the analysis, Pearson's product moment correlations were compared to Kendall's tau, a nonparametric rank order correlation coefficient, with very similar results (e.g., the correlation between current occupation and respondent's education for the Mexican Americans in San Antonio is 0.29 with both Pearson's *r* and Kendall's tau). Also, note the similarity between Pearson's *r* and Kendall's tau *b* in Tables 3.3 and 3.4.

25. See John R. Weeks and Joseph Spielberg Benitez, "The Ethnodemography of Midwestern Mexican Americans," in Stanley A. West and June Macklin, eds., *The Chicano Experience* (Boulder: Westview, 1979), pp. 229–51. An interesting evaluation of the fertility/socioeconomic status relationship can be found in Leo R. Chavez,

"From Labor Camps to Chicana Feminism: Recent Research on Chicanos," *Contemporary Sociology* 10 (November 1981): 765–67.

26. Recall that occupation is measured on a four-point scale from unskilled (low-status) to professional/managerial (high-status) jobs. (See note 24). Therefore, the higher the median or mean for a particular group, the larger the proportion in high-status occupations, and vice-versa.

27. Evidence is also available on the experience of grandfathers in the Shifflett sample. About 84 percent of the grandfathers ended their occupational careers where they started, mostly as unskilled laborers. The number of cases is so small ($N = 45$), however, that this finding must be treated with caution. Nevertheless, the overwhelming static pattern is consistent with other studies, and it seems safe to conclude that grandfathers were much less mobile than subsequent generations. These findings may indicate that opportunities have improved for each succeeding generation. No comparable data are available for Anglos.

28. See note 4 for the discussion of the index of dissimilarity.

29. Shifflett with Harris, *Occupational Mobility and the Process of Assimilation.*

30. See, for example, Blau and Duncan, *The American Occupational Structure;* Duncan, Featherman, and Duncan, *Socioeconomic Background and Achievements;* Sewell and Hauser, *Education, Occupation, and Earnings.*

31. Gordon, *Assimilation in American Life;* Murguia, *Assimilation, Colonialism;* and Arnold M. Rose, *Migrants in Europe: Problems of Acceptance and Adjustment* (Minneapolis: University of Minnesota Press, 1969).

32. These variables are correlated with each other at -0.52, and language problems are correlated with education at -0.71.

Chapter Four

1. Norton Long, "Aristotle and the Study of Local Politics," *Social Research* 24 (Autumn 1957): 287–310.

2. David C. Perry and Alfred J. Watkins, eds. *The Rise of the Sunbelt Cities* (Beverly Hills: Sage, 1977).

3. Ricardo Gonazlez Cedillo, "The Impact of Restrictive Deed Provisions on Racial/Ethnic Segregation Patterns in the San Antonio Metropolitan Area" (Unpublished paper, Department of Urban Studies, Trinity University, 12 May 1975).

4. Charles L. Cotrell, *Municipal Services Equalization in San Antonio, Texas: Exploration in Chinatown* (San Antonio: Department of Urban Studies, St. Mary's University, 1976).

5. Ibid., pp. 12–13.

6. Bill Crane, "San Antonio: Pluralistic City and Monolithic Government," in Leonard E. Goodall, ed., *Urban Politics in the Southwest* (Tempe: Arizona State University Institute of Public Administration, 1967), pp. 127–42, and "San Antonio Liberalism: Piecing it Together," *Texas Observer,* May 27, 1966, pp. 1–5; Arnold

Fleischmann, "Sunbelt Boosterism: The Politics of Postwar Growth and Annexation in San Antonio," in Perry and Watkins, *Rise of the Sunbelt Cities*, pp. 151–68; Charles Cotrell and R. Michael Stevens, "The 1975 Voting Rights Act and San Antonio, Texas: Toward a Federal Guarantee of a Republican Form of Government," *Publius* 8 (Winter 1978): 79–100.

7. See Booth and Johnson, Chapter 1 in this work, on the origin of the GGL; Gibson, Chapter 6, on aspects of GGL rule; Baylis, Chapter 5, for details on the GGL's composition and eventual demise; and Jones, Chapter 2, and Plotkin, Chapter 8, on how the GGL shaped the city's development patterns and furthered the economic interests of its supporters.

8. The four exceptions to this general pattern are the 1971 council races, when the GGL fielded Leo Mendoza, Gilbert Garza and Felix Trevino, and the 1975 race, when GGL-sponsored Olivia Garza, widow of former councilman Gilbert Garza, ran against D. Ford Nielsen. In none of these races did the GGL candidates have formidable Mexican-American opponents.

9. See Rudolph O. de la Garza and Charles Cotrell, "Internal Colonialism and Chicanos: A Reconceptualization" (Paper delivered at the International Studies Association Convention, Toronto, Canada, 1976); Joe Sekul, "The Birth of a Movement: A Study of the Formation of C.O.P.S. in San Antonio, Texas" (Studies in Politics Series, University of Texas at Austin, 1978); and Paul Burka, "The Second Battle of the Alamo," in *The Texas Monthly Political Reader* (Austin: Sterling Swift, 1978), pp. 244–56.

10. The GGL devoted substantial financial resources to quelling its opposition. From 1971 to 1975, the GGL spent an average of $1.07 per vote in the preliminary elections (an average total of $109,000 per election). In runoff elections held during this same period, the GGL funneled an average of $61,466 to support its candidates, or $0.69 per vote. By contrast, $0.41 was spent per vote in the 1977 elections. See Charles L. Cotrell and Arnold Fleischmann, "The Change from At-Large to District Representation and Political Participation of Minority Groups in Fort Worth and San Antonio, Texas" (Paper presented at the annual meeting of the American Political Science Association, Washington, D.C., August 30–September 3, 1979).

11. Joining the dissident north side businessmen in their effort to defeat the GGL were Glen Hartman, a local TV weatherman who ran on the plank of a need for a city master plan; Nielsen, who ran and lost on the reform slate four years earlier; Al Rhode, a south side businessman; Rev. Claude Black, a prominent black minister who had bolted the GGL shortly after the 1973 election; Richard Teniente, a west side pharmacist; and Bob Billa, a south side businessman.

12. The term "overnight coalition" was coined by the members themselves and obtained in an interview with Glen Hartman.

13. U.S. v. Texas, 384 U.S. 155. For a chronology of historic obstacles to voting in Texas, see U.S. Congress, House Committee on the Judiciary, *Extension of the Voting Rights Act: Hearing before a Subcommittee on Civil and Constitutional Rights on*

H.R. 939, H.R. 2148, H.R. 3247, and H.R. 3501, 94th Cong., 1st sess., 1975, pp. 360, 398, 519, 799, 800 and 853.

14. Carrington v. Rash, 380 U.S. 89 (1965).

15. Kramer v. Union Free School District No. 15, 395 U.S. 621.

16. Hill v. Stone, 421 U.S. 289 (1975).

17. Dunn v. Blumstein, 405 U.S. 330 (1972).

18. Beare v. Smith, 321 F. Supp 1100.

19. Cotrell and Fleischmann, "The Change from At-Large to District Representation."

20. We may easily illustrate the new law's potential for altering the character of the electorate in San Antonio. A comparison of the change in levels of new registrations in San Antonio since 1970 shows a noticeable increase in the number of persons added to the city's voter rolls since 1975, the year of the VRA. Prior to 1975, in years when the major election was for mayor/city council, the average number of new registrations was about 20,000. For years in which Congress is the focus of political interest, approximately 30,000 new registrants become eligible to vote; and about 50,000 joined the rolls in a presidential year. After 1975 new registrations for mayor/council election years rise to nearly 30,000, the number of new voters in a congressional year jumps to over 50,000 and 86,500 were added in the presidential election year. The potential of these new voters to alter completely the character of politics becomes more apparent if we recall that the total number of votes cast in the last five mayor/council races in San Antonio has not exceeded 114,000. An organization that can mobilize only one-fourth (or 20,000) of the 86,500 new voters added in 1976 could clearly shift the balance in a mayoralty contest and would need far fewer numbers to influence the smaller single-member district elections of council persons.

21. U.S. Attorney General, Objection Letter to City of San Antonio. April 2, 1976.

22. Cotrell and Stevens, "The 1975 Voting Rights Act and San Antonio, Texas."

23. Voter registration counts are from official voter registration lists for 1976 provided by the Trinity University computer center. Population counts are from 1970 census tract reports for San Antonio.

24. See Roy Young, *The Place System in Texas Elections* (Austin: Public Affairs Institute of the University of Texas, 1965).

25. A recent survey of Texas home rule cities indicates that 179 of 214 have at-large elections, 156 of 214 employ the numbered place arrangement, and 124 of 214 require a majority runoff. See Charles Cotrell, *A Report on the Participation of Mexican Americans, Blacks, and Females in the Major Political Institutions and Processes of Texas, 1968–78,* vol. 1 (prepared under contract for the U.S. Commission on Civil Rights, San Antonio, Texas, January 1980), chap. 10.

26. The reasons for disproportionately fewer Mexican Americans among registered voters as compared to the overall population might be a combination of (1) the younger average age of the Mexican-American population, yielding proportionately

fewer persons of voting age; (2) lower registration rates—only 41% of the registered voters in San Antonio in 1978 were Spanish-surnamed; and (3) lower turnout rates in Mexican-American precincts—in 1977 30.4% voted in precincts of more than 70% Spanish-surnamed registered voters, and 32.2% voted in precincts of less than 30% Spanish-surnamed registered.

27. Cotrell and Fleischmann, "The Change from At-Large to District Representation," pp. 24–25.

28. The council passed a moratorium on new construction over the Edwards Aquifer recharge zone for eighteen months in June 1977 and later rescinded it when it was declared unconstitutional. See Chapter 8 by Sidney Plotkin in this volume for a historico-political analysis of the aquifer controversy.

29. The percentage of Spanish-surnamed registered voters was computed from voter registration tapes provided by the county clerk's office and a computerized master list of Spanish surnames from the U.S. Bureau of the Census.

Chapter Five

1. Robert Putnam, *The Comparative Study of Elites* (Englewood Cliffs, N.J.: Prentice-Hall, 1976), pp. 165–214.

2. E.g., W. L. Guttsman, *The British Political Elite* (London: MacGibbon and Kee, 1968); Wolfgang Zapf, *Wandlungen der deutschen Elite* (Munich: Piper Verlag, 1966); John A. Armstrong, *The European Administrative Elite* (Princeton: Princeton University Press, 1973).

3. M. Kent Jennings, reexamining the power structure of Atlanta some years after Floyd Hunter's classic study, considers the possibility that his substantially different findings simply reflect changes in the city over time; he largely rejects this explanation, however. See *Community Influentials* (New York: Free Press, 1964), pp. 161–62.

4. Suzanne Keller, *Beyond the Ruling Class* (New York: Random House, 1963).

5. This formulation combines elements of the "nondecision" critique with the decisional approach. See Robert A. Dahl, "A Critique of the Ruling Elite Model," *American Political Science Review* 52 (June 1958): 463–69; Dahl, *Who Governs?* (New Haven: Yale University Press, 1961); Peter Bachrach and Morton Baratz, "Two Faces of Power," *American Political Science Review* 56 (December 1962): 947–52; Robert Presthus, *Men at the Top* (New York: Oxford University Press, 1964), esp. chap. 2.

6. L. Tucker Gibson, "Mayoralty Elections in San Antonio" (Paper delivered at the annual meeting of the Southwestern Political Science Association, Houston, April 12–15, 1978). In 1977 the figures were estimated to be 52.16% Spanish surnamed, 38.8% other white, and 9.04% nonwhite. San Antonio Metropolitan Health District, *Vital Statistics 1973–1977* (San Antonio, 1978), p. 1.

7. See F. Chris Garcia and Rudolph O. de la Garza, *The Chicano Political Experience* (North Scituate, Mass: Duxbury, 1977), pp. 178–85, for a listing and brief

discussion of San Antonio's Chicano organizations as of 1975. A more complete, but older listing (1968) is contained in John Hart Lane, *Voluntary Associations among Mexican-Americans in San Antonio, Texas* (New York: Arno, 1976).

8. See Chapter 9 and the following: Calvin Trilling, "U.S. Journal, San Antonio: Some Elements of Power," *New Yorker*, May 2, 1977, pp. 92–100; Paul Burka, "The Second Battle of the Alamo," *Texas Monthly*, December 1977, pp. 138–43, 218–38; E. D. Yoes, Jr., "COPS Comes to San Antonio," *Progressive*, May 1977, pp. 33–36.

9. Although COPS does not formally endorse candidates, it demands that they appear before its forums and unambiguously support its position on key issues. Those who do not appear, or who qualify their endorsement of COPS' positions, are sharply attacked and have been decisively beaten in the areas in which COPS is active.

10. Nearly 40% of the Anglo work force was classified as professional or managerial by the 1970 census, as opposed to 12% of both the Mexican-American and black workers. However, 36.3% of the Mexican Americans and 28.6% of the blacks were classified as white collar workers (professional, managerial, sales, and clerical) and an additional 14.5% of the Mexican Americans and 29.1% of the blacks were service workers (cleaning, health, food, personal, and protective services). See Chapter 3.

11. *San Antonio*, July 1980, p. 6.

12. See Charles L. Cotrell and R. Michael Stevens, "The 1975 Voting Rights Act and San Antonio, Texas," *Publius* 8 (Winter 1978): 79–99.

13. L. Tucker Gibson, Jr., and Robert R. Ashcroft, "Political Organization in a Nonpartisan Election System" (Paper delivered at the annual meeting of the Southwestern Political Science Association, Dallas, Texas, March 30–April 2, 1977).

14. See ibid. and Luther Lee Sanders, *How to Win Elections in San Antonio the Good Government Way, 1955–1971* (San Antonio: Department of Urban Studies, St. Mary's University, 1975).

15. In 1973 the GGL lost four of nine contests; in 1975, six of nine.

16. See Sanders, *How to Win Elections*, pp. 10–12.

17. Leo Mendoza, who was elected as a GGL councilman in 1971 but left the organization and was reelected in 1973 as an independent, is now a county commissioner.

18. See Kemper Diehl in the *San Antonio Express-News*, February 17, 1974, p. 69. Diehl mentions Bob Sawtelle and Ellis Schapiro as particularly valuable advisors.

19. See Gibson and Ashcroft, "Political Organization," p. 25.

20. See Paul Burka, "Power Politics," *Texas Monthly*, May 1975, pp. 68–97.

21. See the *San Antonio News*, November 24, 1972; *San Antonio Express*, November 23, 1972.

22. *San Antonio Light*, April 28, 1974.

23. *San Antonio News*, April 27, 1973.

24. See the *San Antonio Express*, April 18, 1973, p. 3-A.

25. *San Antonio News*, February 16, 1973, p. 11-A. The process became still more publicized in 1975.

26. The immediate impetus for this demand was the firing, supported by the five, of City Manager Sam Granata, who had originally been appointed at the behest of Becker.

27. *San Antonio Express,* February 15, 1977, p. 9-F.

28. For an alternative interpretation, see Booth, Chapter 10.

29. See Rick Casey, "Council Elections as Important as Race for Mayor," *San Antonio Express-News,* March 15, 1981, p. 1-A.

30. *San Antonio,* August 1980, p. 14.

31. See Rick Casey, "The Seductive Henry C.," *San Antonio Express-News,* February 15, 1981, pp. 1-H, 5-H, 12-H.

32. See Ben King, Jr., "Bernardo Eureste: Bandit or Savior?" *San Antonio Style* (in *San Antonio Express-News*), September 13, 1981, pp. 20–30.

33. "The action is at City Hall. That's where the big decisions are made. That's where the future of this community rests." Former county judge Blair Reeves, quoted in the *San Antonio Express-News,* April 13, 1977, p. 6-H.

34. In 1971, perhaps in an effort to defeat the incumbent independent Mexican-American Councilman, Pete Torres, Gonzalez did endorse the entire GGL ticket. *In Search of Good Government* (San Antonio: Good Government League, 1972), p. 45. In 1981 he announced that he would vote for Cisneros after his son went to work for a rival Mexican-American candidate. *San Antonio Express-News,* March 1, 1981, p. 6-A.

35. Of those listed who are no longer members of the council, only one was defeated for reelection (Ortiz). The rest (Hartman, McDaniel, Pyndus, Steen, Cockrell, Canavan), all Anglos, either resigned in mid-term or chose not to run for reelection. None appear to have left for primarily financial reasons.

36. The important City Public Service Board, which supplies electricity and natural gas to the city, appoints its own members; the mayor, however, is a voting member *ex officio.*

37. See Booth, Chapter 10, who argues that these changes, combined with the decline of the GGL and rising citizen participation, have at least partly democratized San Antonio politics.

38. E.g., Becker, Jim Dement, Cliff Morton, Frank Manupelli, and Ed Harrington.

39. E.g., Ray Ellison, H. B. Zachry, and John Schaefer. "Red" McCombs, an automobile dealer with extensive real estate, publishing, and other interests, is also among the most active and generous supporters of a variety of political candidates.

40. I am grateful to Mr. James Kobersky for some of the following information.

41. See articles by Jim Dolan in the *San Antonio Express-News,* October 26, 1975, pp. 1-H, 3-H.

42. Kemper Diehl in the *San Antonio Express-News,* February 17, 1974, p. 69.

43. "Four days after Cisneros had announced, fellow Councilman John Steen went looking for support and knocking on doors. Steen discovered Cisneros already had been there." *San Antonio Express-News,* December 27, 1981, p. 5-H.

44. See Marina Pisano, "The Kingdom Crowns Its Queen," *SA Magazine*, April 1978, pp. 42–50; Marina Pisano, "Inside San Antonio's High Society Clubs," *SA Magazine*, June 1977, pp. 29–34, 56–57.

45. See Marina Pisano, "The Conservation Society," *SA Magazine*, April 1979, pp. 24–33.

46. On the apparent hostility of San Antonians to unions, particularly in the political arena, see John A. Booth and Richard A. Gambitta, "Myth and Reality in San Antonio Politics," *SA Magazine*, July 1977, pp. 12–13.

47. See Jeff Franks, "S.A.'s Industrial Revolution Stirs Union Ambitions," *San Antonio Express-News*, April 5, 1981, p. 1-G.

48. As it was in the Callaghan era (1885–1912) and under the commission machine (1925–52). See Booth and Johnson, Chapter 1.

Chapter Six

1. For a discussion of commission government and of the events related to the adoption of the current city charter and the development of the Good Government League, see Booth and Johnson, Chapter 1; and *In Search of Good Government* (San Antonio: Good Government League, 1972).

2. San Antonio, *Charter of the City of San Antonio*, Art. V, Sec. 47.

3. Ibid., Art. II, Sec. 9.

4. For an extended discussion of city council and mayoralty elections in San Antonio, see L. Tucker Gibson and Robert R. Ashcroft, "Political Organization in a Nonpartisan Election System" (Paper delivered at the annual meeting of the Southwestern Political Science Association, Dallas, March 30–April 2, 1977); and L. Tucker Gibson, "Mayoralty Elections in San Antonio" (Paper delivered at the annual meeting of the Southwestern Political Science Association, Houston, April 12–15, 1978). See also Brischetto et al., Chapter 4, and Booth and Johnson, Chapter 1.

5. All voting data are taken from the computerized data files maintained by the Data Resource Center of Trinity University, San Antonio. For more on the GGL split, see Baylis, Chapter 5.

6. Luther Lee Sanders, "Nonpartisanism: Its Use as a Campaign Appeal in San Antonio" (Master's thesis, St. Mary's University, 1974), pp. 56–91.

7. "Anglo" is not an official census designation, but it is used extensively in South Texas in describing the white non-Spanish population.

8. U.S. Bureau of the Census, *1970 Census of Population: Characteristics of the Population*, vol. 1, tables 120, 125, 130; San Antonio, Planning and Development Department, Comprehensive Planning Division, *Population Update, September, 1975*, table J. Ethnic distribution of registered voters is based on a series of preelection polls and a computerized list of registered voters with Spanish surnames.

9. Allen M. Shinn, Jr., "A Note on Voter Registration and Turnout in Texas, 1960–1970," *Journal of Politics* 33 (November 1971): 1126.

10. From available data on financial reports from past elections the GGL slates spent well over $100,000 in any given election year. Opposition candidates or mini-slates spent only a small fraction of this amount.

11. Catherine Powell and Thomas F. Brereton, "COPS and APA: A Minority Environmental Alliance" (Unpublished paper, Trinity University, San Antonio). See also Chapter 8 by Plotkin for a detailed account of this process.

Chapter Seven

1. *San Antonio Independent School District* v. *Rodriguez*, 411 U.S. (1973).

2. Don José Francisco de la Mata, "Petition to the Cabildo," cited in translation in Frederick Eby, ed., *Education in Texas: Source Materials* (Austin: University of Texas, 1918), pp. 9–10. Also see J. J. Cox, "Education in San Antonio under the Spanish Regime," in C. W. Raines, comp., *Yearbook for Texas*, 2 vols. (Austin: Gammel-Statesman, 1902), 1: 124; idem, "Educational Efforts in San Fernando de Bexar," *Quarterly of the Texas State Historical Association* 6 (July 1902): 50.

3. Eby, *Education in Texas;* Frederick Eby, *The Development of Education in Texas* (New York: Macmillan, 1925), pp. 62 ff.

4. Coahuila and Texas, *Constitution*, (1827); Hans P. N. Gammel, comp., *The Laws of Texas, 1822–1897* (Austin: Gammel Book Co., 1898), 1: 451–52; Eby, *The Development of Education*, p. 66.

5. José Antonio Saucedo, San Fernando de Bexar, to Governor of Coahuila and Texas, April 18, 1825, in Eby, *Education in Texas*, pp. 56–70.

6. Saucedo to Governor Gonzales, January 21, 1826, trans. W. A. Whatley, in Eby, *Education in Texas*, pp. 61–63.

7. Eby, *Education in Texas*, p. 65; Eby, *Development of Education*, p. 64; Cox, "Educational Efforts in San Fernando de Bexar," pp. 52–63.

8. Republic of Texas, *Constitution*, General Provisions, sec. 5; Gammel, *Laws of Texas*, 1: 1079; Eby, *Education in Texas*, p. 131.

9. *Laws of the Republic of Texas*, 2 vols. (Austin: Printed by order of the Secretary of State, 1838), 2: 37–39; Gammel, *Laws of Texas*, 1: 1380 (legislation signed into law by Sam Houston, December 14, 1837).

10. Gamel, *Laws of Texas*, 2: 1297; *Journals of the Convention Assembly at the City of Austin on the Fourth of July, 1845* (reprint, Austin: Shoal Creek, 1974), pp. 361–62; Eby, *Education in Texas*, pp. 212–13.

11. Eby, *Education in Texas*, p. 246.

12. *Austin State Times*, January 14, 1851; Eby, *Education in Texas*, p. 246.

13. Eby, *Development of Education*, pp. 127 ff.

14. Ibid., p. 115, and Kenneth W. Wheeler, *To Wear a City's Crown: The Beginning of Urban Growth in Texas, 1836–1865* (Cambridge: Harvard University Press, 1968). Also see E. W. Winkler, *Platforms of Political Parties in Texas*, Bulletin no. 53 (Austin: University of Texas, 1916); *Laws of Republic of Texas, Fifth Legislature*, pp. 17–21; Eby,

Education in Texas, pp. 284–89, 472 ff.; *Journal of the House of Representatives of the State of Texas,* 6th Legis., pp. 401–12; Eby, *Development of Education,* pp. 120, 150 ff.

15. Eby, *Education in Texas,* p. 475; Eby, *Development of Education,* pp. 150 ff; "E. M. Wheelock, Superintendent of Public Instruction, Report to His Excellency E. M. Pease, Governor of Texas, May 30, 1868," in Eby, *Education in Texas,* pp. 483–88.

16. Eby, *Education in Texas,* p. 534.

17. Eby, *Development of Education,* pp. 160 ff.; R. A. Gambitta and R. M. Stevens, "Law and the Politics of Educational Deprivation in Nineteenth-Century Texas" (Paper delivered at the annual meeting of the Law and Society Association and the International Sociological Association, Madison, Wis., June 5–8, 1980), pp. 17–18.

18. Gambitta and Stevens, "Law and the Politics of Educational Deprivation," pp. 17–18; Eby, *Development of Education,* pp. 161 ff.

19. Gambitta and Stevens, "Law and the Politics of Educational Deprivation," pp. 18–19; Eby, *Education in Texas,* pp. 580 ff.

20. See Eby, *Development of Education,* pp. 171 ff., for further discussion. Texas, *Constitution,* Art. 7; Gammel, *Laws of Texas,* 8:809–13.

21. Texas, *Constitution,* Art. 7; Gammel, *Laws of Texas,* 8: 809–13. Section 29 stated: "Parents and guardians . . . in order to avail themselves of the benefits of the available school fund . . . may organize themselves into school communities, embracing such population as may agree to avail themselves of the benefits of the available public free school fund, on the following terms, *viz.:* They shall make out a list to be signed in person by such parents and guardians as desire to avail themselves of the available school fund." Part of the section, though of symbolic, not realistic, value, stated: "The Assessor, when taking the scholastic census, shall also ascertain to what community each child belongs; and if it appears that any child is not included in any community list, the County Judge shall assign such child to the most convenient and appropriate community, and set apart to said community such a child's *pro rata* of the fund."

22. Gammel, *Laws of Texas,* 8: 1376–77; *General Laws of the State of Texas passed at the Regular Session of the Sixteenth Legislature* (Austin: State of Texas, 1879); *General Laws of the State of Texas, passed at the Special Session of the Sixteenth Legislature* (Austin: State of Texas, 1879), pp. 49–50; and Eby, *Education in Texas,* pp. 723–24.

23. Texas, *Constitution,* Art. 7, Sec. 29; Gammel, *Laws of Texas,* 8: 809–13; Gambitta and Stevens, "Law and the Politics of Educational Deprivation," pp. 21–23.

24. Eby, *Development of Education,* pp. 216–21; William Seneca Sutton, *Bulletin: Some Wholesome Educational Statistics* (n.p., 1904).

25. Eby, *Development of Education,* p. 229.

26. Governor's Committee on Public School Education, *The Challenge and the Chance* (Austin: State of Texas, 1968), appendix C; American Association of School Administrators, *School Administration in Newly-Reorganized Districts* (Washington, D.C.: Government Printing Office, 1965), pp. 12–13.

27. It must be remembered that Texas operated *de jure* segregated, separate

school systems for blacks and whites until 1955. In reality, browns and whites were separated on a *de facto* basis in education because of the ethnic and class separation in housing. As we will see, *de jure* segregation via restrictive covenants in property deeds maintained homogenous racial/ethnic communities.

28. This relationship holds for San Antonio districts as well.

29. This information and much of the following was obtained from interviews beginning October 31, 1978, with Clyde Smith, Bexar County Superintendent for thirty-one years (1947–78), and from documents he provided. Smith, an immensely knowledgeable person on school affairs in Bexar County, coordinated the reorganization and consolidation efforts in the post–World War II San Antonio/Bexar County area.

30. E. E. Arnaud, "History of Edgewood Common School District Number 41" (Master's thesis, St. Mary's University, 1942), pp. 5–9.

31. Ricardo Gonzales Cedillo, "The Impact of Restrictive Deed Provisions on Racial/Ethnic Housing Patterns in San Antonio" (Unpublished study in the files of the Mexican American Legal Defense and Education Fund [MALDEF], 1975). MALDEF planned to use the study in litigation that never reached fruition.

32. See Corrigan v. Buckley, 371 U.S. 323 (1926); Liberty Annex Corporation v. City of Dallas, 289 S.W. 1067 (1926); Shelley v. Kraemer, 334 U.S. 1 (1948).

33. Cedillo, "Impact of Restrictive Deed Provisions"; Arnaud, "History of Edgewood," pp. 5–9.

34. *San Antonio Light*, November 15, 1949, p. 2-A.

35. Ibid.; and December 11, 1949, p. 2-E.

36. Rae F. Still, *The Gilmer-Aikin Bills: A Study in the Legislative Process* (Austin: Streck, 1950), p. 150.

37. R. A. Gambitta and R. A. Milne, "Assessing the Impact of Judicial Decision Making: The Rodriguez Case" (Paper delivered at the annual meeting of the Southwestern Political Science Association, Houston, April 12–15, 1978); Governor's Committee on Public School Education, *The Challenge and the Chance*, p. 35; J. Coons, W. Clune, and S. Sugarman, *Private Wealth and Public Education* (Cambridge: Harvard University Press, 1970), pp. 48–49.

38. Still, *The Gilmer-Aiken Bills*, p. 150.

39. "Answers to Interrogatories," Northside Independent School District, Rodriguez v. SAISD, from the private papers of Arthur Gochman (hereafter cited as Gochman Papers).

40. Minutes of the Bexar County School Board, August 3, 1949, San Antonio, Institute of Texan Cultures Archives. Seven districts combined to form Northeast Rural High School District, later becoming Northeast ISD: Blanco Road CSD No. 6, Sealy CSD No. 7, Olmos CSD No. 9, Lookout Valley CSD No. 10, Salado Valley CSD No. 10-1/2, Serna CSD No. 11, and Coker CSD No. 50. For further data see also "Answer to Interrogatories," Judson Independent School District, Gochman Papers; Order of the Bexar County School Board, November 14, 1949; Minutes of the Bexar County School Board, November 14, 1949; ibid., May 31,

1949; Minutes of the Bexar County School Board, February 3, 1949, and March 6, 1950; and *San Antonio Express,* February 2, 1950, and March 7, 1950.

41. For additional treatment, see the *San Antonio Express,* April 3, 1949, p. 1.

42. Petition dated October 15, 1949, San Antonio, Institute of Texan Cultures Archives.

43. Interview with former Edgewood superintendent E. E. Arnaud, November 27, 1978.

44. Edgewood CSD No. 41 Board of Trustees, Minutes of Meeting, November 8, 1949, and particularly, Minutes of the Bexar County School Board, March 22, 1950.

45. *San Antonio Light,* November 15, 1949, p. 2-A.

46. The petitions were approved on March 22 and May 29, respectively. See Minutes of the Bexar County School Board, March 22, 1950 and San Antonio Independent School District, "Answers to Interrogatories," 1969, Gochman Papers.

47. Sample drawn from City of San Antonio, 1950 Federal Census, Housing Block Statistics.

48. *San Antonio Express,* March 24, 1955. Edgewood superintendent E. E. Arnaud, however, disagreed with this assessment. Interview quoted in *San Antonio News,* January 20, 1956.

49. *San Antonio Express,* March 10, 1960.

50. Correspondence to M. Maverick, Jr., Gochman Papers.

51. The independent school districts were San Antonio, Edgewood, Harlandale, Northside, Northeast, Alamo Heights, and South San Antonio. The State of Texas is shorthand for the State Board of Education and its members, the commissioner of education, and the attorney general of Texas.

52. Rodriguez v. San Antonio ISD, U.S.D.C., W.D. of Texas, San Antonio Division, Civil Action no. 68-175-SA, order filed October 15, 1969.

53. Texas, Senate Bill 4 of the 59th Legis., regular sess., established the Governor's Committee on Public School Education.

54. The previous committees were the Texas Educational Survey Commission (1925); the Texas Statewide School Adequacy Survey (1938); the Gilmer-Aikin Committee Study (1948); and the Hale-Aikin Committee Study (1958).

55. *A Revenue System for Texas Public Schools* (Austin: Texas Advisory Commission on Intergovernmental Relations, 1974).

56. Rodriguez et al. v. San Antonio ISD et al., 337 F. Supp. 280 (1971).

57. Ibid, at p. 284.

58. Ibid, at p. 286.

59. *Texas Observer,* December 5, 1972.

60. Figures compiled by the Texas Research League, with editorial correction made from *Texas Observer,* December 5, 1972.

61. For a general accounting of the dynamics of this transition, see Bob Woodward and Scott Armstrong, *The Brethren* (New York: Simon and Schuster, 1979).

62. SAISD v. Rodriguez, at pp. 71–72.

63. Ibid.

64. Statistics are from 1967–68, the school year in which *Rodriguez* originated.

65. *Public School Finance Study: A Preliminary Report of Findings and Recommendations,* (Austin: Governor's Office of Education Resources, 1976).

66. Robert Brischetto, testimony before Texas Senate Education Committee regarding Texas's 1975 School Finance Law, "How Far Are We on the Road to Equity?" (Unpublished document in Mr. Brischetto's personal files), p. 1.

67. Ibid, pp. 1–2.

68. José Cardenas, former Edgewood ISD superintendent of schools, interview by Richard A. Gambitta and Anne F. Crawford, December 1977.

69. Richard A. L. Gambitta, "Litigation, Judicial Deference, and Policy Change," *Law and Policy Quarterly* 3 (1981): 141, reprinted in Richard A. L. Gambitta et al., eds., *Governing through Courts* (Beverly Hills: Sage, 1981), pp. 259–82.

70. Ibid.

71. Richard A. L. Gambitta and J. Craig Youngblood, "Harmful Effects of Hold-Harmless Legislation" (Paper delivered at the American Section of the International Association of Philosophy of Law and Social Philosophy, Westminister Institute, London, Ontario, April 1981).

72. Texas Session Law Service, 1st spec. sess., chap. 1, sec. 14, at p. 26, (1977). The State Equalization Aid formula, separate from the FSP, is figured as follows:

$$SEA = 1 - \frac{DAPV/ADA}{SAPV/ADA \times 1.10} \times ADA \times \$185$$

where

" 'SEA' is the state equalization aid guaranteed to district;

"*DAPV/ADA* for districts offering a full K–12 grade instructional program is the average of the district's full market value of property and agricultural use value of property as determined by the Governor's Office, Education Resources for the 1977–1978 and 1978–1979 school years and thereafter as determined pursuant to Section 11.86 of this code divided by the number of students in average daily attendance in the district. '*DAPV/ADA*' for districts where the full K–12 grade instructional program is not offered shall include the average daily attendance of eligible students transferred to other school districts in grades not taught by the resident district;

" '*SAPV/ADA*' is the average of the total statewide full market value of property and the total statewide agricultural use value of property and the total statewide agricultural use value of property as determined by the Governor's Office, Education Resources for the 1977–1978 and 1978–1979 school years and thereafter as determined pursuant to Section 11.86 of this code divided by the number of students in average daily attendance in the state; and

" '*ADA*' is the number of students in average daily attendance in the district." Ibid., at p. 27.

73. Gambitta and Youngblood, "Harmful Effects of Hold-Harmless Legislation."

74. Governor's Committee on Public School Education, "A Tale of Two Districts," 1968, referenced in and elaborated upon in Affidavit by Dr. José Cardenas, November 30, 1971, in proceedings of Rodriguez v. SAISD. The two districts compared were Northeast and Edgewood ISD.

Chapter Eight

1. Many studies have documented the intersection of private enterprise, residential interests, and government in the fashioning of land use policy. See, for example, Alan Altschuler, *The City Planning Process* (Ithaca: Cornell University Press, 1965); Richard F. Babcock, *The Zoning Game* (Madison: University of Wisconsin Press, 1966); Edward Banfield and Martin Meyerson, *Politics, Planning, and the Public Interest* (New York: The Free Press, 1955); Michael N. Danielson, *The Politics of Exclusion* (New York: Columbia University Press, 1976); William Worthy, *The Rape of Our Neighborhoods* (New York: William Morrow, 1976). Conventional researchers and journalists, however, tend to accept, without much critical reappraisal, market forces as the principal dynamic of land use. The operation of the political economy as a contradictory structure framing and spawning spacial conflicts is not itself called into question. This study highlights the formative and structuring role of the urban political economy in the battle over aquifer protection. For purposes of this paper, the urban political economy is treated as a complex of economic, social, and political forces projected out of the underlying capitalist social structure. Thus, government structure, social values, and economic practices can be seen to have what Robert Lynd has called a common drift "so that, like loaded dice, events tend to roll with a bias that favors property." "Power in the United States," in G. William Domhoff and Hoyt B. Ballard, eds., *C. Wright Mills and the Power Elite* (Boston: Beacon, 1968), p. 111; "Power in American Society as Resource and Problem," in Arthur Kornhauser, ed., *Problems of Power in American Society* (Detroit: Wayne State University Press, 1966). Conflicts are fought, questions raised, and dissent manifest in the urban setting—but in a framework whose impersonal logic favors the private accumulation and production of capital. Scholars have shown increasing concern for this structural imperative in the urban setting. Examples include Manuel Castells, *The Urban Question* (Cambridge: MIT Press, 1979); David Harvey, *Social Justice and the City* (Baltimore: Johns Hopkins University Press, 1974); William K. Tabb and Larry Sawyers, eds., *Marxism and the Metropolis* (New York: Oxford University Press, 1978). Also see the debate over the virtues and weaknesses of such an approach generated by Harvey Boulay, "Social Control Theories of Urban Politics," *Social Science Quarterly* 59 (March 1979): 605–21 and the replies in the same issue by Ira Katznelson, "Logical Heresies and Theoretical Possibilities," pp. 622–27 and David M. Gordon, "Social Control and Capitalist Cities," pp. 628–35.

2. For an analysis of the relation between expansion of the scope of conflict and

change in power relations, see E. E. Schattschneider, *The Semi-Sovereign People* (New York: Holt, Rinehart and Winston, 1960). Also see Roger W. Cobb and Charles D. Elder, *Participation in American Politics: The Dynamics of Agenda Building* (Baltimore: Johns Hopkins University Press, 1972).

3. James W. Ingram and Chia Shun Shih, "Utility Analysis for the Urban Growth inside the Recharge Zones of the Groundwater Resources of San Antonio, Texas" (Unpublished manuscript, Division of Environmental Studies, University of Texas at San Antonio, 1977), pp. 1–2, 18.

4. In 1972, when the conflict over the aquifer began to expand and intensify, the city's water costs came to a bit more than two cents per thousand gallons as compared with thirty cents in most other large U.S. cities. Although inflation has, of course, raised this amount, San Antonio's comparative advantage remains. "The Big Trouble at San Antonio Ranch," *Business Week,* November 3, 1973.

5. The English Rule of Absolute Ownership governs ownership and use of groundwater in Texas. "This rule gives each landowner complete freedom to withdraw and use the water beneath his land without restriction." Owners are prohibited only from wasting groundwater resources. Ingram and Shih, "Utility Analysis," p. 52. As Richard Bath has concluded, "Texas has no groundwater policy," at least insofar as policy is equated with resource conservation. "Texas Groundwater Policy" (Paper presented at the Southwestern Political Science Association Meeting, Houston, Texas, April 14, 1978), p. 2. Of course Texas does have a policy of encouraging the use of groundwater to support private economic development. Thus Rule 20 of the Texas Railroad Commission has been interpreted by the courts to mean that a property owner is entitled to damages "once pollution" of his groundwater "has occurred." But "no precedent has been set giving a landowner injunctive relief from the threat of *potential* groundwater pollution." Ingram and Shih, "Utility Analysis," p. 53. The assumptions underlying the policy are not unique to Texas. For discussion of this bias in the fabric of U.S. legal history see Morton J. Horwitz, *The Transformation of American Law* (Cambridge: Harvard University Press, 1977); James Willard Hurst, *Law and the Conditions of Freedom in the Nineteenth-Century United States* (Madison: University of Wisconsin Press, 1956).

6. For a classic satiric description of the real estate market in the "American Country Town," see Thorstein Veblen, *Absentee Ownership,* introduction by Robert Lekachman (Boston: Beacon Press, 1967), pp. 142 f.

7. Harvey, *Social Justice and the City,* p. 165.

8. The tale of the University of Texas at San Antonio's siting is told by Ronnie Dugger, *Our Invaded Universities* (New York: W. W. Norton, 1974), pp. 283–88. See also Chapter 2 by Jones.

9. For an analysis of land use conflicts centering on the disposition of downtown space see John Mollenkopf, "The Post-War Politics of Urban Development," in Tabb and Sawyer, *Marxism and the Metropolis;* also Robert Goodman, *After the Planners* (New York: Simon and Shuster, 1971), and Worthy, *Rape of Our Neighborhoods.*

10. For an historical overview of elite dominance of San Antonio government see John Booth and David Johnson, in Chapter 1. Contemporary currents are discussed by Thomas Baylis, Chapter 5, and Tucker Gibson, Chapter 6.

11. Edward Banfield and James Q. Wilson, *City Politics* (Cambridge: Harvard University Press, 1965), p. 170.

12. For a somewhat testy discussion of the social consequences of at-large elections see Chandler Davidson, "At-Large Elections and Minority Representation," and Susan A. MacManus, "At-Large Elections and Minority Representation: An Adversarial Critique," *Social Science Quarterly* 60 (September 1979): 336–37, 338–40. The debate is based on Susan A. MacManus, "City Council Election Procedures and Minority Representation: Are They Related?" *Social Science Quarterly* 59 (June 1978): 153–61.

13. Charles L. Cottrell and Michael B. Stevens, "The 1975 Voting Rights Act and San Antonio, Texas; Toward a Federal Guarantee of a Republican Form of Local Government," *Publius* 8 (Winter 1978): 79–99; *San Antonio Light,* October 31, 1976; Luther Lee Sanders, *How to Win Elections in San Antonio the Good Government Way, 1955–1971* (San Antonio: Department of Urban Studies, St. Mary's University, 1975), p. 1. See also Brischetto et al., Chapter 4.

14. Banfield and Wilson, *City Politics,* p. 171.

15. Ingram and Shih, "Utility Analysis," p. 4.

16. The men behind Ranchtown included close friends of John Connally, then secretary of treasury in the Nixon administration. They included George Christian, Lyndon Johnson's press secretary, and Hayden Head, South Texas lawyer and rancher who owned half of the 9,000-acre site. Several San Antonio politicians charged that shady insider dealings were behind the project. Mr. Head replied, however, that "I gave only $3,000 to the President's campaign last year (1972) and that doesn't get you any points in Washington." "The Big Trouble at San Antonio Ranch," pp. 78–79. The national, state, and local connections of wealth and power revealed by Ranchtown's backers suggest the truth of C. Wright Mills' observation that we risk misunderstanding "the upper levels of local society" if we fail to recognize that "all these cities are very much part of a national system of status, power and wealth." C. Wright Mills, *The Power Elite* (New York: Oxford University Press, 1956), p. 39.

17. *San Antonio Light,* October 12, 1972; "The Big Trouble at San Antonio Ranch," pp. 78–79.

18. Al J. Notzen, Jr., executive director, Alamo Area Council of Governments, interview, March 1978.

19. Glen Hartman, city councilman, San Antonio, interview, March 1978.

20. I would like to thank Dr. Michael Stevens for making me aware of this fact.

21. G. E. Harrington, former president, Greater San Antonio Home Builders Association and former chairman, City Planning Commission, San Antonio, interview, March 1978.

22. Ibid.

23. Jan Jarboe, "Who Pulls the Strings in San Antonio?" *San Antonio,* March 1977, pp. 46–48.

24. Cipriano F. Guerra, Jr., director of planning and community development, San Antonio, Memorandum to Directors of Public Works, Building and Planning, Traffic and Transportation, City Attorney, November 7, 1975. Emphasis added.

25. Frank G. Vega, "Activity Report for Edwards Aquifer Protection Office" (San Antonio, October 1975).

26. The State Water Quality Board's reluctance to press for strong land use controls reflects the preeminence of Texas's individualistic political culture. Daniel Elezar, *Cities of the Prairie* (New York: Basic Books, 1970), pp. 259–62; V. O. Key, Jr., *Southern Politics* (New York: Vintage Books, 1949), pp. 254–76. Jack Bass and Walter DeVries, in their updating of Key's classic, *The Transformation of Southern Politics* (New York: Basic Books, 1976), entitle their chapter on Texas "Still the Politics of Economics" (pp. 305–38). Kirkpatrick Sale takes a similar, if more bitter, view in *Power Shift* (New York: Vintage Books, 1975). Beneath ideology lays material interest. Thus it should be noted that the board's diffidence might be explained by then governor Dolph Briscoe's ownership of nearly one million acres of Uvalde County, source of the recharge waters of the aquifer. Briscoe was a conservative property owner whose views were shared by his rural neighbors. Uvalde and the remaining agricultural counties were also strongly represented on the board of the Edwards Underground Water District. Composed of two elected representatives from each county, the board was also disinclined to antagonize San Antonio's politically potent builders. Sidney Plotkin, "The Edwards Aquifer Controversy: A Study of Private Controls, Government Power, and Political Change in San Antonio, Texas (Paper presented at the Southwestern Political Science Meeting, Houston, April 14, 1978), pp. 9–23.

27. Sylvan Rodriguez, "The Aquifer Controversy: Is It Really about Clean Water?" *San Antonio,* September 1977, p. 23.

28. Another federal danger signal to private control of urban development was congressional consideration of a national land use policy aimed at financing state land use regulatory agencies. San Antonio businessmen were well alerted to this threat after the bill twice passed the Senate. The U.S. Chamber of Commerce spurred local land merchants to oppose the measure in the House. In 1974 and 1975 the bill failed to reach the floor. Sidney Plotkin, "Policy Fragmentation and Capitalist Reform: A Study of the Defeat of National Land Use Policy," *Politics and Society,* forthcoming.

29. Luther Sanders, *How to Win Elections,* p. 11, describes the GGL philosophy of public government by private decision: "Rational decisions cannot be made in open public debate because most individuals seek public approval or will use public pressure in order to force their beliefs on others. Therefore, debate on public issues must be removed from public view in order to reach a workable consensus on a best course of action."

30. Glen Hartman, interview, March 1978.

31. Sheldon Wolin, *Politics and Vision* (Boston: Little, Brown, 1960), pp. 16–17 passim. In a recent article Wolin suggests the dismal fate of the sense of place in Jimmy Carter's political philosophy. See "Carter and the New Constitution," *New York Review of Books*, June 1, 1978, pp. 16–19.

32. Saul D. Alinsky, *Reveille For Radicals* (New York: Vintage Books, 1969), esp. chap. 8.

33. Paul Burka, "The Second Battle of the Alamo," *Texas Monthly*, December 1977, p. 221.

34. Ibid., p. 226.

35. The mall's backers were not entirely accurate. For example, a study completed for the U.S. Geological Survey in 1972 concluded that accelerated development over the recharge zone would produce "deterioration of the chemical and bacteriological quality" of Edwards water unless "stringent precautions are . . . taken to prevent the increased waste load from reaching the Aquifer." Cited by Ingram and Shih, "Utility Analysis," p. 19.

36. *San Antonio Light* and *San Antonio Express*, June 25, 1975.

37. Rodriquez, "The Aquifer Controversy," p. 24.

38. In one sense the mall issue rested on a base of economic make-believe. As the City Planning Commission chairman, himself a builder, pointed out, the mall's backers "weren't ready to build" and probably intended to sell out in a few years in hopes of reaping a giant "unearned increment," perhaps on the order of a 10,000 percent—from 30¢ to $30.00 per square foot!" G. E. Harrington, interview, March 1978.

39. *San Antonio Light*, January 23 and February 2, 1976.

40. *San Antonio Express*, February 13, 1976.

41. Ibid., March 9, 1976.

42. After two years of lobbying organized by the Alamo Area Council of Governments, the Texas Water Quality Board, in January 1975, published an aquifer protection ordinance drawn heavily from the federal government's Ranchtown standards. It closely regulated septic tank and sewage system siting and construction and introduced a number of other regulations on land use in the area. According to environmentalists, its major deficiency lay in the absence of standards for control of storm water runoff from large parking lots. This was, of course, the main environmental criticism of the mall project.

43. Undoubtedly though, the basic factor at work in the 10–1 election was the federal presence. Probably some Anglo voters stayed away from the polls not because of faith in COPS but because in one form or another change was a foregone conclusion determined by the Justice Department. Just as federal support for Ranchtown placed the growth issue on San Antonio's agenda in the first place, it was the national government's power that fortified, at a key stage in its development, the pattern of democratic change so intimately tied to the aquifer's fate. One need not agree with Schattschneider's use of the word "inevitably" to see the relevance of the following comment to San Antonio: "The nationalization of politics inevitably

breaks up local power monopolies and sectional power complexes . . . the new dimension produces so great a change in the scale of organization and the focus of power that it may take on a semi-revolutionary character." *Semi-Sovereign People*, p. 11.

44. Cottrell and Stevens, "The 1915 Voting Rights Act," p. 87.

45. *San Antonio Express*, May 26, 1977.

46. Ibid., June 4, 1977.

47. *San Antonio Express* and *San Antonio Light*, various issues, June 10–30, 1977.

48. *San Antonio News* and *San Antonio Light*, June 11–12, 1977.

49. *San Antonio News*, June 25, 1977.

50. *San Antonio Express*, January 26 and July 20, 1978.

51. In the report's words, "development of various types does generate pollutant runoff; . . . the aquifer is highly accessible to that runoff; . . . present regulations do not adequately protect against the potential for ground water pollution due to that accessibility." Metcalf and Eddy, "Proposed Development Controls for the Edwards Aquifer: Report to the City Council of San Antonio, Texas" (Boston, 1980), pp. 4–5.

52. Ibid., p. I-4–9.

53. *San Antonio Express*, October 21, 1979. Revival of interest in north side real estate is also evidenced by two long Sunday supplement pieces on prospective growth in the area. See "How Site-Seekers Spot Malls" and "The UTSA Land Boom Bust: There's money buried in the hills around UTSA. The question is: How do investors dig it up again?" *San Antonio Express*, September 30 and November 18, 1979.

54. Ibid., January 30, 1979.

55. Ibid., August 16, 1979.

56. Ibid., January 1–4, 1980.

57. "The Runaway Economy," *Business Week*, March 10, 1980, pp. 102–12; Robert Goodman, *The Last Entrepreneurs*, (New York: Simon and Schuster, 1979). Nationally oriented businessmen should not be expected wholeheartedly to support uncoordinated intergovernmental rivalry for investment. They perceive the social ills which flow from uneven development, especially the potential for political instability. Thus the above article prints a recipe for economic renewal offered by Felix Rohatyn, a major architect of New York City's rescue. Rohatyn calls for a new Temporary National Economic Committee to generate "an integrated economic strategy, both domestic and international, for the next two decades." This would include "reducing the Regional divisiveness between the have and have-not states by providing a permanent burden-and-revenue sharing on the national level" (p. 112). Northern and midwestern Congressmen, meanwhile, are busy trying to establish legal roadblocks to constrain corporate flight from the "frostbelt." See "Can Congress Control Runaways?" *Dollars and Sense*, November 1979, p. 9. In Cleveland, a federal district judge went so far as to order U.S. Steel to keep open a Youngstown plant it expected to close. The judge ruled that "a property right has arisen from

this . . . long-established relationship between U.S. Steel [and] the community in Youngstown." This right justifies labor's claim to keep the plant open. "A Tightening Vise on Plant Shutdowns," *Business Week*, March 17, 1980, pp. 38–40. It is not a legal theory likely to be embraced in San Antonio. Unity aside, one town's "common interest" is another's sacrifice.

58. Sidney Plotkin, "Limits to Urban Political Change: The Abating of Pluralism in San Antonio" (Paper presented at the Southwestern Political Science Association Meeting, Houston, April 4, 1980).

59. "Read this list—this is S.A. unity" (editorial), *San Antonio Express*, January 4, 1980.

Chapter Nine

1. Beatrice Gallego, former president of COPS, interviews, San Antonio, February 1980 and September 29, 1981. For additional information on the meeting with Granata see Paul Burka, "The Second Battle of the Alamo," *Texas Monthly*, December 1977, p. 222; see also Jan Jarboe, "Building a Movement," *Civil Rights Digest*, Spring 1977, p. 43.

2. *San Antonio Light*, June 20, 1976, p. 2-B.

3. See, for example, "Uprising in Texas: Control of San Antonio Is Slowly Being Won by Mexican Americans," *Wall Street Journal*, July 13, 1977, p. 1; Calvin Trillin, "U.S. Journal: San Antonio, Some Elements of Power," *The New Yorker*, May 2, 1977, pp. 92–100; Jarboe, "Building a Movement," pp. 39–46; Burka, "Second Battle," p. 139; E. D. Joes, Jr., "COPS Comes to San Antonio," *The Progressive*, May 1977, p. 33–36; "COPS Beginning to Reach Their Goals," *San Antonio Express*, November 16, 1975, p. 2-B.

4. See, for example, Robert L. Lineberry and Ira Sharkansky, *Urban Politics and Public Policy*, 2nd ed. (New York: Harper and Row, 1974); and Charles R. Adrian and Charles Press, *Governing Urban America*, 4th ed. (New York: McGraw-Hill, 1972).

5. Information on Cortes's early organizational activities has been pieced together from written accounts such as Burka, "Second Battle," and Jarboe, "Building a Movement," and from various interviews and conversations with COPS leaders.

6. Father Albert Benavides, former executive vice president of COPS, interview, San Antonio, November 3, 1981.

7. A few years later in Los Angeles, where Cortes was involved in organizing another community group, he found an even more easily overlooked problem at the top of people's lists of grievances: car insurance rates. *Los Angeles Times*, May 17, 1979, Part II, p. 7.

8. Gallego interview, September 29, 1981.

9. Constitution of Communities Organized for Public Service, adopted November 23, 1975.

10. Each church is assessed annual membership dues based on the size of its budget. Members of the clergy are eligible for election as officers in COPS, although thus far a cleric has never been elected president. Also COPS' constitution requires that two clerics (a priest and a nun) be elected each year to represent the clergy. Finally, the current chief organizer and staff director of COPS, Christine Stephens, is a nun.

11. Benavides interview, November 3, 1981.

12. For one of the authoritative texts on liberation theology see Gustavo Gutierrez, *A Theology of Liberation* (Maryknoll, N.Y.: Orbis Books, 1973).

13. Benavides interview, November 3, 1981.

14. On business relocation see Edgar M. Hoover and Raymond Vernon, *Anatomy of a Metropolis,* (Cambridge: Harvard University Press, 1959; Anchor Books, 1962), chap. 2. Census figures as of 1970 show that 54.2% of the residents of metropolitan areas lived beyond the boundaries of the central cities. Dennis R. Judd, *The Politics of American Cities* (Boston: Little, Brown, 1979), p. 159.

15. Arnold Fleischmann, "Sunbelt Boosterism: The Politics of Postwar Growth and Annexation in San Antonio," in David C. Perry and Alfred J. Watkins, eds., *The Rise of the Sunbelt Cities* (Beverly Hills: Sage, 1977), p. 159.

16. Between 1950 and 1980 San Antonio's population grew from 408,442 to 788,002; its land area increased from 70 square miles to 267 square miles. *San Antonio Light,* April 12, 1981, p. 1-D.

17. For a concise history of major government subsidies to business see H. H. Liebhafsky, *American Government and Business* (New York: John Wiley and Sons, 1971), chap. 8.

18. *San Antonio Light,* May 25, 1976, p. 1-A.

19. *San Antonio Express,* January 11, 1977, p. 5-H.

20. Michael D. Reagan and John G. Sanzone, *The New Federalism,* 2nd ed. (New York: Oxford University Press, 1981), chap. 5.

21. Office of Budget and Research, City of San Antonio, "CDBG Status Report" (October 1981), p. 1.

22. "CDBG Status Report" and various request sheets submitted at public hearings by COPS.

23. Confidential interview, San Antonio.

24. Memorandum submitted by Roy E. Robbins, principal planner of the Office of Planning and Community Development, City of San Antonio, to Roy Montez, assistant director of the Office of Community Planning and Development, December 4, 1975.

25. For a brief history and analysis of the UDAG program see Jerry A. Webman, "UDAG: Targeting Urban Economic Development," *Political Science Quarterly* 96 (Summer 1981): 189–96.

26. *San Antonio Light,* June 27, 1979, p. 8-C.

27. Reagan and Sanzone, *The New Federalism,* chap. 4.

28. City of San Antonio, "Annual Report of Grant-In-Aid Funds of San Antonio for the Fiscal Year Ended July 31, 1980," pp. 314–62.

29. San Antonio, "Annual Report" and various request sheets submitted at public hearings by COPS.

30. *The News*, April 20, 1978, p. 1-A. See also *Southside Sun*, July 6, 1978, p. 1.

31. San Antonio, "Annual Report," pp. 314–62.

32. *San Antonio Light*, July 28, 1978, p. 1-A.

33. Computed from an untitled document drawn up at the author's request by John Rinehart, capital program manager, Department of Public Works, City of San Antonio, and from "The City of San Antonio, Proposed Capital Budget (1981–1982)—Capital Improvement Program (1982–1987)," pp. 42–172.

34. *San Antonio Express*, November 25, 1981, p. 2-A.

35. Ibid., July 12, 1977, p. 1-A.

36. Beatrice Cortez, president of COPS from 1980 to 1982, interview, San Antonio, December 9, 1981.

37. *San Antonio Light*, August 28, 1977, p. 1-A.

38. For an in-depth discussion of the scandal see Rich Casey, "Scandal at SAC," *SA Magazine*, March 1980, pp. 50–57.

39. *San Antonio Light*, April 4, 1980, p. 2-A.

40. Ibid., July 29, 1977, p. 6-A.

41. Carmen Badillo, former president of COPS, interview, San Antonio, September 24, 1981.

42. *San Antonio Express*, April 9, 1976, p. 1-A.

43. *San Antonio Light*, May 5, 1980, p. 19-A. Oddly, the plant has yet to be built. COPS leaders speculate that their challenge to the permit forced some expensive antipollution equipment on Barrett that made the cost of constructing the plant prohibitive.

44. *San Antonio Express*, July 20, 1979, p. 1-A.

45. *San Antonio Light*, January 16, 1977, p. 5-H.

46. Ibid.

47. Ibid., February 17, 1982, p. 1-A.

48. Ibid. The CWDF is a revolving fund whereby the city advances the developers money for approach water mains and the developers reimburse the city from the proceeds of the sale of the houses.

49. Ibid., January 16, 1977, p. 5-H.

50. *San Antonio Express*, July 31, 1977, p. 3-B.

51. Ibid., May 20, 1981, p. 1-A.

52. Ibid., January 23, 1982, p. 2-A.

53. Ibid.

54. Charles E. Lindbloom, *Politics and Markets* (New York: Basic Books, 1977), pp. 173–74.

55. Badillo interview, September 24, 1981.

56. *National Catholic Reporter,* December 16, 1977, p. 2.

57. "Joint Statement of San Antonio Communities Organized for Public Service (C.O.P.S.) and the San Antonio Economic Development Foundation (E.D.F.)," May 30, 1978.

58. Gallego interview, September 29, 1981.

59. Benavides interview, November 3, 1981 and Cortez interview, December 9, 1981.

60. Robert McDermott, "United San Antonio" (Personal papers of Beatrice Gallego, November 11, 1979), p. 2. This document is a proposal for the establishment of United San Antonio submitted to COPS and various other persons and groups in San Antonio.

61. Andres Sarabia, former president of COPS, interview, San Antonio, September 19, 1981 and Cortez interview, September 22, 1981.

62. *San Antonio Express,* January 21, 1982, p. 1-B.

63. Ibid., January 22, 1982, p. 2-A.

Chapter Ten

1. L. Tucker Gibson and Robert R. Ashcroft, "Political Organization in a Nonpartisan Election System" (Paper presented at the annual meeting of the Southwestern Political Science Association, Dallas, March 30–April 2, 1977).

2. Luther Lee Sanders, *How to Win Elections in San Antonio the Good Government Way, 1955–1971* (San Antonio: Department of Urban Studies, St. Mary's University, 1975).

3. For detailed discussions of the nature, means, and policy results of control by this elite, see Baylis, Chapter 5; Plotkin, Chapter 8; Brischetto, Cotrell, and Stevens, Chapter 4; Gibson, Chapter 6; and Gambitta, Milne, and Davis, Chapter 7.

4. Baylis, Chapter 5, provides extensive detail concerning the issues and personalities involved in this schism. Brischetto, Cotrell, and Stevens, Chapter 4, elaborate on the electoral consequences of the GGL–Independent split. See also Scott Bennett, "Texas' Great Hispanic Hope," *Texas Business,* June 1981, pp. 24–27, 109.

5. See also Charles L. Cotrell and R. Michael Stevens, "The 1975 Voting Rights Act, Annexation Policy, and Urban Growth in the Sunbelt," *Urban Law Review* 3 (Spring/Summer 1979); John A. Booth, "The Impact of the Voting Rights Act in San Antonio, Texas," in *Bilingual Elections at Work in the Southwest* (San Antonio: Mexican American Legal Defense and Education Fund, March 5, 1982), pp. 62–119; Brischetto, Cotrell, and Stevens, Chapter 4; Gibson, Chapter 6; and Plotkin, Chapter 8.

6. Paul Burka, "The Second Battle of the Alamo," *Texas Monthly,* December 1977, pp. 138–43, 218–38; Sekul, Chapter 9; Joseph D. Sekul, "Grass-Roots Power in a Businessman's Town: An Analysis of the Political Methods of Communities Organized for Public Service" (Paper presented at the annual meeting of the South-

western Political Science Association meeting, San Antonio, March 18, 1982); and Bennett, "Texas' Great Hispanic Hope," pp. 109–10.

7. Although the city council followed the referendum's guidance, COPS and the city eventually lost their decision on appeal to the U.S. Supreme Court. A detailed discussion of the implications of this decision for water policy formulation, development policy, and San Antonio city politics may be found in Sidney Plotkin, "Limits to Urban Political Change: The Rise and Abating of Pluralism in San Antonio" (Paper presented at the annual meeting of the Southwestern Political Science Association, Houston, April 4, 1980).

8. This history of the rise of Chicano participation and representation is drawn mainly from Booth, "Impact of the Voting Rights Act," pp. 67–77. See also Bennett, "Texas' Great Hispanic Hope," pp. 27, 109–13.

9. Booth and Johnson, Chapter 1; Baylis, Chapter 5; Brischetto, Cotrell, and Stevens, Chapter 4; Gibson, Chapter 6; Plotkin, Chapter 8; and Booth, "Impact of the Voting Rights Act," pp. 80–89.

10. Booth, "Impact of the Voting Rights Act," pp. 80–89.

11. Quoted in John A. Booth and Richard A. Gambitta, "Myth and Reality in San Antonio Politics," *SA Magazine*, July 1977, pp. 12–14.

12. Booth and Johnson, Chapter 1; John A. Booth, "San Antonio: From Machine to Coalition Politics, 1925–1979," in Ernest Crain, Charles Deaton, and William Earl Maxwell, *The Challenge of Texas Politics* (St. Paul: West, 1980), pp. 359–63; and Booth, "Impact of the Voting Rights Act," pp. 66–77.

13. Gambitta, Milne, and Davis, Chapter 7; Burka, "Second Battle of the Alamo"; Charles L. Cotrell, *Municipal Services Equalization in San Antonio, Texas: Exploration in Chinatown* (San Antonio: Department of Urban Studies, St. Mary's University, 1976).

14. Quoted in *An Inquiry into Voting Irregularities in Texas* (San Antonio: Southwest Voter Registration and Education Project, 1980), p. 130.

15. Robert L. Ashcroft, political consultant and adviser to a member of the 1977–79 council, interview, 1978.

16. For example, see Sanders, *How to Win Elections*.

17. Carl Cohen, *Democracy* (New York: Free Press, 1973); Carole Pateman, *Participation and Democratic Theory* (Cambridge: Harvard University Press, 1970); Carl Cohen, ed., *Communism, Fascism, and Democracy: The Theoretical Foundations*, 2nd ed. (New York: Random House, 1972).

18. Thomas Jefferson to John Taylor, May 28, 1816, in C. M. Wiltse, *The Jeffersonian Tradition in American Democracy* (Chapel Hill: University of North Carolina Press, 1935), p. 83.

19. A. J. Lindsay, *The Essentials of Democracy* (1929), quoted in Cohen, *Communism, Fascism, and Democracy*, pp. 542–43.

20. Thomas Jefferson to Benjamin Waring, March 23, 1801, in Cohen, *Communism, Fascism, and Democracy*, p. 440.

21. Lindsay in Cohen, p. 545.
22. Gibson and Ashcroft, "Political Organization," p. 7; Booth, "Impact of the Voting Rights Act."
23. See Plotkin, "Limits to Urban Political Change," pp. 8–18.
24. Booth and Gambitta, "Myth and Reality."